Dreamweaver® 4
f/x & Design

Laurie Ulrich

President, CEO
Keith Weiskamp

Publisher
Steve Sayre

Acquisitions Editor
Beth Kohler

Product Marketing Manager
Patricia Davenport

Project Editor
Jennifer Ashley

Technical Reviewer
Connie Myers

Production Coordinator
Meg E. Turecek

Cover Designer
Jody Winkler

Layout Designer
April E. Nielsen

CD-ROM Developer
Chris Nusbaum

Dreamweaver® 4 f/x and Design

Limits of Liability and Disclaimer of Warranty

The author and publisher of this book have used their best efforts in preparing the book and the programs contained in it. These efforts include the development, research, and testing of the theories and programs to determine their effectiveness. The author and publisher make no warranty of any kind, expressed or implied, with regard to these programs or the documentation contained in this book.

The author and publisher shall not be liable in the event of incidental or consequential damages in connection with, or arising out of, the furnishing, performance, or use of the programs, associated instructions, and/or claims of productivity gains.

Trademarks

Trademarked names appear throughout this book. Rather than list the names and entities that own the trademarks or insert a trademark symbol with each mention of the trademarked name, the publisher states that it is using the names for editorial purposes only and to the benefit of the trademark owner, with no intention of infringing upon that trademark.

The Coriolis Group, LLC
14455 N. Hayden Road
Suite 220
Scottsdale, Arizona 85260

(480)483-0192
FAX (480)483-0193
www.coriolis.com

Library of Congress Cataloging-In-Publication Data
Ulrich, Laurie Ann.
    Dreamweaver 4 f/x and design / by Laurie Ulrich.
        p.   cm
    ISBN 1-57610-789-2
    1. Dreamweaver (Computer file) 2. Web sites--Authoring programs. 3. Web publishing.   I. Title.

TK5105.8885.D74 U47   2001
005.7'2--DC21   2001028056
                                                                            CIP

 **CORIOLIS**

Printed in the United States of America
10 9 8 7 6 5 4 3 2 1

A Note from Coriolis

Thank you for choosing this book from The Coriolis Group. Our graphics team strives to meet the needs of creative professionals such as yourself with our three distinctive series: *Visual Insight*, *f/x and Design*, and *In Depth*. We'd love to hear how we're doing in our quest to provide you with information on the latest and most innovative technologies in graphic design, 3D animation, and Web design. Do our books teach you what you want to know? Are the examples illustrative enough? Are there other topics you'd like to see us address?

Please contact us at the address below with your thoughts on this or any of our other books. Should you have any technical questions or concerns about this book, you can contact the Coriolis support team at **techsupport@coriolis.com**; be sure to include this book's title and ISBN, as well as your name, email address, or phone number.

Thank you for your interest in Coriolis books. We look forward to hearing from you.

Coriolis Creative Professionals Press
The Coriolis Group
14455 N. Hayden Road, Suite 220
Scottsdale, AZ 85260

Email: **cpp@coriolis.com**

Phone: (480) 483-0192
Toll free: (800) 410-0192

Visit our Web site at **creative.coriolis.com** *to find the latest information about our current and upcoming graphics books.*

Other Titles for the Creative Professional

Flash™ 5 f/x and Design
By Bill Sanders

Flash™ 5 Cartoons and Games f/x and Design
By Bill Turner, James Robertson, Richard Bazley

Flash™ ActionScript f/x and Design
By Bill Sanders

Fireworks® 4 f/x and Design
By Joyce J. Evans

Photoshop® 6 In Depth
By David Xenakis and Benjamin Levisay

Illustrator® 9 f/x and Design
By Sherry London

GoLive™ 5 f/x and Design
By Richard Schrand

Painter® 6 f/x and Design
By Sherry London and Rhoda Grossman

Adobe InDesign™ f/x and Design
By Elaine Betts

This book is dedicated to my grandmother, Betty Talbot, who I miss very much. She gave me my first eyelash curler (at 12), and was the only woman I know who could wear bright pink lipstick (Revlon's "Cherries in the Snow") and not look like a tart. She tried to teach me to "Say yes, and then do as you damn well please!" and told me (on the sly) not to listen to my parents. Grandmothers don't get much better than that.

ᐧ🌢

About the Author

An art major in college, **Laurie Ulrich** planned on a career as an artist. After college, however, she accepted a job in the business sector and found herself in front of a computer for the first time. This introduction led to a fascination with software and uncovered a talent for helping businesses use computers to chart their progress, market themselves, and plan for the future. As a result, Laurie has been working with computers since 1981 and has spent the last 10+ years teaching thousands of students of all backgrounds and skill levels, writing training materials and computer books, and consulting to growing businesses, nonprofit organizations, and home users.

In 1992, Laurie established her own firm, an organization specializing in technical documentation and software training. In 1997, her firm expanded to offer Web design and Web-site hosting, enabling her to provide a comprehensive set of computer-related services and also put her creative nature and graphic design skills to work. Since 1998, Laurie has written and coauthored 13 nationally published books on topics ranging from business software to Web design and has contributed to and edited several other books as well. She can be reached at **laurie@planetlaurie.com**, and invites you to visit her rather self-absorbed Web site, **www.planetlaurie.com**, where her complete bibliography and bio can be found.

Acknowledgments

I must first thank Robert, my partner in all things. He patiently provided technical advice and design suggestions, put up with my singing while he tried to work, and continues to love me, even though I get very crabby when I'm under stress. He also fed the cat and taped my soaps while I was writing, for which Jasper and I are eternally grateful.

I'd like to thank Beth Kohler for giving me the opportunity to write this book. She and the rest of the editors at Coriolis (namely Jennifer Ashley and Michelle Stroup) were very helpful throughout the project. I'd also like to thank those who worked behind the scenes at Coriolis: Meg Turecek, production coordinator; Jody Winkler, cover designer; April Nielsen, layout and design and Color Studio designer; and Chris Nusbaum, CD-ROM developer.

I'd also like to thank my students, especially BADG Groups A and B (you know who you are). Helping you achieve your Web-design certification was great fun, and I learned a lot.

I must also thank my clients. From the inspired to the bizarre—their marketing and Web-design goals, needs, and ideas have been a significant source of content for this book. I obviously wouldn't have a Web-design business without clients, and without the business, I'd have more opinion than experience to share with my readers.

Finally, I must thank my agent, Margot Maley, for her guidance and support. She's just the best—that's all I can say.

—*Laurie Ulrich*

Contents at a Glance

Table of Contents

Introduction

If you've been using the Web for a while, you'll know that the source for a Web page can be viewed through your browser, by selecting View|Page Source or View|Source. The resulting lines of HTML code are what the browser sees and uses to display the Web page. Well, there are sources, and then there are *sources.* To me, the source of Web designs is the creative heart of every (yes, every) Web designer, from the person who feels they have no creativity at all, to the true *artiste* who sees the Web as yet another canvas to be filled with colors and ideas.

The *f/x and Design* series is a valuable combination of these two source elements—the technical how-to information, and the more conceptual when-to and where-to information that people need to satisfy both sources of Web design. Artists need brushes and canvas, the tools of their trade, but they also need ideas and pictures in their heads so they have something to put *on* the canvas. When it comes to Web design, a designer needs software to take his or her ideas and get them onto the computer screen. *Dreamweaver 4 f/x and Design* provides that combination of procedural instruction and creative influence that most books, even those pertaining to creative software, don't usually attempt to offer. Dreamweaver is the perfect application to be covered in an *f/x and Design* format, because it, too, is a powerful combination of art and science—every color you apply, font you choose, and image you insert is turned into HTML code before your eyes (or in a hidden window, if the artist in you can't bear to look).

Who Will Enjoy This Book

While this book assumes some knowledge of Dreamweaver, you don't need to be a veteran user to appreciate this book. New users will find the book helpful in that it doesn't just show you how to do something, but why to do it, and in some cases, why not to do it. Examples of good design and bad design abound, along with clear descriptions of how and why each example fell into one category or the other. Typical readers of this book might see themselves in these profiles:

- *Web Designer*—You're a freelance designer, or you work for someone else, designing a specific site or many sites. You are tasked with coming up with new ideas and original artwork, or perhaps you are given specific ideas and images and have to find ways to make them work on the Web. Chances are, your life as a Web designer is some combination of all of these things. You may or may not have any formal art training, and may not have any experience with design beyond or before the Web, so concepts relating to color and type may be new to you. If you come from the print world, you may know a lot about color and type, but be confused about how (or even if) what you know can be applied to the Web. This book will help you figure out what's possible and effective on the Web, and how to turn your visions (or the visions someone else is foisting upon you) into a Web reality.

- *Webmaster*—Maybe you aren't the designer, but you maintain the pages that the designer creates and need to understand Web design from a designer's perspective. If you're working with designers who don't know much about creating art for the Web, you have your work cut out for you in terms of reining them in and making sure color, text, and images are all in a suitable format for Web use. This book will help you talk to the designer and make your needs (which are the Web's needs) understood.

- *Graphic Artist*—You've been designing for print media and see that many of your clients who came to you for brochures and business cards are looking to carry their marketing materials into cyberspace. They want a Web site, and they want it now. They also want it to look like the printed marketing materials they already have, or maybe they're looking at their debut on the Web as a chance for a marketing makeover. You don't want someone else nabbing this client, after you've spent time getting to know them, their business, and their customers. This book will help you take what you know about designing for print work and apply it to designing for the Web—what colors and type you can and can't use (and why), and how designing for a computer screen is a lot different than designing for paper. You'll be happy to learn that designing for the Web is often easier, more freeing (it's *deep*, literally), and you can make some very nice money at it.

- *Creative Soul*—You aren't a professional designer, but you're good at designing things. Maybe you designed the cover of your local symphony's concert guide, or you draw your own Christmas cards every year. Perhaps you've dabbled in design software at work, using products like QuarkXpress or PageMaker to design your company's catalog, or you create signs and product labels with CorelDRAW. Maybe you've scanned and retouched some family photographs with Photoshop, and fooling around with all the cool features awakened that artist that's lurking somewhere inside of you. The Web is probably calling you, and whether it's a Web site for your family, your church, your school, or for you as a professional—somewhere to post your resume and list of accomplishments—you want it to look great. This book will help you unleash all that creative stuff and give it some direction so that you're happy with the results of your foray into Web design.

How This Book Is Organized

Not surprisingly, this book is divided into chapters—13 of them, to be exact—and each of the chapters has one or more projects to help you use the skills discussed and demonstrated in the chapter. The files needed to complete the projects are on the CD-ROM that accompanies this book, and Appendix D describes how the project files are organized on the CD so you won't have any trouble finding them when you need them. The chapters are as follows:

- *Chapter 1: Working with the Dreamweaver Environment*—Learn about the workspace and tools at your disposal so you won't waste time looking for things when you decide to dive in and start designing.

- *Chapter 2: Understanding Sites vs. Pages*—Dreamweaver wants to help you build Web sites, not just ad hoc Web pages, and the site management tools are considerable. They're also pretty easy to use and appear in a very handy window that this chapter will help you use to your advantage.

- *Chapter 3: Working with Text*—You wouldn't think you'd need much help beyond some tips for typing, but that would be underestimating Dreamweaver's text-formatting tools and the Web's requirements for text. This chapter explains what a designer needs to know in terms of using text to convey information, thoughts, and ideas in an effective, visually appealing way.

- *Chapter 4: Effective Use of Graphics*—The old saying, "a picture's worth a thousand words," is certainly true on the Web. Beyond how to insert images and what kind of images work best on the Web, this chapter focuses on what your images should look like, where to put them on the page, and how many is too many.

- *Chapter 5: Connecting with Hyperlinks*—What would the Web be without links? A lot of pages that don't go anywhere, that's what. From links between a site's pages to links that connect sites, generate email messages, and download files, this chapter shows you how to create real depth within and between your Web pages.

- *Chapter 6: Structuring a Web Page with Tables*—Need to lay out a page quickly and effectively and not worry that only the latest versions of browsers will be able to display your final product? Tables are your answer, and this chapter shows you how to build, format, and fill them with the stuff pages are made of.

- *Chapter 7: Controlling a Page with Frames*—The love-hate relationship many designers have with frames is described in this chapter, along with the nuts and bolts of building framesets and controlling how frames look and work for your site's visitors.

- *Chapter 8: Positioning Page Content with Layers*—Layers are a very cool feature, but browsers don't always display them as we'd like. Despite this drawback, this chapter acknowledges and explains the creative freedom that layers provide for a Web designer.

- *Chapter 9: Using Color Effectively*—This chapter explains primary colors, secondary colors, complementary colors, why opposites "attract," and when white is wrong and black is bad (in a good way). You'll learn which colors are Web-safe and how to match the Web-safe palette to print colors.

- *Chapter 10: Creating Forms*—"Sign on the dotted line" has been replaced by "Click the Submit button." Add interactivity to your pages, turning your site visitors into a source of information and/or giving them access to your data. As always, the focus is on design, so you'll learn to create attractive, easy-to-fill-out forms that gently pry the information you want out of the most private of site visitors.

- *Chapter 11: Working with Dreamweaver Assets*—That title is almost redundant when it comes to Dreamweaver—it's such a powerful product. In this chapter, you'll learn to store and access Assets—colors, images, URLs—to speed up your design process and make it easy to keep pages consistent throughout a site.

- *Chapter 12: Creating and Using Style Sheets*—This often-neglected source of control and consistency is demonstrated through practical design examples. Learn to build styles that apply uniform type and color formatting throughout your site's pages.

- *Chapter 13: Using Multimedia Objects*—Even if your average visitor is still connecting to the Internet via a slow modem, you may want to jazz things up with some sound and motion on your pages. Learn how to add Flash and Shockwave movies, sound files, and connect events (like the user's mouse movements) to multimedia effects. You'll also learn how to apply multimedia objects without creating a circus-like atmosphere, helping to keep any tendency to go overboard safely in check.

- *The Color Studio*—Sixteen pages of images from real Web sites will show you how the design concepts taught throughout the book can be applied to actual pages, in fabulous color.

- *Appendix A: What's New in Dreamweaver 4?*—If you used Dreamweaver 3, you'll notice some changes immediately. You may also be confused when some subtle changes make themselves known as you start to work in the new version. Forewarned is forearmed!

- *Appendix B: Do I Have to Know HTML to Use Dreamweaver?*—Knowing HTML can't hurt and probably will help you at some point. If you've been wincing at the thought of even reading a line of HTML code, this Appendix can ease your fears by showing you the basic constructs of this ubiquitous programming language. Once you see how HTML code is built and works, you won't be afraid of it anymore.

- *Appendix C: The Basics of Macromedia Fireworks*—Because so many people buy Dreamweaver packaged with Fireworks, it made sense to provide a little primer in this handy application. Learn to create buttons and other graphic images for your pages, and to use Fireworks to retouch existing line art and photographic images.

- *Appendix D: Using Project Files for This Book*—Take a tour of the CD-ROM that accompanies this book, and discover where the files for each chapter's projects are stored and how to get at them when you need them.

Each chapter begins with a brief description of what you can expect to learn, and ends with a description of what you'll find in the next chapter. There is a concerted effort to create flow from the beginning of the book to the end, as topics increase in complexity and your skills build on one another. This is not to say, however, that the book must be read cover-to-cover in order to be enjoyed or utilized—it's not. You can look up a topic at random, read about it and do the related project (or not) and close the book until you need it again.

Chapter 1

Working with the Dreamweaver Environment

The Dreamweaver interface gives you all the tools you need to create and edit dazzling Web pages. Knowing which palettes do what and how to display and rearrange the palettes is a big part of mastering Dreamweaver and letting your creativity flow.

The Dreamweaver Palettes

Like a blank canvas, the empty, white Web-page-to-be stares back at you, awaiting your first action. There to assist you are three boxes, each loaded with tools—buttons for adding objects to the Web page, buttons for changing your view of the environment and adding more tools to the workspace, and buttons for formatting everything from text to images on the page. Aptly referred to as *palettes*, these three boxes give you just about everything you need to create any sort of Web page.

Identifying the Palettes

The three palettes that appear as soon as you open Dreamweaver are:

Figure 1.1

Set to the Common objects view by default, the Objects palette has seven different faces that offer seven different groups of tools.

- *Objects*—You use the Objects palette for adding objects to the Web page— objects such as typographical symbols, tables, frames, and form fields. By clicking the Common button at the top of the palette (see Figure 1.1), you can choose from seven different views of this palette: Characters, Common, Forms, Frames, Head, Invisibles, and Special. As you select each view from the list, the palette changes to offer the tools associated with that object's palette view.

- *Properties*—This palette, known as the *Properties Inspector*, is something of a chameleon, changing its tools to match the formatting options of whatever element you have selected on the Web page. If you have selected text, an assortment of tools for changing the appearance and placement of text appears (see Figure 1.2). If you're in a table cell, options are offered for both the content of the cell and the cell itself. If you have selected the table (rather than its contents), you can change the placement and size of the table and its cells. If you're working with images, you can adjust their placement and size, turn them into links to other pages or sites, and even chop out hotspots (parts of the graphic that have been made into hyperlinks) on the images to create multiple links on the surface of a single image. Of the three palettes, you'll find yourself frequently using the Properties Inspector, relying on it to help you make the Web page you have envisioned an on-screen reality.

Figure 1.2

The Properties Inspector, which changes to match the formatting needs of whatever on-screen element is selected, offers a comprehensive set of formatting tools.

- *Launcher*—As its name implies, the Launcher starts things. It opens any of seven different dialog boxes, which you can use to:

    1. create a Site map,

2. list your page's Assets (links, objects, graphics, templates, libraries) and view Reference materials that define various HTML tags and attributes,

3. display HTML (Hypertext Markup Language),

4. display Cascading Style Sheet (CSS) styles,

5. view Behaviors,

6. move through time in your page's development History and view Layers and Frames,

7. and check underlying HTML code with the Code Inspector.

Figure 1.3 shows several of these dialog boxes on screen.

Figure 1.3
Display various dialog boxes and leaf through their tabs to unveil a series of powerful features and views.

Displaying Palettes

By default, all three palettes—Objects, Properties, and the Launcher—appear when you open the Dreamweaver application. If you turn the palettes off during your session and then exit the software without restoring the palettes to view, they won't appear the next time you open the Dreamweaver application.

To display the palettes—one, two, or all three—use the Window menu, and select the palettes by name. You can also use the following keyboard shortcuts to display them:

Note: When you redisplay a palette, it appears on screen where it was positioned the last time you used it.

- Ctrl+F2 brings back the Objects palette.

- Ctrl+F3 calls up the Properties Inspector.

- F2 restores the Launcher to view.

Moving and Resizing Palettes

As you're working on your Web pages, you'll no doubt need to move the palettes out of the way from time to time, if only to see something they're currently obscuring. The Properties Inspector is the largest of the three and is often covering the very object you want to format. I like to place this palette off to the right, with just its title bar showing, so I can pull the palette back into view when I need it, but keep it out of the way while I'm typing page text or formatting a table.

To move any of your palettes, drag them by their title bars. Figure 1.4 shows a convenient configuration of palettes on a page in progress.

You can resize the Launcher to appear vertically or horizontally. Click the button in the lower right corner of the palette to switch between these views (see Figure 1.5).

Collapse and Expand the Properties Inspector

You can shrink the Properties Inspector by clicking the small arrow in the lower left corner. When the arrow is pointing up, the palette is its full size. Click the arrow to reduce the palette's size by half; click the arrow again to expand the palette back to full size with all its tools displayed.

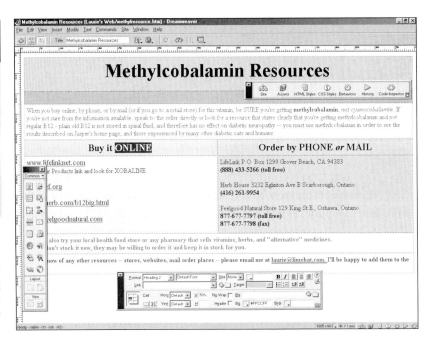

Figure 1.4

If you close a palette to get it out of your way, use the keyboard shortcuts to restore the palette to view.

Figure 1.5

Your personal preference is the only rule that applies when it comes to choosing a horizontal or vertical display mode for the Launcher.

Working with Text Properties

When it comes to your Web page text, the Properties Inspector does everything short of typing and editing the text. The key to using this palette is to select the text you want to format before you use any of the palette's tools—selecting the text first tells Dreamweaver to which text your changes should apply.

For alignment and other paragraph formats, you need only to have your cursor in the paragraph you want to format. If the formatting applies to characters—font, size, color—you must already have selected the text with your mouse or a combination of the Shift and arrow keys, as Figure 1.6 shows (in the figure, *ONLINE* is selected).

Viewing Selected Text Formats

Sometimes, you don't know what was done to text in your Web page. What font has been applied? What size is the font? Is that the green I was supposed to use? You can answer these questions, plus many others, simply by clicking on the text in question and viewing the Properties Inspector. The font, size, color, and alignment all appear in the palette's tools when your cursor is blinking in the text in question (see Figure 1.7).

Figure 1.6

If your cursor is in the text, you can control the text's position, but not its appearance. To control how the text looks, you must select it entirely before you apply formats.

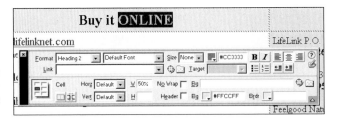

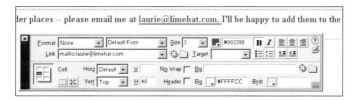

Figure 1.7
Need to check the formatting applied in one place so you can quickly match it in another? View the Properties Inspector to see which formats have been applied to any text on the page.

Understanding Palette Formatting Options

The Properties Inspector's tools come in four flavors, offering choices through a drop list or array, toggle buttons, text boxes, and checkboxes. The number and combination of tools vary, of course, depending on what's selected at the time on the active page. Figure 1.8 shows the Properties Inspector when text in a table cell is selected—tools are offered for adjusting both the table cell and its text content.

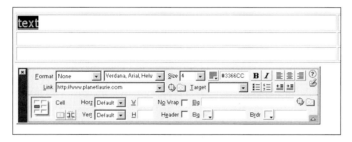

Figure 1.8
With drop lists, checkboxes, text boxes, and buttons that turn formats on and off, the Properties Inspector makes changing the appearance of text quick and easy.

Some of the Properties Inspector tools do double duty—you can make selections from a drop list/array, or you can manually type your own entry. For example, if you know the color name or number that you want to apply, you can type that information in the color text box, or you can select a color from the array of colors that appears when you click the color button that accompanies the text box. You can apply links, fonts, and sizes in these two ways, as well.

When you type your entries (rather than choosing options from a list), you must be accurate. Although entering a misspelled font name won't do much harm—the software won't apply a font it doesn't recognize—entering the wrong color number will apply the wrong color. And if a subtle shade difference exists between what you meant to type and what you actually entered, you won't notice the error until later, when you notice that two things that should be the same color aren't.

Controlling Image Properties

Images can be photographs, clip art, scanned drawings, or even a text object you create in an application such as Photoshop for use as a graphic object on a Web page. The Properties Inspector offers tools for adjusting the placement, position, or source location of the image file; a location that the image links to; image alignment; and any border around the image. This palette also lets

Interpreting Displayed Properties

If your text is obviously formatted beyond the default settings, yet the palette shows None for the font size, Default Font for the font, and no color selected, either you haven't selected the text that you think you have, or you have selected text that contains more than one font, size, or color setting—thus disabling the palette's ability to display a single set of formats. Reposition your cursor, and check the palette again.

you create hotspots on the image, so that portions of a graphic can point to different locations on the page or within the site, or to a URL on the Web.

Unlike text, the fact that the image is within a table cell—or simply placed on the page—has no effect on the tools that appear in the palette (see Figure 1.9).

Figure 1.9
The Properties Inspector offers 25 different image-formatting tools.

Viewing Selected Image Settings

To view the settings already applied to a given image, click once on the image. The Properties Inspector will display the default settings if you haven't adjusted anything about the image since its insertion. If you have made changes, you can see those changes reflected as well in the palette.

If your image has hotspots in it, you can view the settings for those by clicking the individual spots with the hotspot Pointer tool. When a hotspot is selected, small handles appear around its perimeter, and the Properties Inspector's offerings are reduced to show only Link, Target, and Alt (alternate text) settings for that hotspot (see Figure 1.10, in which the Cat hotspot is selected).

Figure 1.10
Check your hotspot links by selecting individual spots and viewing their properties, one by one.

Changing Image Size, Position, and Links

You can manually adjust the size of your images by dragging the object's handles, which appear when the object is selected. To make an object larger, drag the handles outward; to make it smaller, drag the handles inward. If you want to keep the object's current *aspect ratio* (proportionate width and height), drag from a corner handle. Of course, depending on the type of image you're working with, enlarging the image can create distortion and a choppy appearance (see Figure 1.11). If you need to adjust the size of an object beyond a 2 percent or 3 percent increase, resizing it in an image editor is better because, that way, you can maintain the image quality.

You can adjust image position by changing the object's alignment, and you can adjust only the object's horizontal alignment. If you want to adjust its vertical alignment, you must add or remove blank lines (paragraphs) above

Figure 1.11
Tiny changes in size are possible from within the Dreamweaver environment, but major increases in size can create distortion and a choppy appearance.

and/or below the image. If the image is in a table cell, you need to display the Properties palette tools for the table cell by selecting the cell and *not* the image inside it. When the cell's properties are displayed, adjust the Vert alignment to Top, Middle, Bottom, or Baseline.

If you want the image to serve as a hyperlink, you can enter the exact URL in the Link text box. If you've linked other text and images on the active page, you can select one of the URLs from the Link drop list rather than retyping the address. Once you have used the Link box, you can enter Target information. The Target specifies the frame or window in which the linked page should load, such as a floating window spawned by the link.

Note: An often-neglected tool is the Alt box, in which you can type alternate text that you want to appear when someone moves the mouse over the link image (or text). The Alt text won't appear until you preview the page in a browser or view it online.

The Quick Tag Editor is always present in the Properties Inspector. On the right side of the palette, the button displays a tiny HTML-tag editing window, which offers the tag that would be your most likely choice, depending on the position of your cursor, or what object is selected at the time (see Figure 1.12). You can get further, context-sensitive assistance by clicking the Help button in the palette. Doing so opens your default browser and displays the Help article that explains the feature you're using.

Figure 1.12
Enter HTML code with the Quick Tag Editor.

Using the Objects Palette

As the name implies, you use the Objects palette to insert objects. You can choose from seven different object types (by clicking the button at the top of the box to display a list), and you insert the objects in each type by clicking the palette buttons. If you're not sure which object a given button will insert, move the mouse over the button, and pause to view the screen tip (see Figure 1.13).

By default, the Common objects buttons are displayed, from which you can insert such common items as tables, frames, Flash movies, horizontal rules, dates, and email links. The palette's six other categories enable you to add anything your Web-designing heart desires, from typographical symbols to scripts.

At the bottom of the Objects palette are Layout and View options, which control how you create layout tables and cells. In Standard view, you cannot draw tables and cells with your mouse. In Layout view (see Figure 1.14), however, you can use the Draw Layout Cell and Draw Layout Table tools to draw tables, tables within tables, cells within cells, and cells within tables. Whew!

Figure 1.13

Although most Dreamweaver buttons are well illustrated, you can display a button's name if you're not sure.

Working with the Launcher

The Launcher opens windows and panels, through which additional Dreamweaver tools become available. The default group of Launcher buttons includes:

- *Site*—Opens the Site window, through which a site map can be made, and you can view the contents of a remote Web site and local folders (see Figure 1.15).

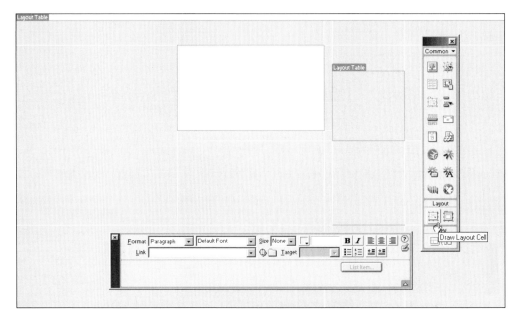

Figure 1.14

If your page design requires a complex table structure, use the Draw Layout Table and Draw Layout Cell buttons to draw the table configuration you need.

- *Assets*—This window contains two tabs, Assets and Reference. The Assets tab lets you view all the assets available to your site, including Web-safe colors, and objects such as Flash movies, scripts, and templates. The Reference tab contains searchable text definitions of HTML tags and attributes (see Figure 1.16).

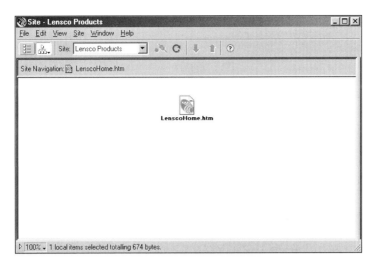

Figure 1.15
If you're building an entire Web site, use the Site window to manage it.

Figure 1.16
Read all about your site's assets, and its HTML tags and attributes, in the context-sensitive Reference tab.

- *HTML Styles, CSS Styles, and Behaviors*—These three tabs are available in a single window (see Figure 1.17). View a list of styles and behaviors that you can use in the active page.

- *History*—In addition to the History tab, this window contains Layers and Frames tabs that list the layers and frames used in the active page (see Figure 1.18).

Figure 1.17
(Left) To speed formatting, you can apply HTML and CSS styles.

Figure 1.18
(Right) The History button on the Launcher opens this three-tab window on your page's layers, frames, and the steps you've taken to build the page.

• *Code Inspector*—The Code Inspector provides a floating window that displays the underlying HTML code for the active page in general and the selected portion of the page specifically (see Figure 1.19). You can edit code through this window (you can also edit code and access the Reference tab in the Assets window to read about selected HTML code).

Figure 1.19

In Dreamweaver's WYSIWYG (what-you-see-is-what-you-get) environment, view and edit the HTML code your actions have created.

Working with the Menu and Toolbar

The menus give you access to all the tools Dreamweaver's palettes and windows provide. Also, you can access a significant number of commands only through the menus, although the most frequently used commands are represented on the palettes, if only for the sake of convenience. As Figure 1.20 shows, you can use Dreamweaver's menus to access important commands not available through the palettes.

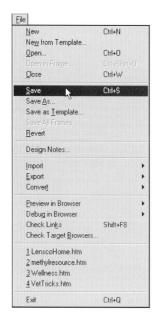

Figure 1.20

You can access the Open and Save commands only through the menu or via keyboard shortcuts.

The toolbar provides a series of 10 tools for changing the layout of your workspace:

- Code view

- Design and Code views

- Design view

- Page Title command

- File Status menu

- a button that lets you preview the active page in a browser

- Refresh button

- a button that lets you access the Reference window and that displays context-sensitive Help

- Code Navigation button (for debugging HTML code)

- Options Menu button

The Options menu contains a list of helpful features that change the way your page and its elements look and work (see Figure 1.21).

Figure 1.21

Through the Options menu, turn on helpful screen elements, such as Table Borders, and a Ruler and Grid that make setting up a page, aligning objects on it, and resizing tables and images much easier.

Achieving Control with the Ruler and Grid

You can tell that the ruler and grid are powerful features—Dreamweaver gives you two ways to apply the ruler and grid, and to customize how they look. You can turn these features on through the View menu or through the Options Menu button on the toolbar. Through the View menu, you can choose the measurement method the ruler will use (inches or pixels), and the color and dimensions of the grid.

If you want your grid to assist and control you as you move images around on screen, make sure the Snap To option is on. Choose View|Grid|Edit Grid to access the options for the grid's appearance and function (see Figure 1.22).

Note: The grid appears in a bright blue color with 50-pixel spacing. You might find that the bright color is visually distracting,and that a more muted shade (that you can still see if you apply a background image or color) is easier to work with. You can also choose to display the grid as dots rather than lines.

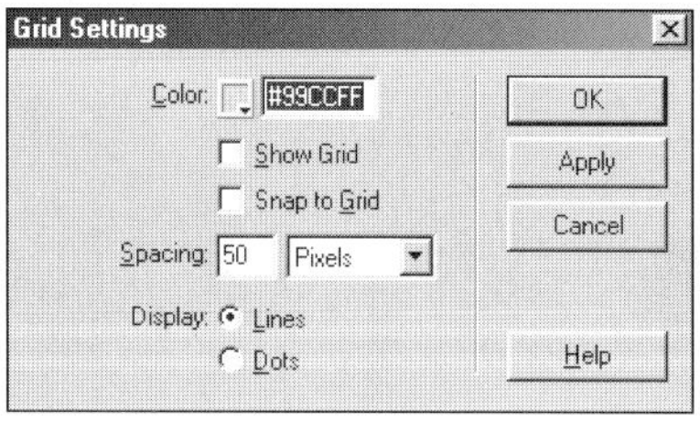

Figure 1.22
Customize the grid to meet your
design needs.

Moving On

Now that you have more than a nodding acquaintance with the Dreamweaver
environment, you can move on to starting a new Web site. You can build Web
sites page by page, or as a cohesive group of related pages. The next chapter
focuses on these two approaches and explains the tools that help you create a
Web site.

Chapter 2

Understanding Sites vs. Pages

A Web site is made up of one or more Web pages. With that universally accepted fact stated, you might be wondering what the big deal is about understanding the difference between sites and pages. Chapter 2 will take you on a tour of Dreamweaver's site-creation and -management tools, and explain the big deal about sites.

Sites and Pages Defined

If a site is a group of pages, are you creating a site by creating individual Web pages? Not as far as Dreamweaver is concerned. Dreamweaver sees the creation of several ad hoc pages as an entirely different pursuit from the creation of a Web site. Dreamweaver offers you the capability to build a Web site in a series of pre-existing folders, which you create and populate with pages, and which contain the images that will appear on those pages. By building your pages within an established site, you are able to take advantage of Dreamweaver's site management tools. Dreamweaver automatically inserts the source and link information for all your pages and their content into each page's properties, and ties that information to the site's folders.

But aside from some automatic insertions of image sources and link information, what do these capabilities do for you? By creating a site and establishing a folder hierarchy for that site, Dreamweaver makes posting your pages and their images to a remote Web server much easier. Just copy the main site folder to the server, and that folder, along with its subfolders and their contents, will be posted, with the relationships between the pages and their images intact.

Because the folder hierarchy on the Web server will be the same as the one you used to store the page files and graphic images, you can perform a one-step upload and know your images will appear and your intersite page links will work—no need to set up folders on the remote server and copy individual pages and images to them. Further, you can use Dreamweaver's Site Map feature to move pages and images around, and the links between everything will update automatically. This interrelationship is impossible if you're creating piecemeal pages for a Web site—you will have to manually establish and maintain any links between individual pages (and, certainly, any changes to those links).

Creating a site, rather than just building a series of disparate pages, can feel a little constricting the first time. The idea of having to plan and create folders ahead of time to store your files in might seem foreign to you. Making sure all your images are in the appropriate folder might not be something you're used to worrying about until you're ready to post your pages to the Web. Dreamweaver's site tools do impose and require some level of control, yes. But those tools free you in many other ways. Of course, the site folder names can be anything you want, and you can store your images in a folder right along with your pages, rather than in a separate Images folder. Dreamweaver doesn't have too many hard and fast rules. What's important is that Dreamweaver's site-creation and -maintenance tools quicken and simplify the process of building your site and posting it to the Web. The tools also help you become accustomed to an important part of the Web site creation process that's often overlooked: making a plan and sticking to it.

Web Site Creation

Creating a Web site involves two main steps—building the folders on your local computer (the computer you'll be using to build your pages), and telling Dreamweaver what to call your site and which folders to use for storing site pages and images. Of course, you'll want to set up your site folders before you use Dreamweaver's Site Menu tools, so that the folders you want to designate for your site are already in place. As you go on to build your site's pages, you can create new folders at the same time you save the pages. But setting up your main folders ahead of time is still a good idea.

Setting Up Site Folders

You can set up your site folders through the Windows Explorer or My Computer programs. Planning your folder names and relationships before you sit down to actually create them is a good idea. Some folder setup suggestions include the following:

- Start with a Sites (or similarly named) folder, and create subfolders for each new site you create.

- Each new site's main folder (whether it's a subfolder of Sites or a new folder off the root of your C: drive) can contain folders for each page, or a single Pages folder that holds them all.

- If you'll be using graphic images on your pages, you'll want to create an Images or Pictures folder in which to store those files.

- Keep it simple (see Figure 2.1, which shows the Src [Source] box in the Properties Inspector). Remember that despite Dreamweaver's automatic updating of links between pages and source information for graphic images, you will sometimes have to edit the HTML code or the content of the Properties Inspector, and you won't enjoy having to type or edit long, complex paths.

Figure 2.1

Set up your folders and subfolders in a logical way so you can easily remember which content is stored in which folder.

To use the Windows Explorer or My Computer programs to build your site folders, follow these steps:

1. Open the tool of your choice—Windows Explorer or My Computer.

2. Select and display the local drive (C: in most cases).

3. Choose File|New|Folder.

4. Type a name (such as Sites) for your new folder in the New Folder box that appears. This new folder can be the starting folder for a variety of future site folders that you can store in subfolders of this main folder (see Figure 2.2).

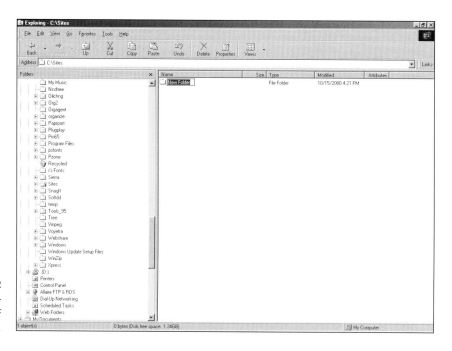

Figure 2.2
Replace the generic New Folder with a folder name of your choice.

5. Repeat Steps 3 and 4 for each site folder you want to create (if you'll be building multiple sites) and for subfolders of the main site folder(s). To ensure that you designate the site folder as the home of new subfolders as you create them, select the site folder *before* you issue the File|New|Folder command.

Creating a Web Site

To create a Web site in Dreamweaver, simply open the application and, from the Site menu, choose New Site. The Site Definition dialog box opens (see Figure 2.3), through which you can name your site, designate the site's main (Local Root) folder, and even enter the site's URL (HTTP Address).

As soon as you enter this information and click OK to close the Site Definition dialog box, a prompt appears, indicating that the site will be created, and that Dreamweaver's tools for tracking links between site pages will begin operating for the site. Click OK to close the prompt and continue the site-creation process.

You can always go back and update the site information—changing the site's name, moving the information to a new folder, or changing the Web address with which the site is associated. You can also go back to the Site Definition

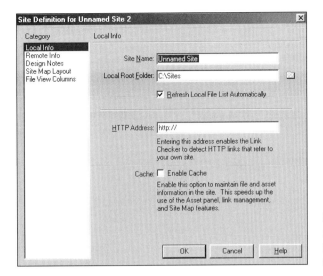

Figure 2.3
Name your new site and, if a URL has been established, enter the address in the HTTP Address box.

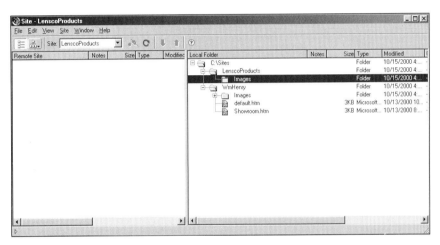

Figure 2.4
Looking very much like the Windows Explorer window, the Site window shows a folder tree for your new site.

dialog box to designate which page is the home page. Designating a home page is the first step in creating and using a site map, which is a graphical representation of the hierarchy and relationship among your site's pages. Figure 2.4 shows a new site with an Images folder.

Creating a Site Map

A site map is created as soon as you select a particular page within your site to be the home page. Of course, the page must already exist and have been saved, even if you haven't done anything with it. If you don't have any pages for your site yet, simply save the new, blank Web page that appeared when you opened Dreamweaver; save the page as index.htm or default.htm—whichever your Web server requires for the home page of a site. Note that the file will automatically be saved with an .htm extension, so you needn't type that yourself. Figure 2.5 shows the Save As dialog box.

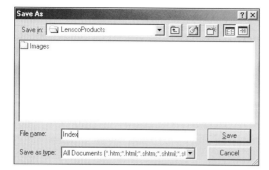

Figure 2.5
Save your home page to the
site's main folder, and name the
page index.htm or default.htm—
whichever your Web server or
host requires.

Once you've created the page you intend to use as your home page, you must officially designate it as the home page. To do this, follow these steps:

1. Choose Site|Define Sites. The Define Sites dialog box opens, as shown in Figure 2.6.

Figure 2.6
Choose the site you want
to set up.

2. Select the site (by the name you gave it in the Site Definition dialog box), and click the Edit button.

3. The Site Definition dialog box reopens, displaying your settings for the selected site.

4. From the Category list on the left side of the dialog box, select Site Map Layout.

5. On the right side of the dialog box, click the folder next to the Home Page text box to browse to the page that will serve as the selected site's home page. The Choose Home Page dialog box opens to help you select the page (see Figure 2.7).

6. After you have selected the page and clicked the Open button, you are returned to the Site Definition dialog box. Click OK to close that dialog box, and then click the Close button (X) to close the Define Sites dialog box.

After you close the Define Sites dialog box, Dreamweaver creates a site map, viewable through the Site Window. If you choose Map and Files from the view option buttons (see Figure 2.8), you can see your new map (which consists of a home page icon) in one pane and your folder tree in the other.

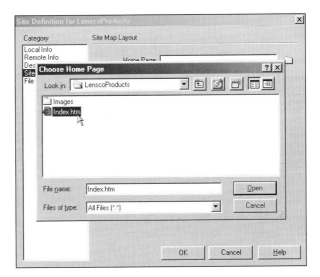

Figure 2.7
Use the Choose Home Page dialog box to select the page you'll use as your site's home page.

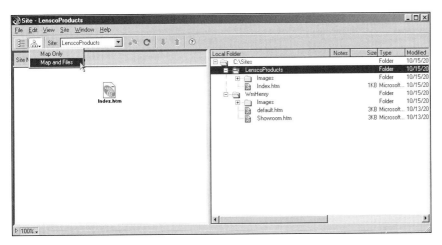

Figure 2.8
View your fledgling site map and folder tree in the Site window.

Now that you have started your site map, you can create new pages and store them in the site folder. Once they're stored there, you can add the pages to the site map by dragging the home page Point to File button onto the pages in the folder tree, as Figure 2.9 shows.

Using the Site Map

The site map gives you a graphical environment for creating page associations, and for updating relationships between pages within a site and between sites. By dragging the Point To File button for any page selected within the site map, you can link that page to other pages, graphics, Flash movie files, sounds—to any file you have stored within the displayed folder tree. When you drag the Point To File button from a page in your site to a Flash movie file, for example, you add a link to that movie right on that page. As Figure 2.10 shows, you can create links between pages and files by dragging the Point To File button from a page in the site map to a page not yet included, or to a file to which that

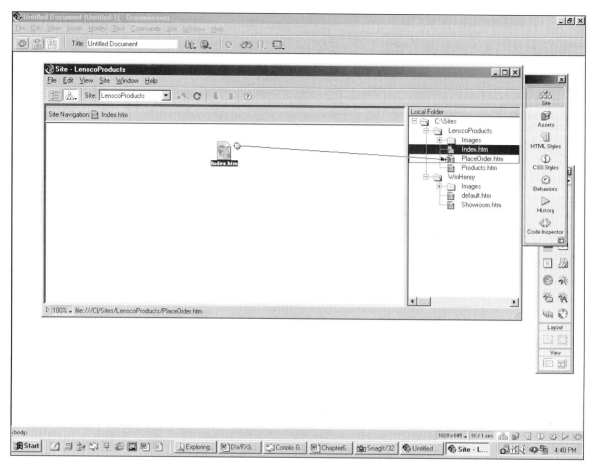

Figure 2.9

Figure 2.9

Point to the page you want to connect to the home page, and your site map grows to include the beginnings of a new level of pages in the site.

Figure 2.10

Build your site map by creating links between pages and other files. Dreamweaver's site tools will maintain these links for you as your site grows and changes during development.

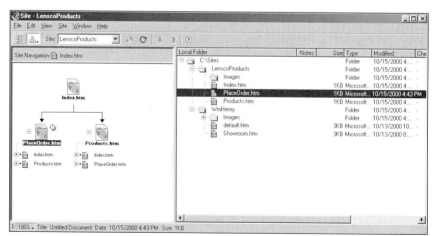

page should link. Once you have connected the page or file through this dragging method, the page or file becomes part of the site map and is linked within the site until and unless you delete it from the map.

Moving On

Now that you've read about Dreamweaver's site-creation and -management features, you're ready to begin creating Web pages. The next chapter focuses on the first steps you'll take in building a new Web page—inserting and formatting text for headings, paragraphs, and bulleted lists. In addition, you'll learn to position large pieces of text and to separate sections of a text-heavy Web page with horizontal rules.

Switching between Sites

If you're working on more than one site at the same time, you can switch between sites and view each site's map through the Site window. Simply click Site, and choose the site you want to view and work on from the drop-down list. You can then use the site map to open any of the chosen site's pages—just double-click the page icon, and that page opens, ready for editing.

Chapter 3

Working with Text

The text on your Web page needs to be accurate, well-written, and visually effective. No software can help you with the first two, but Dreamweaver can make it easy to enter, position, and format your text. Chapter 3 will show you how to get your point across and make your words have the impact you desire.

A picture may be worth a thousand words (as the old saying goes) and interesting to look at, but a Web site that consists entirely of pictures might not be terribly effective in terms of sharing information or selling a product or idea. Conversely, Web pages that consist entirely of text can be rather dull to look at, however riveting the content may be. Your Web pages should be legible, attractive, and positioned properly. Dreamweaver provides a simple, yet comprehensive, set of tools for controlling the appearance and placement of text.

Effective Headings

Headings tell us what to expect from the text or graphic content we find below the headings, just as the headings on this book's pages tell you what to expect within sections of each chapter. Within a Web page, single words and short phrases perform this very important role, and we must rely on their size and color to make them stand out. Appropriate word size and color allow site visitors to spot and read the headings first. Because the heading text is larger than the rest of the text on the page and normally comprises five or fewer words, the site visitor isn't really conscious of *reading* those words—headings don't require intense concentration to digest (see Figure 3.1). The headings, therefore, must be large enough to stand out from surrounding text and graphics, and the heading fonts must provide instant legibility.

Nix the Caps

When you are typing heading text, use sentence or title case—never all capital letters. Why? Because text in "all caps" is difficult to read. In addition, the use of all capitals implies that the writer is yelling at the audience, and that's rarely a perception you want to encourage.

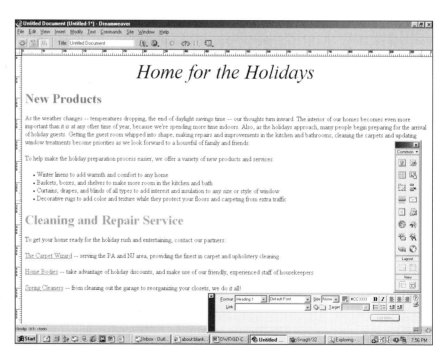

Figure 3.1
Headings work like short headlines, announcing the content to be found beneath them and/or on a linked page (if the heading functions as a hyperlink to another page or Web site).

Dreamweaver's Properties Inspector, displays the formats for any text on your Web page and gives you tools for changing those formats. As shown in Figure 3.2, you can apply Heading styles, which automatically change the font and size of

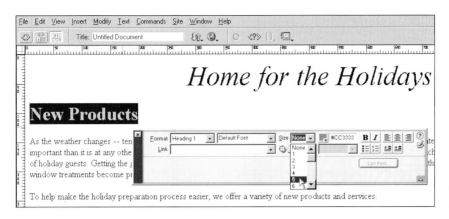

Figure 3.2

Choose a Heading style for your selected text.

the designated text, or you can customize the heading text with fonts and sizes you choose.

Typing Heading Text

When you type your heading text, keep it short and simple. You can go into detail in the subsequent paragraphs. Remember, headings are supposed to act as headlines—short references to the text or other content that follows them. To be effective, headings should be single words or short phrases rather than complete sentences—single words and short phrases take up less room on the page, and they're quick and easy to read.

To format your headings, type the text first, and then go about formatting it—don't turn on a format and then type the text. Why? Because you're doubling your efforts. If you apply formats to existing text, you need to make your formatting selections only once. If you apply the formats and then type the text, you have to turn the formats off so they don't continue to apply to text typed on the next line on the page.

As you type text, use the Enter key sparingly. Of course, you want to use the Enter key at the end of a heading that should appear on a line by itself. But if you're typing paragraph text, using the Enter key (which indicates the end of a paragraph) interferes with the natural wrapping of the text on the page, or within a table cell or layer. Using the Enter key to control the flow (or *wrap*) of text within a paragraph is tempting, but if you've forced paragraph breaks within a group of lines or sentences, this approach might create undesirable effects when you resize the window that contains the text. Rather than rewrapping to fit the new window size, your paragraph will end up with odd gaps wherever you used the Enter key to force text onto the next line (see Figure 3.3).

Selecting and Editing Headings

After you type your heading text, you can select the text with your mouse or use the Shift and arrow keys. When you use your mouse, you can drag through the text or simply click in the left margin to select the entire line to the right of

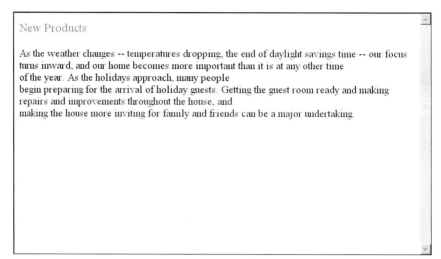

Figure 3.3

Let your paragraph text flow naturally so that when visitors resize the Web page window the text wraps nicely within the reduced confines of the page.

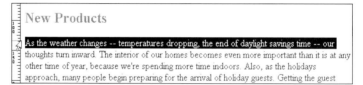

Figure 3.4

You can select a heading that is by itself on a line with a single click in the left margin.

your mouse pointer (see Figure 3.4). You can drag down the left margin with your mouse to select a series of lines or paragraphs, stopping when you have all the text you want. You can hold down the Shift key and press the arrow key(s), or hold the Shift key and click with your mouse, to extend or reduce your selection if you dragged too far or stopped before you selected everything you needed. To select a single word, double-click it.

After you've selected the text you want, you can apply formats, or you can edit the text. While text is selected, the very next thing you type will replace the selected text. For this reason, be careful when you select text—you can easily bump a key on your keyboard and find that you've replaced your heading (or any selected text) with a random character (or with a blank line if you accidentally bumped the Enter key). This instant swapping of content is a great feature, however, if you want to replace text—a name or date, for example. Simply select the content that needs replacing, and type the replacement text. (Whether the replacement and original text were of the same length doesn't matter.)

If you need to correct a misspelling or make some small change to your heading text, position the cursor within the text and use the Backspace or Delete keys; don't select the entire heading.

Text Formatting

When your text is selected, you can format it using the Properties Inspector. The Format option lets you apply up to six different Heading styles, plus None (which means text remains in the default font and size), Paragraph (which is

A Is for All

To select all of your page content, press Ctrl+A. Bear in mind that this technique will select everything, including graphics. So for the purposes of text formatting, it's best to use this shortcut if your page consists solely of text and if you can apply the format you want to all of that text.

essentially the same as None), and Preformatted, which puts your text in a bare-bones Courier font and turns off word wrap.

If you don't like any of the styles available through the Format option (or, if you want to tweak what the selected style has done to your selected text— perhaps increasing the font size of text formatted as Heading 1), you can use the Font and Size options to change the appearance of your text. The fonts acceptable to most Web browsers are few in number. The list of fonts you see when you click the Font option are the fonts that are safe to use with any browser—even the older versions of those browsers that some of your site's visitors might be using (see Figure 3.5).

You can add to the list of fonts by choosing Edit Font List from the list of available fonts. The Edit Font List dialog box opens, through which you can select any font installed on your computer and add that font to the Font list. Once a font is on that list, you can apply it to any text in your Web page. Bear in mind, however, that the font might not display properly in some (or any) browsers. Always use Dreamweaver's Preview In Browser button to verify that your content and its formatting look right when viewed through Netscape and Internet Explorer—and don't assume that if things look OK in one browser they'll look the same way in another—always check both.

Spelling and Saving

Unlike current word-processing applications (such as Microsoft Word) to which many of us have become accustomed, Dreamweaver doesn't give you the option to check your spelling as you type. You must remember, therefore, to run spell check before you post any page to the Web, or submit it to a client or co-worker for approval. Choose Text|Check Spelling (or press Shift+F7) to begin the spell-checking process. Remember to repeat the process as you add or edit text within your document, and to save the document after each spell check.

Figure 3.5

For text you type in your Web page (as opposed to text you insert as a graphic), stick to the basic fonts: Times New Roman, Verdana, Arial, and Courier.

Applying Fonts and Sizes

If you're a seasoned word processor, perhaps familiar with applications such as Microsoft Word or Corel WordPerfect, you're used to the point system for font sizes. You're accustomed to using 10- and 12-point text for business letters, and you know that an inch contains 72 points, which means that each character of 14-point text is roughly one-fifth of an inch high. When you're formatting text on a Web page, however, you won't be using the point system. Instead, Dreamweaver offers font sizes 1 through 7, which are sizes above and below the *base font* size of 3 (sizes +1 through +7, and –1 through –7). Size 3 is the equivalent of whatever your default font size is, as set in your default Web browser software. Unlike the Heading style numbers, in which the smaller the heading number is, the larger the text, the font size numbers are truly indicative of size. As shown in Figure 3.6, a small font-size number results in small text, and a large font-size number results in large text.

One's Not the Loneliest Number—It's the Biggest

The smaller the Heading format number is (Heading 1, for example), the larger the font size. Heading 6 is the largest heading style number, but this heading style results in tiny text. You can also apply text formats from the Dreamweaver menu, using the Text|Paragraph Format command to view a submenu of the same formats offered through the Properties Inspector.

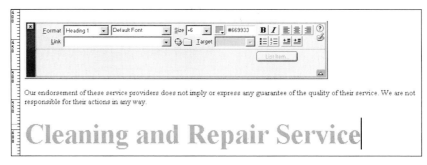

Figure 3.6

Apply font size +6 to text you want to be very large. Size 1 or 2 results in tiny text, great for copyright information at the bottom of a page, or for the "fine print" on a legal document.

Fancy Fonts Need Not Apply

If you want to use a font that's not on the list, don't take the risk that your visitors' browser software doesn't support that font. Create the text as a graphic through a program such as Adobe PhotoShop, and insert the graphic where you want the text. As you'll learn in Chapter 4, this approach lets you create artistic text objects that don't fall prey to the limitations of Netscape and Internet Explorer in their various versions for PC and Macintosh computers.

Clicking for Clues

A blank Font and/or Size option means that you have text selected that's been formatted with more than one font or size. For this reason, don't select text if all you want to do is check the existing formats—just click within the text in question to position your cursor.

To apply a font or size, simply select the text to be formatted and make a selection from the Font and/or Size drop lists. If you're not sure what font or size is in use for existing text, click your mouse to position your cursor in the text in question, and observe the Properties Inspector—it will display the font and size for the text in which your cursor is located.

Applying Text Color

When you type text onto a blank Dreamweaver page, the text appears black by default, but you can change it to any Web-safe color. Dreamweaver offers only Web-safe colors in the Properties Inspector, thus preventing you from applying a color that won't display properly on the Web.

If you know a color's number, you can type that number into the color name box, or you can select a color from the color palette. As you move the mouse pointer (which looks like an eye dropper while the color palette is displayed), the numbers of the colors appear as you hover over them. This display makes using the palette easy (and lets you avoid typing) to choose a color you know by the number. If you don't have a specific color in mind, you can use the palette to select one that works with your page color scheme, and you can make note of the number for use in matching other elements to the text (see Figure 3.7).

Applying Bold and Italic Styles to Text

Making text bold or italic in Dreamweaver couldn't be easier—simply select the text you want to format, and click the B or I button on the Properties Inspector, as shown in Figure 3.8. You can also press Ctrl+B or Ctrl+I to apply these styles with the keyboard. Both techniques work like toggle switches: Apply the format once, and it's "on"; apply the format again (to the same text), and it's "off."

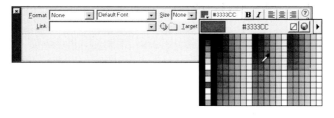

Figure 3.7

Choose a color by eye or by number, using the Properties Inspector and the text color palette within it.

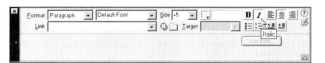

Figure 3.8
The use of bold or italics within a paragraph can draw attention to specific words or phrases. Apply these formats sparingly so their use retains its effectiveness.

The keyboard technique for applying bold or italic is especially useful when you're typing longer paragraphs and want to use either style for emphasis. As you're typing, and you come to the word you want to format, press the keyboard shortcut, and then type the word. Before typing the next word in the sentence, press the keyboard shortcut again to turn the formatting off, then continue typing.

Text Alignment

A hallmark of a well-designed Web page is consistent horizontal alignment throughout the page. If the main elements of the page—the items that immediately pull the visitor's focus—are centered, for example, virtually everything else on the page should be centered, too—at least within each element's region of the page. For that reason, you'll want to make use of Dreamweaver's alignment tools to adjust the position of text on the page, within table cells, and inside layers and frames, as well.

Vertical alignment is another story, and your choices for aligning items vertically (within table cells, layers, and frames) are dictated not so much by a desire for consistency, but for reasons related to composition. A logo or button might be centered within a table cell in one part of your page, but the text might be aligned to the top of a cell somewhere else (if only to eliminate dead space above the text). Each text element should be aligned so that it is close to any graphic to which it relates (or that the text explains/defines), yet far enough from contiguous items (other text, graphics) that nothing impedes a visitor's reading the text.

Choosing Horizontal Text Position

Aligning text horizontally is simple. Select the text, and click the appropriate alignment button on the Properties Inspector, choosing from Align Left, Align Center, or Align Right (see Figure 3.9). The alignment you choose will apply to all of the text in the paragraph if your text is on the page, or to all of the text within the active cell if your text is in a table.

You can apply alignments through the menu by choosing Text|Align and making an alignment selection from the submenu. On the submenu,

What's Your RGB?

You can use a product such as Adobe PhotoShop to find the Web-safe equivalent of colors to use for print work. If, for example, you have brochures or other printed marketing materials and you want your Web site's colors to match, get a color's Pantone number used in the materials (or, if another color model/system was used, get the color's CMYK [cyan/magenta/yellow/black] or RGB [red/green/blue] levels). You can then use PhotoShop to display that color, switch to Web-safe colors, and find the closest match to the original color. Unlike printed materials, for which you can compare one piece to another in the same light—and even spot the slightest differences in color—you won't be able to discern a slight variation between the color of your printed materials and your Web site colors.

Text That Moves Ahead

Using italic text in headings implies action, because the text is leaning to the right, which represents forward motion. With italic font, you can also achieve the appearance of some font variety in your Web page without having two different fonts in use at all. Apply italic font to the headings, and use the same font, without italics, for the paragraphs that follow the heading.

you'll see the following keyboard shortcuts, which you can also use to align selected text:

- *Ctrl+Alt+L*—applies left alignment

- *Ctrl+Alt+R*—applies right alignment

- *Ctrl+Alt+C*—applies center alignment

Figure 3.9

Align your text within the page or a table cell by clicking the alignment buttons in the Properties Inspector.

Aligning Text Vertically

You'll most often apply vertical alignment to text in table cells, and the tools for adjusting the text will appear only when your cursor is in a table cell. When the cursor is in a cell, rather than clicking a button to choose an alignment, you can choose Default, Top, Middle, Bottom, or Baseline from the Properties Inspector's vertical alignment drop list (Vert). The Default setting places your cursor in the vertical center of the cell, which has the same effect as if you choose Middle. Remember that the alignment you choose applies to the cell—not to the text itself. Whatever alignment you apply to the cell will apply to anything placed in the cell—text you type, or a graphic you insert. Figure 3.10 shows text that is vertically aligned to the top of a table cell, which is beneath a centered heading outside of the table.

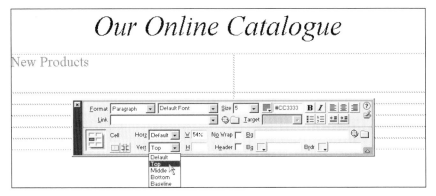

Figure 3.10

Make sure your text starts at the top of a table cell, or right in the center of the page, by clicking the correct alignment button.

The Cell settings in the Properties Inspector also include a Horz (horizontal) alignment option. This option, too, applies to the cell and as a result, to the cell's contents. You can, therefore, apply Align Left to the text, then choose Center for the cell's alignment, and have left-aligned text, together with a centered graphic image, in the cell (see Figure 3.11). When you're aligning text, use the text-alignment buttons. Use the Horz setting for graphic cell content.

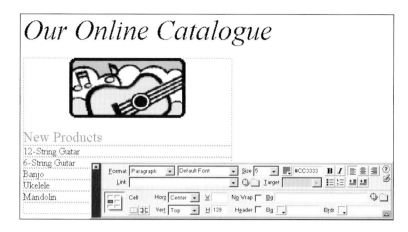

Figure 3.11
Horizontal cell alignment is best applied to graphics in cells, not to text.

PROJECT Create Eye-Catching Web-Page Headings

If you can grab your site visitor's attention in the first few seconds after his or her arrival at your site, you've accomplished a great deal. Many sites don't make clear what information/products/services they're offering. Because the text is vague—even if the visitor is compelled to spend the time to try to figure it out—he or she might end up leaving, never to return. With the abundance of Web sites available to anyone these days, you must do your best to make your point—and make it clearly and quickly.

This project takes you through the process of starting a new Web page, entering heading text, and formatting that text so that it's easy to read and large enough to be seen immediately—it stands out among the paragraph text and any graphics you might add later.

Start a New Web Page

When you open the Dreamweaver application, a new, blank Web page is provided automatically. If you already have Dreamweaver open and need a new page, choose File|New. A new page appears on top of any currently open pages, and a Taskbar button is added to represent the new page, too.

Type Your Headings

Create the page you see in Figure 3.12 by typing a series of three (3) headings:

```
Our Mission
Our Subscribers
Join Today!
```

Format Your Headings

Once you've typed them, you need to format your headings as headings—either by choosing a Heading 1 or Heading 2 style from the Format list, or by applying a preferred font and large font size to the heading text.

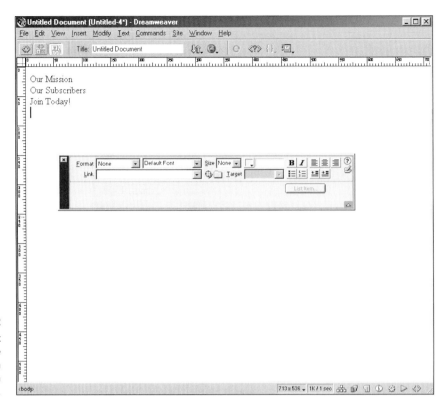

Figure 3.12

Three simple headings represent the beginning of an informative Web page that describes a news-gathering and -distribution Web site.

1. Format the three headings (as Figure 3.13 shows).

2. For the font, choose Verdana.

3. Choose 6 for the font size.

4. Apply center alignment to all three headings.

5. Enter a color number for the text using #3333CC—a bright, but dark, shade of blue.

6. Apply the italic style to the Join Today! heading. This heading asks the visitor to take an action, and italic text implies action through its forward slant.

Insert Paragraphs below Each Heading

Using the Project3A document you will find on the CD-ROM, copy the appropriate paragraphs from the document and paste them below each heading. To paste and format the paragraphs properly, follow these steps:

1. Open the Project3A document on the CD-ROM.

2. Select the paragraph below the Our Mission heading.

3. Copy the selected paragraph to the clipboard by pressing Ctrl+C or by choosing Edit|Copy.

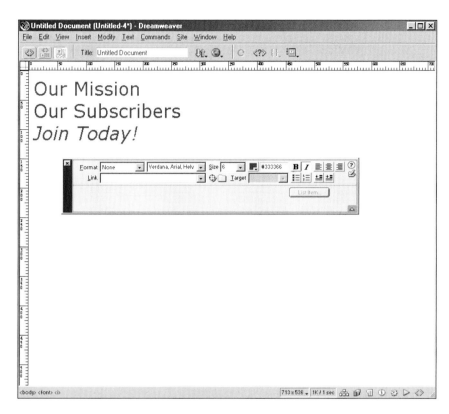

Figure 3.13

Choose a clean, crisp font, and make it big enough to stand out.

4. Switch back to your Web page, and click at the end of the Our Mission heading.

5. Press Enter to move down one blank line, inserting a paragraph break.

6. Paste the paragraph by pressing Ctrl+V, or by choosing Edit|Paste. Note that the paragraph appears in the style of the heading, because the formatting of the heading has been carried forward to the new paragraph.

7. Select the paragraph text, and apply the Paragraph format to it.

8. Change the text color of the paragraph to black (#000000).

9. Repeat Steps 2 through 8 for the Our Subscribers and Join Today! paragraphs in the Project3A document, pasting the paragraphs beneath the Our Subscribers and Join Today! headings, respectively.

Figure 3.14 shows the Web page after you have pasted and formatted the paragraphs as described in Steps 1 through 8.

Save the Page

Save the page you've just created—always an important step. For the purposes of this project, call the saved page mainpage.htm.

Figure 3.14

Copy the Our Mission paragraph, and paste it below the Our Mission heading, paste the Our Subscribers paragraph below the Our Subscribers heading, and insert the Join Today! paragraph below the Join Today! heading.

Indents, Bullets, and Numbering

Although most Website text is either headings or simple paragraph text, you will at times need to visually demote text, either by indenting it or by creating lists—of items, steps in a procedure, or terms and accompanying definitions. Dreamweaver gives you the capability to indent text and create these lists, making it possible to include driving directions or step-by-step instructions, to create bulleted lists, and to build lists with no bullets or numbers (known as *unordered lists*) on your Web site.

The Properties Inspector is your primary tool for indenting text and for creating bulleted and numbered lists. You can also use the Text menu, choosing Text|List, and then selecting the type of list you want to create. The Text menu provides the only access to Unordered and Definitions lists, while the more common bulleted and numbered (Ordered) list tools are represented on the Properties Inspector, along with the Text Indent and Text Outdent buttons, as Figure 3.15 shows.

When you use the menu (Text|List), select from the following submenu items:

- *None*—Apply this option if you want to remove existing indent or list settings.

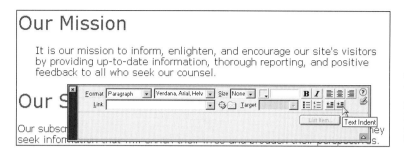

Figure 3.15

Indent text 35 pixels at a time with the Text Indent button. The Text Outdent button moves text back toward the left margin, removing indents you have applied with the Text Indent button.

- *Unordered List*—An unordered list is simply a bulleted list. You can apply Unordered List to a series of words (each word on its own line, as Figure 3.16 shows) or a series of paragraphs. The text is indented, and the default bullet appears in front of it.

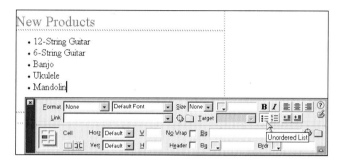

Figure 3.16

Bulleted lists are great for products, services, or features you want to highlight on a Web page.

- *Ordered List*—You will use ordered lists for words, sentences, or paragraphs that must appear in a particular order, or that represent instructions or tasks that must be performed in order (see Figure 3.17). The numbers 1, 2, 3, and so on precede the text in an ordered list and, if you remove or add text to the list, the numbering is automatically updated.

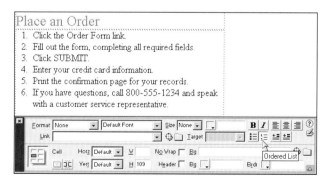

Figure 3.17

If your Web page includes instructions or a list of prioritized items, apply an Ordered (numbered) List format.

- *Definitions List*—A Definitions List lets you type a term at the margin, and the subsequent paragraph will be indented 35 pixels. In word-processing lingo, this process creates the equivalent of a *hanging indent*. You can use this formatting for lists of defined terms, product descriptions, or clauses in a legal document. Figure 3.18 shows a list formatted as a Definitions List.

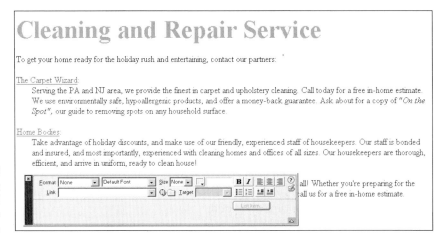

Figure 3.18
The first line of a Definitions List paragraph is not indented, but all subsequent wrapped lines in the paragraph are.

Indenting Text

To indent text, you must select the text to be indented, and then employ one of the following methods:

- Click the Text Indent button on the Properties Inspector.

- Choose Text|Indent on the menu.

- Press Ctrl+].

You can apply indents repeatedly, moving the text farther and farther toward the page center in 35-pixel increments. If you've indented text too far, use the Text Outdent button on the Properties Inspector, choose Text|Outdent from the menu, or press Ctrl+[. Each issue of the command—be it from the palette, menu, or keyboard—moves the text 35 pixels toward the left margin. Once you're back at the margin, the command has no effect.

Creating Ordered Lists with Custom Bullets

To bullet a list, select the text, and then choose one of the following methods to turn the selected text into an *unordered* list:

- Click the Unordered List button on the Properties Inspector.

- Choose Text|List|Unordered List.

You can change the default bullet (a small, filled circle) through the use of HTML (hypertext markup language) attributes. If you want a square bullet, add the following to your <**ul**> tag:

```
type="square"
```

To turn your bullets to small, unfilled circles, add this to the <**ul**> tag:

```
type="circle"
```

Designating no attribute, of course, leaves the default filled circle.

Numbering and Customizing an Ordered List

You employ the same process that creates an unordered or bulleted list to create an ordered or numbered list. Simply select the text to be numbered, and click the Ordered List button on the Properties Inspector. If you prefer to use the menu, choose Text|List|Ordered List.

By default, the list is numbered in Arabic numbers 1, 2, 3, and so on. If you want to use uppercase or lowercase letters of the alphabet, or Roman numerals (also in uppercase or lowercase), you can use the following HTML attributes, added to the <**ol**> tag at the beginning of the list.

For uppercase letters of the alphabet, add:

```
type="A"
```

For lowercase letters of the alphabet, add:

```
type="a"
```

When you want your numbered list to be preceded by Roman numerals, use the following attribute for uppercase:

```
type="I"
```

For lowercase, use:

```
type="i"
```

Creating Outlines with Bullets or Numbers

Obviously, creating a simple list of bulleted or numbered words or paragraphs is quite easy. But what if you need to create a list that indicates levels, or a hierarchy, within the list? You can achieve this result using indents and ordered or unordered lists. The number of indents you insert in front of a paragraph (remember that a single word followed by the Enter key is technically a paragraph) indicates the paragraph's rank in the outline.

For example, text with no indents in front of it is at the first level of the outline, text with a single indent is at the second level, text with two indents is at the third level, and so on. Figure 3.19 shows a typed series of items, indented in preparation for creating a numbered (ordered) outline list.

After you type and indent the items in the list, select the entire list, and apply an Ordered List if you want the outline to be numbered (in Arabic numbers, Roman numerals, or letters of the alphabet), or an Unordered List if you want bullets. When you apply an Unordered List, your outline levels will have different bullets—circles for the second level and squares for the third and subsequent levels (see Figure 3.20).

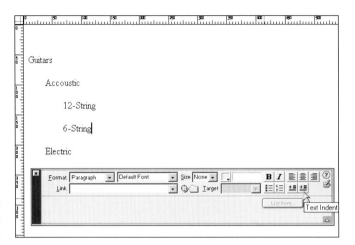

Figure 3.19
Assign rank within the outline by indenting items in your list.

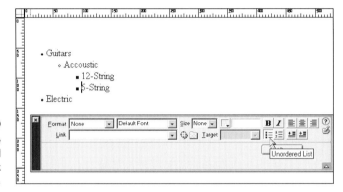

Figure 3.20
An Unordered List outline uses different bullet points (and indentation) to indicate rank within the outline.

Show Us the Code

Don't forget the Code view and Design view buttons on the Dreamweaver toolbar. The inclusion of this split-screen view is one of Dreamweaver 4's most useful enhancements. Through this view, you can easily select the text in your outline, then view the code and add the necessary attributes.

When you apply an Ordered List to a series of items, the process becomes a little more complex in terms of having the numbers (or letters) increment properly throughout the ranked items in the list. Each time you indent a line, a new <ol> tag is created in HTML, and you have to insert the type="A" (using uppercase Roman numerals as an example) attribute into the <ol> tag. Figure 3.21 shows the split Design and Code views, and an outline that's been formatted properly for each level in the outline.

Defining Text with Horizontal Rules

Horizontal rules provide simple, graphical breaks between sections of your Web page. Horizontal rules are especially useful for breaking up paragraphs of text, and you can use them in conjunction with an accompanying heading to further emphasize a change in topic, thus increasing the effectiveness of the heading. Figure 3.22 shows a horizontal rule that helps define the sections on a Web page.

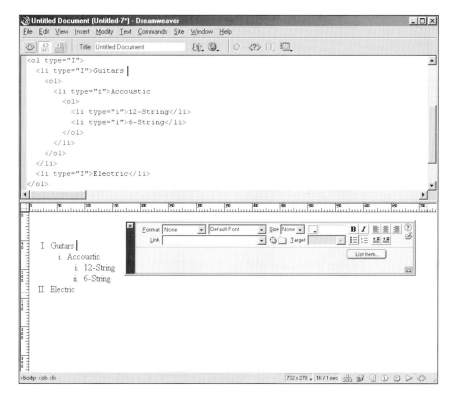

Figure 3.21

An outline with uppercase Roman numerals for first-level items and lowercase Roman numerals for second-level items is easy to create with a little HTML editing.

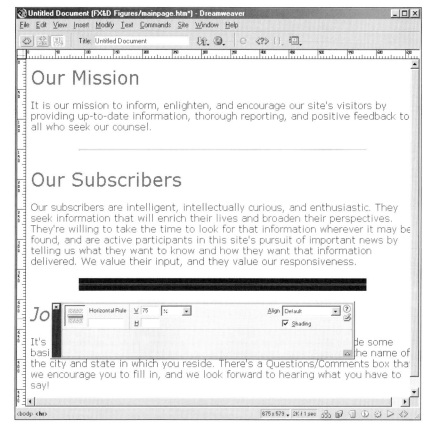

Figure 3.22

Horizontal rules can create a visual break between topical areas of your Web page.

Inserting a Horizontal Rule

To add a horizontal rule to your Web page, choose Insert|Horizontal Rule. Depending on the other formatting and content of the page at the point where you choose to insert the rule, it should span the width of your page and be a single pixel thick. If an ordered or unordered list is in force at the point where you insert the rule, the rule will be indented to match the surrounding text. Figure 3.23 shows a horizontal rule that spans the entire Web page, following a paragraph of text.

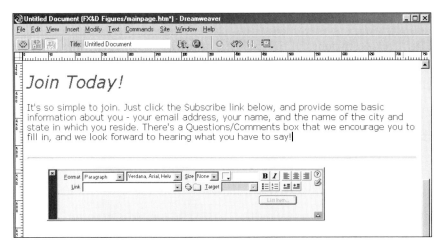

Figure 3.23

By default, a horizontal rule spans 100 percent of the width of your Web page. You can easily shorten the rule, then change its alignment, as needed.

Customizing a Rule

You can change three things about a horizontal rule—its length, its height (thickness), and its alignment on the page. You can make all these changes through the Properties Inspector, which changes to offer horizontal-rule tools when a horizontal rule is inserted and selected on the page (see Figure 3.24).

Figure 3.24

When a horizontal rule is selected, the tools you'll need to customize it are displayed on the Properties Inspector.

You can define the rule's width (W) in pixels, or as a percentage of the page. Your choice depends on how you think about the rule's role on the page. If the rule should be exactly as wide as an existing, centered heading, for example, display the ruler (View|Rulers|Show), and note the pixel width of the heading. Enter that same pixel width in the Properties Inspector for the selected rule, and choose Center from the Align list.

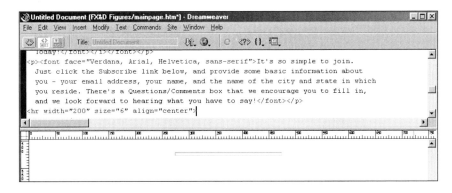

Figure 3.25
You can make your horizontal rule short or long, thick or thin, and position it horizontally to the left, right, or center of your page.

To adjust the height (H), or thickness, of a horizontal rule, enter the pixel height into the Properties Inspector. Figure 3.25 shows a horizontal rule that's 200 pixels wide and 6 pixels high.

To change the color of your horizontal rule, you can add a color attribute to the <**hr**> tag, such as this:

```
hr color="red"
```

You can, of course, use a color number in the attribute, such as #CC3333 for a purple shade.

HTML Text Handling

As evidenced by the procedures for entering, editing, and formatting text as I've described them in this chapter, you need to do very little of your text handling through HTML—Dreamweaver is more than capable of generating the appropriate HTML code and executing your commands for the content and appearance of your Web page text. What happens, however, if you're forced to edit your Web page on a computer that doesn't have Dreamweaver installed on it? And how do you handle the situation when you want to apply formats, but Dreamweaver doesn't give you the tools or commands to do so?

In the first case, you'll simply need a text-editing program, such as Notepad (a Windows Accessory), or TextPad, a popular shareware program. If you have Dreamweaver at your disposal, and you simply find HTML easier or faster for applying a format, you can easily use HTML from right within the Dreamweaver window. One of Dreamweaver 4's new features is a group of three view buttons, and each gives you a unique environment in which to build your Web page:

- Code view

- Design and Code views

- Design view

Browser Rules

Only Internet Explorer (versions 4 and 5) will display colored horizontal rules. Netscape will ignore your <**hr**> color attribute and display a gray rule. Because of this, Dreamweaver's Design view will show a gray rule, no matter what color you apply. If you decide to apply a color anyway, and you want to see the color you've applied in use, preview your page in Internet Explorer.

The first two views give you access to your HTML code for the open page; the second of these two views shows you both the Code and Design views at the same time. You can select content within the page before you invoke either of these two views, and the code pertaining to the selected content will be highlighted, as shown in Figure 3.26.

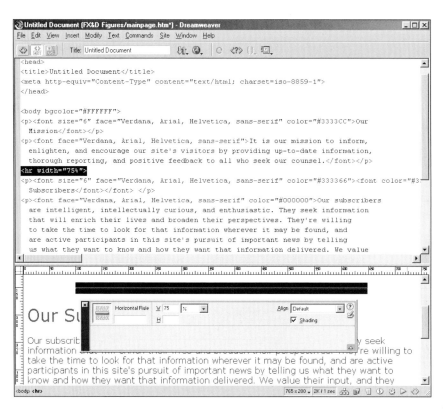

Figure 3.26
If you need to enter a color attribute for your horizontal rule, select the rule, and then click the Design and Code views button to see both your code and the rule in separate panes within the Dreamweaver window.

Editing Text in HTML

Once you're viewing your HTML code, you can edit it. You can add new tags, insert attribute code and of course, edit your text content. You can insert text, delete text, and change the case of text. Through HTML code, you can add and remove paragraph breaks and indents, create ordered and unordered lists, and apply heading styles to text. Figure 3.27 shows Code view and a paragraph with too many paragraph breaks preceding it.

Using Breaks and Spaces to Control Text Flow

Each time you press the Enter key in Design view, you insert a paragraph break. This action inserts a blank line and creates a relatively large vertical space between paragraphs. If you're typing paragraphs of text, and you want to insert a break, but you don't want a big, blank line between your current line of text and the next one, press Shift+Enter instead of Enter. Doing so

Take a Break When You Need One

Not all page breaks are unwanted. You might find page breaks useful when you need extra space at the top of a table cell (when you want vertical space, but you don't want to use a Middle vertical alignment, for example), or when you want to create a distinct visual space between paragraphs.

Figure 3.27
Get rid of unwanted paragraph breaks by deleting the <**p**> and <**/p**> tags that encompass your text.

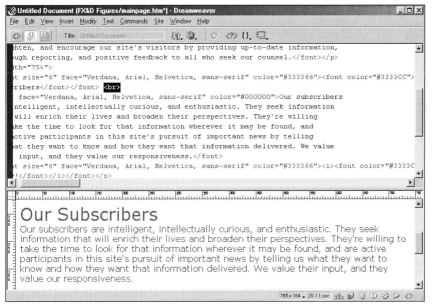

Figure 3.28
A line break creates a visual break between paragraphs but doesn't waste vertical space by adding a blank line.

inserts a <**br**> line-break tag and creates less vertical space than a paragraph <**p**> break (see Figure 3.28). A <**br**> requires no closing tag, so if you're looking at your HTML code for the page, don't assume a closing tag is missing and add one in error.

Build a News and Information Web Page

An online newspaper is a perfect example of a text-heavy Web site, and creating an informative Web page filled with articles that contain a variety of formats is a great way to use the skills you've learned in this chapter.

You might be expecting a newspaper-like layout for this Web page, but you won't find one (see Figure 3.29, which shows how your finished project should look). Instead, you'll find a simple format, with the text of each article filling the width of the page. Why? Because many people have difficulty or are uncomfortable reading large amounts of text onscreen—because of the familiarity of printed documents, of course, and thanks to the computer screen itself—long-term viewing can cause eyestrain. By creating a simple layout, you make your Web page more inviting for people to sit and read, and you make your Web page more printer-friendly (should the site visitor want to print the articles to read later on paper).

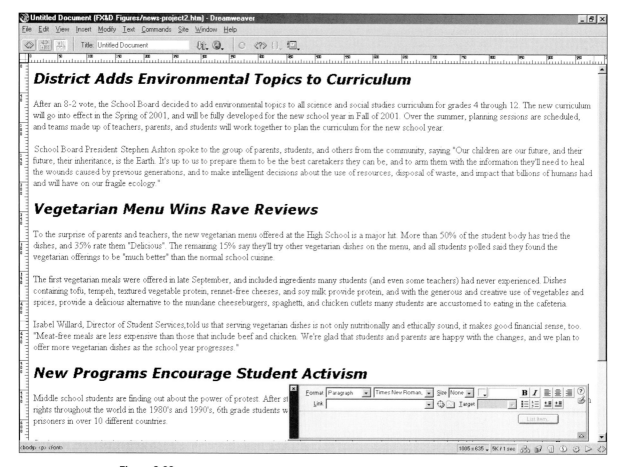

Figure 3.29

Don't make people read snaking newspaper columns onscreen. Give them a simple layout that isn't hard on their eyes.

Create the News Headlines

To start, let's create the headlines:

1. Open a new, blank Web page in Dreamweaver.

2. Type the following headlines, leaving them in the default format (None) for new text on a new, blank Web page:

   District Adds Environmental Topics to Curriculum

   Vegetarian Menu Wins Rave Reviews

   New Programs Encourage Student Activism

3. Press Enter twice after each heading, so that a blank line will separate each heading from its related article text.

4. Save the page as news.htm, and remember to save the page after each phase of the project.

Insert the Article Text

You'll find the text for each article on the CD-ROM, in a file called Project3B. Copy the text for all three articles from this document, and paste the text into the Web page as follows:

1. Select the article under Environmental Topics, and copy that selection to the Clipboard (Ctrl+C or Edit|Copy).

2. Click on the second blank line below District Adds Environmental Topics to Curriculum, and paste the article (Ctrl+V or Edit|Paste).

3. Returning to the Project3B document, select the article under Vegetarian Menu, and copy the selection to the Clipboard.

4. Switch back to Dreamweaver, click on the second blank line below the heading pertaining to a vegetarian menu, and paste the article there.

5. Switch back to Project3B, and copy the text under Activism.

6. Back in Dreamweaver, paste the copied article under the activism-related heading.

7. Apply Heading 1 formats to each heading, and change the font to Arial.

8. Italicize the first and third headings. Leave all three headings left-aligned.

Create Bulleted Lists

The Vegetarian Menu article includes a list of ingredients in the second paragraph. Separate that list from the paragraph with a paragraph break. Then within the list, use Shift+Enter to insert line breaks between each item in the list, which will create an unordered list from the list of meals, as Figure 3.30 shows.

Add Horizontal Rules to Create Visual Sections

Following each article's text, insert horizontal rules that are 75 percent of the page width. Make the rules blue, and make them 3 pixels high. Your project should look like the page you see in Figure 3.31.

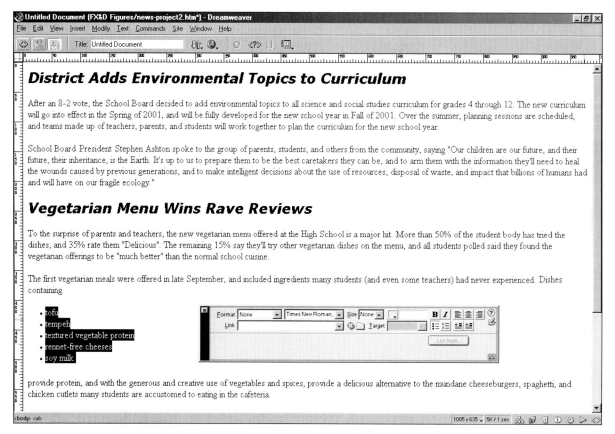

Figure 3.30

Break out the list (remove the commas) and turn it into an unordered, bulleted list. To save vertical space, use line breaks instead of paragraph breaks between each item.

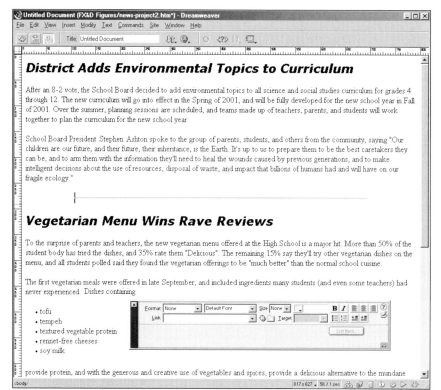

Figure 3.31

Headings, articles with a simple layout, and horizontal rules to visually separate the articles create a news page that's easy to read and a pleasure to look at.

Moving On

The goal of this chapter was to give you a solid foundation in the techniques for entering, editing, and formatting text for maximum legibility and visual impact. Now that your Web page text is in place and looking great, you can begin inserting well-chosen graphics to add visual interest and information to your Web page. Chapter 4 will help you choose the right file formats, keep the size of your graphic files under control (to speed the page-loading process for your site's visitors), and create movement and texture with rollover images (graphics that change when a site visitor's mouse moves over them) and page backgrounds.

Chapter 4

Effective Use of Graphics

Graphics—photographs, drawings, clip-art images, interesting shapes and lines—on a Web page draw people in and keep their attention. Chapter 4 will help you understand the Web's requirements when it comes to graphics: what file formats work well with popular Web browsers, and how to select and position your graphics for maximum effectiveness.

Appropriate File Formats

Who decides what file formats are appropriate for the Web? The Web browsers do. The World Wide Web Consortium (also known as the W3C) is the closest thing to a governing body for the Web, but in reality, Web designers design for the capabilities of the two main Web browsers: Microsoft Internet Explorer and Netscape. Beyond working with the current versions of these two browsers, Web designers also think about what works in the browsers' previous versions—some visitors have older versions of the browsers, and each version affects how a Web page appears when those visitors display a Web site on their computers.

When it comes to graphics, the current versions of Internet Explorer and Netscape display three bitmapped file formats:

- GIF (Graphic Interchange Format)

- JPEG (named for the Joint Photographic Expert Group, which created the format)

- PNG (Portable Network Graphics)

If you have images that you need to use on your Web site, and the files are not currently saved in one of these formats, you can convert them to GIF, JPEG, or PNG by opening them in an image-editing product such as Adobe PhotoShop or Microsoft Photo Editor (you can also use both of these applications for images other than photographs). Or you can convert the files from within the File menu: Choose a Save command that gives you the choice to save in one of these Web-safe formats.

Understanding Browser Requirements

Why can't browsers display graphic formats other than these three (GIF, JPEG, PNG)? Because other graphic file formats—namely, vector formats—store information differently. Vector file formats (used in files created in such programs as QuarkXpress, Adobe Illustrator, and CorelDraw) store the graphic image as a set of mathematical instructions, and browser software doesn't interpret this information properly. Bitmap file formats, however, store graphic information as a series of color and placement values (for each pixel in the image), which browsers can easily interpret and display. Figure 4.1 shows a close-up view of a bitmap graphic, which clearly shows the individual pixels in the image.

Choosing the Right Format

So you have three formats to choose from for your Web pages. How do you choose which format to use? Your choice depends on the visual content and quality of the image at hand. Different formats are better for different types of images, and within this range of Web-safe formats, you want to choose the one that will give you the highest quality image:

But What's a Bitmap?

Bitmap files (which have a .bmp, .gif, .jpg, or .png file extension, with the latter three being Web-safe) are so named because each bit in the image is mapped. This means that each pixel of the image is stored, and the pixel's position and color information is part of the file's format. This mapping explains why the size (dimensions) of the image dictate the file size. An image that's resized to be 50 percent larger than it was originally will also have a 50 percent larger file size—the enlarged file has more pixels to store, more bits to be mapped.

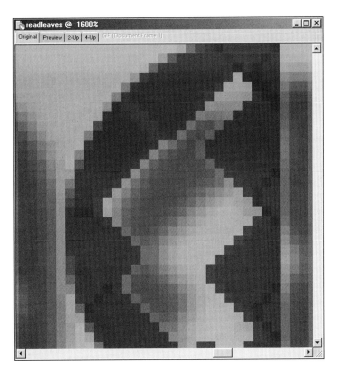

Figure 4.1

Zoom in on a GIF, JPEG, or PNG file and view the individual pixels. Each file's color information is stored as part of the file, and the browser interprets and displays that information.

- *GIF*—For line art, such as logos, drawn shapes and lines, and images without a lot of different colors in them, choose GIF (see Figure 4.2). This is not to say that you can use the GIF format only for simple images—assume no such restriction. Rather, even for complex images with drop shadows, shading, and overlapping colors, the GIF format is quite effective. The GIF format relies on a 256-color palette. So for clip-art images, drawings, or images composed of solid fills and simple patterns, the GIF format is appropriate.

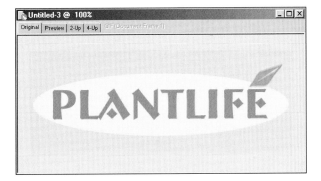

Figure 4.2

A logo composed of text and geometric shapes and lines is a perfect image for the GIF format.

- *JPEG*—Photographs, complex textures, and shapes with picture fills (such as marble or burlap) are best saved in a JPEG format. Why? Because the JPEG format, rather than relying on a fixed palette (as the GIF format does), stores the color information in each pixel. For photographs, in which what appears to be a solid color (as in the leaves shown in Figure 4.3) is made up of hundreds of different colored pixels, this unlimited color capability is essential.

- *PNG*—Slowly gaining popularity (slowly, because it creates challenges for Web programmers), the PNG format is fine for line art or photographs. This format supports both images with a limited palette (which you'd normally save as GIF files) and images that need millions of colors (for which you'd typically choose the JPEG format). This would seem to say that PNG is the best format to choose, but that's not the case. Because only the most recent versions of browsers recognize the PNG format, you don't want to choose this format unless you know that your audience is using only the latest and greatest browser software.

The only environment where you can know absolutely that everyone is using the most current browser is in an *intranet* situation, in which the intranet's Web pages can be viewed only through an organization's computers, under that organization's roof or via password by specific users. If your Web pages will be on the Internet, and available to everyone with a PC, you don't want to risk that the users' browsers won't display PNG files.

When in Doubt

If you're not sure which format to use, use JPEG. The JPEG format will work well for both simple graphics and complex photographic images. You're better off putting more power than necessary behind a graphic than compromising the image's appearance by applying a format that doesn't fully or accurately display the image colors.

Controlling Graphic Size

You won't find too many things that will compromise the effectiveness of your page as reliably as slow-loading graphics. If visitors must wait for images to appear, and if that wait is longer than a second or two, visitors will remember the delay. If alternate sites offer the same content as your site, and their graphics load faster than yours, visitors might not return to your site. To avoid this problem, keep your file sizes as small as possible—all well below 35KB.

Why is 35KB a good limit? Because, to be safe, Web designers should plan for the worst-case scenario—a visitor dialing in at 28.8Kbps. For the 28.8Kbps modem user, every kilobyte of file will take up to 1 second to load, which means that a 5KB file could take 5 seconds to load. Many graphics will be much larger, and you don't want people waiting for 30+ seconds for your images to appear. Thirty seconds isn't a long time to wait for food in the microwave, but in the split-second timeframes we've come to expect from computers, visitors are likely to consider 30 seconds an interminable delay.

Of course, most visitors will be using a 56.6Kbps modem (or a cable modem, a DSL connection, or a T1 line from the office), and you can assume about two-tenths of a second transfer rate per kilobyte of file size. This trend toward faster connections for most users doesn't raise the maximum recommended file size, however. A 50KB file will still take 10 seconds to load, and that's a long time. Planning for the worst case is best, so that none of your visitors are annoyed by a delay and leave your site before the file completely loads—or if they do wait for the file to load, vow never to return.

Interlaced GIFs and Progressive JPEGs

If you have a large file (35KB or larger) and you can't reduce it—either because you need the image to be big on the page, or you feel you can't sacrifice image clarity or detail for faster loading (by reducing the resolution of the image)—save the file as an Interlaced GIF or a Progressive JPEG. These terms mean that the image will appear immediately when the page loads, but it will appear blurry/choppy, and slowly compose (as Figure 4.4 shows), clearing up within the timeframes (seconds per kilobyte) I discussed previously. Using these progressive-loading options when you save your GIF or JPEG files lets the visitor know something's coming; this approach can increase his or her willingness to wait as the image clears up.

Figure 4.4
Even with the graphic in its blurry state, the visitor can tell what's coming and is more likely to wait for the image to compose entirely.

Understanding Resolution and Size

A bitmap file's dimensions (width and height, measured in pixels) and resolution or depth (pixels per inch) dictate its size. These measurements might sound as if they're the same thing, but they're really not. Pixel depth or resolution determines how much detail is retained when an image is scanned or a digital image is captured with a camera. The image dimensions refer to the size of the image when it's measured on screen. You can have a large image in terms of how much room it takes up on the page, but that same image can have very low resolution (resulting in less detail within the image itself). The end result in this case is an image with a smaller file size than an image that has the same dimensions but a higher resolution.

Alternatively, a file that's small in terms of width and height can be very large if the resolution is high—such as a photograph that was scanned at 300 ppi (pixels per inch) so that a detailed pattern or small item within the photo would appear clearly on screen. Figures 4.5 and 4.6 show the same image captured at two different resolutions.

Figure 4.5
(Left) A file of 28KB was scanned at a lower resolution (100 ppi), and the fine details are less visible, giving the user less content to work with when cleaning up the picture.

Figure 4.6
(Right) Scanning at a higher resolution has enhanced the detail in this old, faded photograph. The file size at 300 ppi is 736KB, and the file will be reduced in resolution (and therefore size) after it is retouched.

Adjusting Graphic File Size

When you scan or otherwise capture an image, it's a good idea to use a higher resolution for the scanning/capture than you will want to retain when you save the file for use on the Web. By scanning at a higher resolution, you obtain more of the image—more detail, more color information—which gives you more to work with as you retouch or edit the image. Once the image looks the way you want it to, you can reduce the resolution through your image-editing software. When you use Macromedia Fireworks, for example, you can choose Modify|Image Size and reduce the resolution via the resulting dialog box (as

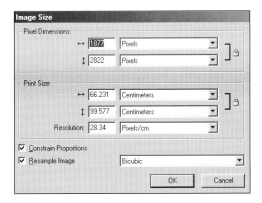

Figure 4.7

After you tinker with the image, reduce the resolution so that the file size is within tolerable limits for fast loading on the Web.

Figure 4.7 shows). By reducing image resolution, you reduce file size, thus increasing the speed at which the image will load when people visit the page.

If you can't reduce the resolution initially, or you can't reduce it further after some reduction (and your file size is still too high), consider reducing the image dimensions. Reducing an image from 300×200 pixels to 200×100 pixels will significantly cut the file size. As Figure 4.8 shows, the graphic is just as clear and will convey the same information in the smaller size as it would have in the larger size; yet because the file size is smaller, the image will load much more quickly.

Figure 4.8

Losing half an inch of width and/or height rarely reduces an image's effectiveness on the Web page, and the increased loading speed more than makes up for any loss of impact.

Using Graphic Text

As you discovered in Chapter 3, a limited list of Web-safe fonts is available to you through Dreamweaver, or through any Web design medium. Certainly, no designer wants to be limited to Times New Roman, Arial, Helvetica, Courier, or Verdana fonts—the restriction would result in every page on the Web looking like every other page on the Web.

So how do you work around the font limitations? Dreamweaver lets you add to the list of fonts you can apply to text in your page by selecting fonts from those you have installed on your computer, but as I discussed in Chapter 3, using those fonts can result in your text not appearing properly in some browsers or versions thereof. The better approach is to create graphic text—text objects that are really graphics. As Figure 4.9 shows, text that plays the role of a heading, or that serves as a link to other pages within the site, benefits from the use of more interesting fonts than those on the Web-safe list. The text you see in this figure was typed and formatted in an illustration application and saved as a graphic file in a Web-safe format.

Figure 4.9

Graphics that consist of text and a background color are so small (this one is just 2KB) that they appear nearly as quickly as text that was typed directly onto the page.

Keeping Images in Site (Sight)

If you're using Dreamweaver's site-management tools, when you choose the image to insert, you'll be prompted if that image is not in the root folder for the site you're building. You'll be asked if you want to copy the file to that folder; if you click Yes, the image is copied to the folder and appears on your page. If you click No, the image is not copied, and it doesn't appear on the page. However, if you've clicked No because you're circumventing the site tools, you can still post the page and the image to the Web. And assuming the image source tag in your HTML code matches the location of the image file on the Web server, the image will appear in your page on the Web.

Inserting Graphic Images

The process of adding a graphic to your Web page is quite simple. You can use any of the following methods, after you have positioned your cursor at the point where the graphic should appear, be it on the page, within a table cell, or inside a layer:

- Click the Insert Image button on the Objects palette.

- Choose Insert|Image on the menu.

- Press Ctrl+Alt+I.

Any one of these techniques will open the Select Image Source dialog box (see Figure 4.10), through which you can navigate to the drive and folder that contains the image you want to insert and from there select the specific image to add to your Web page. Once inserted, the image appears where you left your cursor at the time you invoked the Insert Image command. The image appears in the dimensions that it had when it was last saved.

After you have inserted an image, you can enter new width and height dimensions for the file, but doing so isn't advisable—especially if your intention is to increase the size of the image. Why? Because bitmap files don't survive the resizing

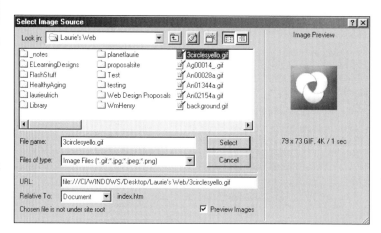

Figure 4.10

Hopefully, you stored your image in an Images folder, or in the root folder for your site. Select the image by double-clicking the file name in the Select Image Source dialog box.

process well when the resizing is done by dragging the image handles to stretch the image horizontally and/or vertically. The edges of the image will become choppy, and on photographs or more complex images, the details of the image will also lose their crisp edges and overall clarity, as Figure 4.11 shows.

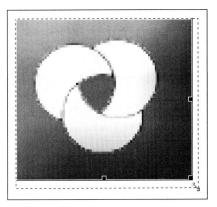

Figure 4.11

If you make an image larger by dragging its handles in the Dreamweaver application window, the image might develop choppy edges and lose overall clarity and crispness.

To avoid this loss of quality, do your image resizing through Fireworks. Choose Modify|Image Size and in the resulting dialog box enter new horizontal and vertical dimensions, as Figure 4.12 shows. If you want to be sure the image retains its current proportions (also known as its *aspect ratio*), make sure you turn on the Constrain Proportions option.

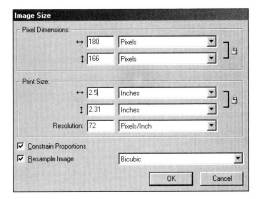

Figure 4.12

Rather than dragging the image handles to stretch the image on the page, resize the image through Fireworks, and save the file.

After you have resized the image through Fireworks, save the new file and return to your Web page. Upon returning to the page, you might notice that the image looks a bit fuzzy—maybe a little choppy or out of proportion (see Figure 4.13). This irregularity results because the size of the displayed image no longer matches the size of the image file. To fix the problem, select the image by clicking on it in the page, then click the Reset Size button in the Properties Inspector. The image is refreshed to the new size.

A File by Any Other Name

If you resize the file but want to leave a version of the image in the original size, give the new-sized file a new name. You'll have to remember to update the image source information for the image in the Properties Inspector by entering the new file name at the end of the path in the Src text box.

Applying a Background Graphic

A background image, rather than a solid page color, can add visual interest to any Web site; a background graphic is especially effective on text-heavy pages that won't include many graphics along with the text. A background graphic is also an effective addition to a site with a lot of graphics—it can provide a cohesive graphical theme on all the pages—to visually tie the pages together.

To apply a background image, follow these steps:

1. With your Web page open in Dreamweaver, choose Modify|Page Properties.

2. In the Page Properties dialog box (see Figure 4.14), click the Browse button to select an image file, or type the path and file name in the Background Image text box.

Backgrounds: Less Is More

Graphic backgrounds should not overwhelm the page content. So on pages with graphics that will appear on top of the background, the background should be as light and simple as possible. If the background will be used with text, avoid using patterns that will interfere with text legibility.

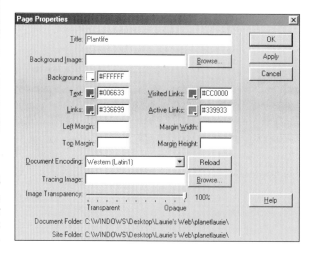

Figure 4.14

Browse to find a graphic image to use as your background, or type the correct path and graphic file name.

3. Click Apply to see the background appear on the page (this action leaves the dialog box open so you can make other page-properties changes), or click OK to apply the background and close the dialog box.

When you apply a background image, the graphic you select is tiled on the page (repeated as many times as necessary to fill the page background), as Figure 4.15 shows. If, for example, your graphic is 100 pixels square and your page is 800 pixels wide by 600 pixels high, the graphic will be repeated eight times across and six times down, to fill the page.

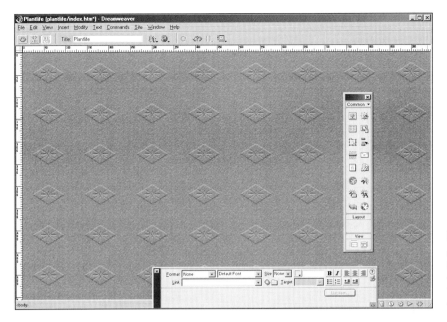

Figure 4.15
A background image is tiled as many times as necessary to fill the page. If your background image is a pattern, the tiling is virtually invisible.

If you don't want your image to be tiled, you have to make the image the same size as your background. Doing this will create a large file, and you might find that the background is the last image to appear when visitors load the page. To avoid that happening, make sure the image has the lowest pixel-per-inch setting—preferably 72 ppi or less.

After viewing the page with its background in place, you can decide whether the background is too bright or busy to work well with the page content, or whether it successfully provides a visually effective backdrop for your page. If the image isn't appropriate, you can use Fireworks to reduce the opacity (make it more transparent) or to apply lighter colors. Figure 4.16 shows a background image that's too intense, and Figure 4.17 shows one that's subtle enough to allow the page content to stand out.

PROJECT Create an Online Catalog

An online catalog can serve as an electronic version of the catalog you've already mailed to customers. The online catalog also saves a company postage and our earth some trees, and it can open up sales opportunities for small companies currently unable to manage the mass-mailing process and/or expense. With what you know about inserting graphic images and positioning Web content, you have the requisite skills to set up an attractive online catalog that provides a structured yet visually interesting collage of product images.

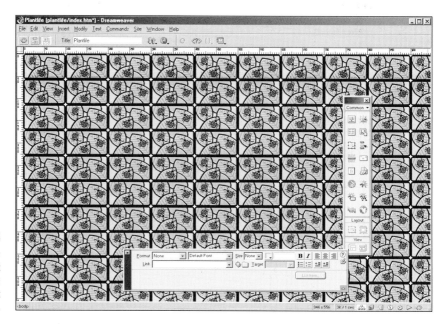

Figure 4.16
A busy pattern or picture with bright colors will make the text hard to read and graphics on top of the background difficult to appreciate.

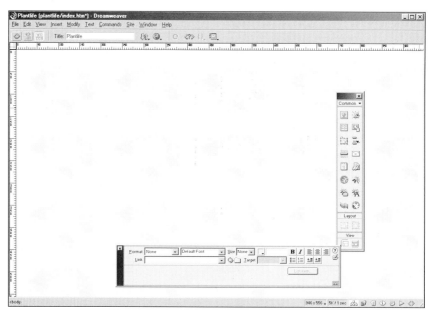

Figure 4.17
An effective background is one that enhances the page but doesn't visually interfere with page content.

Build a Home Page for an Online Catalog

The home page of this online catalog should include the following elements, placed as you see in Figure 4.18:

1. The background image, from the plantlife.jpg file, which you will find in the Project 4A folder on the CD-ROM. The image will tile to fill the entire page.

2. Centered at the top of the page, the graphic from the catalogname.jpg file, which you will find on the CD-ROM in the Project 4A folder.

Figure 4.18
Refer to this image to assist you in setting up your catalog's home page.

3. As Figure 4.18 shows, position the following graphics in pairs: perennials and annuals, herbs and indoor plants. Each image is a JPEG image, and you can find each file in the Project 4A folder on the CD-ROM.

4. Center each pair of images on the page.

5. Across the bottom of the page (on a line below the last graphic), type "For Customer Service or Help Placing an Order, Call 800-555-1234", and format it in the Heading 2 style.

Preview the Catalog in a Browser

To make sure your page will look right online, preview the page in a browser (preferably, use both Internet Explorer and Netscape) to check the formatting of your text, the clarity and position of your images, and the overall look of the page. Choose File|Preview in Browser, or click the Preview/Debug in Browser button, and select the browser you choose to check first from the resulting menu. Figure 4.19 shows the page as it should appear through both Internet Explorer and Netscape.

Save the Catalog Pages

Assuming you like the way the page looks when you preview it (if you don't, go back to the page and make the necessary adjustments), save the page as catalog.htm.

Creating a Rollover Effect

A *rollover image* is so named because the rollover effect occurs when the mouse rolls over the image on the page. Simply pointing to the image will cause it to change. You dictate the image that appears originally, and what the image

Less Is More (Again)

We've all been to Web sites that employ too many rollovers—seemingly anywhere you point your mouse, something moves or changes, which can be disorienting at best, annoying at worst. To avoid this circus-like atmosphere, don't make all of your graphics into rollovers, or people will become immune to their visual and informational effects. Save rollovers for situations in which the movement and change in appearance have an impact.

Figure 4.19

Preview your page to check for correct placement and proper text formatting and to make sure all the page elements look right and work well together.

changes to when the visitor moves the mouse over it, when you set up the rollover effect.

Why use a rollover effect? Consider some of these potential uses:

- *To add visual interest.* An animated GIF image or looping Flash movie running continuously on the page can be distracting. A rollover, on the other hand, provides movement and a change in appearance only when someone points to the original image, so no such distraction occurs.

- *To draw attention to important links.* If you have a graphic set up to work as a link to another page or Web site, unless someone points to the graphic and sees that the mouse pointer turns to a pointing hand, the visitor might not realize the graphic is a link. Even then, the change in the appearance of the mouse is rather subtle—and again the link may remain unexplored. Alternatively, an image that changes when the visitor points to it draws the person's attention, and he or she will then see the mouse pointer change—and follow the link.

Figure 4.20

When someone points to the picture of a person talking on the phone, the image changes to include instructional text.

- *To provide additional information.* Imagine that the graphic that appears when no one is pointing to it is a simple picture, such as a photograph of someone talking on the phone. You hope that visitors will realize this graphic serves as a link to the Customer Service page, on which phone numbers are available. To clear up any confusion, you can turn the image into a rollover. Choose, for example, to have "Customer Service" or "Call Us for More Information" appear on top of the image when someone moves the mouse over the image, as Figure 4.20 shows. How do you do this? You will create two images—one without text on top of the picture, one with text. Read on to find out how to set up these two images to work in concert and create a rollover effect.

Rollover Options and Requirements

Your rollover image is really two images—one image that appears on the Web page when the page first loads and the visitor's mouse is not on the image, and one image that replaces the first image when the visitor points to it. The two images can be completely different—such as a caterpillar and a butterfly—or they can be virtually the same, except that something is added or taken away when the visitor points to the image—such as a whole apple that changes to an apple with a bite taken out of it. Your rollover can be subtle, with two virtually identical images simply changing color, or the latter image acquiring a drop shadow. Or the change can be dramatic, with two completely different (and perhaps unrelated) images being swapped when the visitor's mouse moves onto the image.

While Dreamweaver doesn't attempt to control the content of the two images that make up your rollover image, you do need to keep your images the same size. If you don't, Dreamweaver will do it for you, making the second image the same size as the first. Remember that the size of the image includes any space around the picture or text, so take that into consideration when you're creating images that you will use to create a rollover. Figure 4.21 shows two images in Fireworks, one that will be the first image, and one that will be the second image—the one that appears when someone points to the first image.

To find out more about cropping and resizing images, see Appendix C.

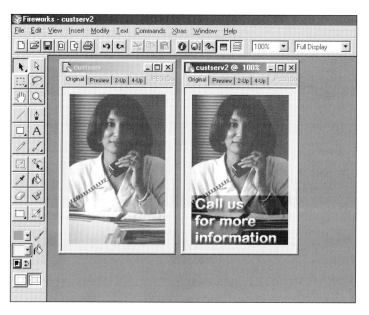

Figure 4.21

The dimensions of the entire image—background and main content—make up the image size.

Creating a Rollover Image

After you've created or otherwise obtained the two graphics you want to use to make your rollover image, you need to tell Dreamweaver which graphics they are. Before you do that, though, make sure you've placed the images in the appropriate folder within your site folders (if you're using Dreamweaver's site-management tools) so that the image source information that is built into the HTML code for your page is accurate and the images are where Dreamweaver expects to find them.

After you've saved or copied the images to the appropriate folder, follow these steps to set up the rollover:

1. Click to position your cursor on the page at the spot where the image should appear. This location can be on the page itself, within a table cell, or inside a layer or frame.

2. Choose Insert|Interactive Images|Rollover Image. The Insert Rollover Image dialog box opens, as you see in Figure 4.22.

Figure 4.22

The Insert Rollover Image dialog box lets you name your image and select the two images that you will use to create the rollover effect.

3. Type a name for the image. This name will appear in the HTML code that's created for your page (see Figure 4.23); the name makes it easier to find this particular rollover image in the code should you need to edit it.

Figure 4.23

References to your figures appear in the HTML code as soon as you name and select the figures through the Dreamweaver dialog boxes.

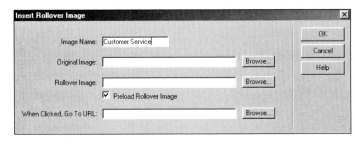

```
<body bgcolor="#FFFFFF" background="plantlife.jpg" onLoad="MM_preloadImages('custserv2.jpg')">
<a href="#" onMouseOut="MM_swapImgRestore()" onMouseOver="MM_swapImage('Customer Service','','custserv2.jpg',1)">
<img name="Customer Services" border="0" src="custserv.jpg" width="165" height="250"></a>
</body>
</html>
```

4. Click the Browse button to the right of the Original Image text box. Of course, if you know the exact path to and file name of the image you want to use, you can type that information into the text box. If you choose to browse for the image, the Original Image dialog box opens, through which you can navigate to and select the image you want.

5. Double-click the image you want to use. This closes the Original Image dialog box and returns you to the Insert Rollover Image dialog box (see Figure 4.24).

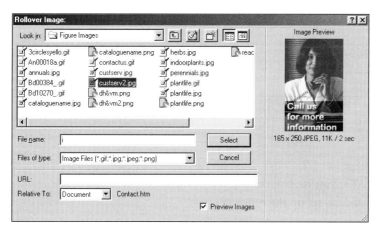

Figure 4.24
Navigate to the folder that contains the image you want to use, then double-click the image name to insert it in the Insert Rollover Image dialog box.

6. Click the Browse button to the right of the Rollover Image text box. Again, if you know the file's location and exact name, type the path and file name in the text box. If not, use the Rollover Image dialog box to locate and select the image you want to use.

7. Double-click the image that you want to use for the rollover. The Rollover Image dialog box closes, and you're back to the Insert Rollover Image dialog box.

8. If your image, when clicked, should take the visitor to another page or Web site, enter the URL of that location in the When Clicked, Go To URL text box (see Figure 4.25). You can also use the Browse button if you want to link the rollover image to another page in your site.

Places, Everyone!

Always put the images (animated and otherwise) in an Images folder, or within the root folder of your site folders, so (a) they're easy to find when you go to insert them, and (b) when you preview the page locally and upload it to the Web, the graphic appears on the page.

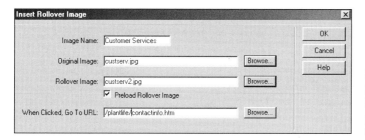

Figure 4.25
Rollover images often function as buttons that are linked to other pages within your site, or to another site entirely.

9. Click OK to create the rollover image based on your file selections. The dialog box closes, and the original image, looking shaded (to indicate that another image is involved), appears on your page, as you see in Figure 4.26.

Using Animated Graphics

Unlike a rollover image, which is two different image files that switch, based on a site visitor's mouse movements, an animated GIF file is a graphic in the GIF format that consists of two or more frames, each containing different

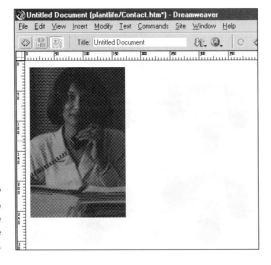

Figure 4.26

When you click on the page to deselect the rollover image, the shading disappears and the original image appears normally.

Testing, Testing, 1, 2, 3

Always test your rollover image in a browser to make sure that you've selected the correct images to serve as your rollover image, and that the rollover's size and placement work well. If you've opted to have the rollover image serve as a link to another page or site, test that, too—click on the rollover image and make sure the proper site or page appears in the browser window. You'll find out more about hyperlinks in Chapter 5.

content. When these frames are viewed in quick succession, they create animation (see Figure 4.27). We've all seen animated GIF files in Web pages—the images that hop, spin, flip, dance—over and over. You can create animated graphics with Macromedia Fireworks (you can find information about how to do that in Appendix C). You can also find animated GIF files, clip art, and fonts on the Web.

Figure 4.27

Through Fireworks, you can create an animated GIF file by placing graphic images in a series of frames.

Animated GIF images are fun, but use them cautiously. Having one animated GIF image spinning/hopping/flipping in the corner of a Web page—perhaps drawing attention to an email link, or one animated GIF image at the top of a page, telling visitors that the site is under construction—is fine. Having more than one animated GIF image on any page (or the portion of a page that can be viewed on screen all at once)—or having one on every page of a Web site— is not so fine, because the movement can be distracting, and you risk making a silly impression. If your Web site advertises your services as a birthday clown, silly can be a good thing. If your site pertains to just about anything else, silly probably isn't an adjective you want to hear used to describe your Web pages.

Inserting an Animated GIF Image

The process of inserting an animated GIF image is the same as inserting any graphic image—the animation is part of the file and is active only when the image is viewed through a Web browser. No special procedure is necessary just because the GIF image is animated. To insert an animated GIF image, choose one of the following methods:

- Choose Insert|Image.

- Click the Insert Image button on the Objects palette.

- Press Ctrl+Alt+I.

From the resulting Select Image Source dialog box, select the GIF file you want to insert (see Figure 4.28). Remember that, once inserted, the image won't animate until you preview the page in a browser or upload it to the Web and view the page online.

> ### Move It or Lose It
>
> If your image doesn't move, that could be because it isn't really an animated GIF image. If the file's extension is .gif, the image might be a simple static image—not one comprising multiple frames. If you have Fireworks, try opening the GIF image in that application, and view the Frames tab in the Layers palette. If you don't see multiple frames, each with different content (or the same content, but in different positions, sizes, and/or colors), the image isn't an animated GIF image.

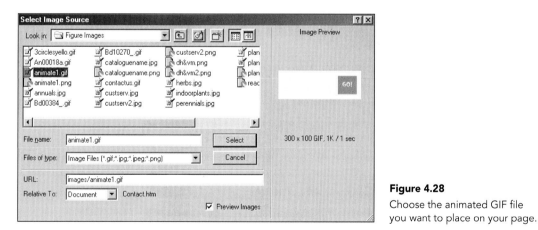

Figure 4.28
Choose the animated GIF file you want to place on your page.

Viewing Animation Effects

To view your animation, click the Preview In Browser button, or choose File|Preview In Browser. When the page opens in Internet Explorer or Netscape (whichever one you've chosen), the animation should start as soon as the image loads.

Create an Advertising Web Page

A Web page that advertises a product or service is a good candidate for movement—both the kind of movement that happens only when the visitor moves the mouse over an image, and the kind of movement that's ongoing, thanks to a looping (repeating), animated GIF image. The use of movement serves two important purposes:

• *Movement immediately grabs the visitor's attention.* Animated graphics, well chosen for content and well placed, grab the visitor's eyes and hold them for a few seconds. The visitor notices surrounding text and graphics more readily because the movement drew focus to that portion of the page.

• *Movement helps move the visitor's eye around the page.* If your page requires scrolling (hopefully, only vertical scrolling), as the visitor scrolls through your page, movement through rollovers, or the discreet use of animated GIF images, can control where the visitor looks. Position important content near animated GIF images so you're sure the visitor reads—or at least skims—the material before he or she moves on.

Figure 4.29 shows the finished page that you'll create in this project. The page consists of a company logo (a nonanimated graphic), heading and paragraph text, rollover images, and animated GIF images. You can transcribe the Heading text from the figure, and you can find the required graphic images on the CD-ROM, in the Project 4B folder.

Figure 4.29
Images, movement, and the requisite text work together to advertise a product and maintain the site visitor's interest.

Insert the Static Logo Graphic

You should insert the company's logo at the top of the page, centered. The logo graphic file is adlogo.jpg and, like the rest of the page graphics, you can find the file in the Project 4B folder on the CD-ROM. Don't resize the graphic or manipulate it in any way beyond centering it horizontally.

Type the Heading and Paragraph Text

Typed one line below the company logo, the heading text serves as a slogan or company statement. Apply the Heading 2 style to the heading text, and change the font to Verdana. You can apply any shade of dark green to the text.

The paragraph text appears next to each of the rollover images, and you can transcribe that text from the figure. Format the text in Verdana font, in Paragraph style.

Create Rollover Images to Add User-Initiated Movement

The rollover images, which you will find down the center of the page, serve as buttons that can be linked to other pages in this company's Web site. Turning the images into links, however, is not important now—the goal is to select the two images for each rollover, as follows:

- For rollover 1, choose bud.jpg for the Original Image and blossom.jpg for the Rollover Image.

- For rollover 2, choose leaftree.jpg for the Original Image and baretree.jpg for the Rollover Image.

- For rollover 3, choose luncheon.jpg for the Original Image and festivefood.jpg for the Rollover Image.

Insert an Animated Graphic for Continuous Activity

The animated graphic you will insert at the foot of the page pulls the visitors' eye down to the bottom of the page, forcing the visitors to look at the entire length of the page. (The logo draws their attention at the top, and then the movement at the bottom of the page draws their focus there.) Insert the callnow.gif file at the bottom of the page, centered. You will find this file on the CD-ROM, in the Project 4B folder.

Test Animations and Rollovers in a Browser

To make sure your rollovers and animated GIF file work properly, preview them in both the Internet Explorer and Netscape browsers.

Save the Advertising Web Page

Save the Web page you have completed as movingad.htm.

Moving On

This chapter's goal was to strengthen your understanding of the role of graphics on Web pages, to help you select the types of graphics that work best on the Web, and to show you how to add graphics to your pages for maximum impact. Chapter 5 will help you use graphics and text as hyperlinks, to create connections to other pages within your Web site and to other Web sites on the Internet.

Chapter 5

Connecting with Hyperlinks

What's a Web page without hyperlinks? A flat page that doesn't go anywhere—literally. This chapter will show you how to create and use hyperlinks to connect the pages within your site, and to connect your pages to other sites, to email addresses, and to files stored on your Web server.

Dreamweaver makes it easy to create the links that give your Web pages both depth and reach, and it also gives you the capability to turn large images into a mosaic of hyperlink regions. You can also use Dreamweaver to provide informative text with any link—text to advise your site visitors about the destination or result of the link they're about to click.

Link Pages within Your Site

Most Web sites consist of several pages—a home page and subpages that contain information about products, services, contact information, and associations. For these pages to function as a cohesive group, visitors must be able to get to one page from another and back again. As anyone who has spent time online knows, hyperlinks (most often referred to simply as *links*) enable this sort of connection between pages. Figure 5.1 shows a home page on the Web, with links that point to subpages within the site.

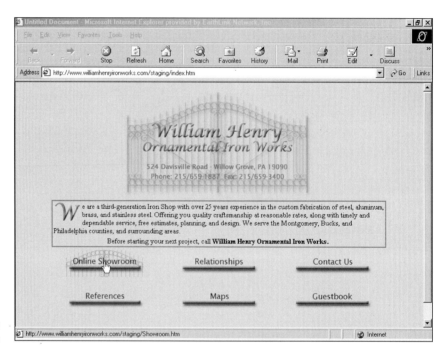

Figure 5.1

You can turn any text or graphic into a link.

Links are easy to establish with Dreamweaver, and you'll do the vast majority of your link setup through the Properties Inspector. You can also establish links using the Site window—but only if you've established a single site for the pages in question, and if you want to create text links (which Dreamweaver inserts automatically) when you connect pages by dragging the page icons within the site map, as shown in Figure 5.2.

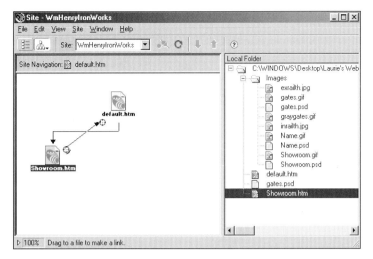

Figure 5.2

You can create text links—new text added automatically and turned into a link—by dragging page icons onto other page icons within the site-map portion of the Site window.

Because you'll probably want to control the placement, content, and appearance of your links, this chapter will concentrate on how to create links from existing text and graphics, using the Properties Inspector and HTML code to do so. Before you set out to create links, you'll want to have a list of your exact page-file names handy—the Site window is a good place to find the names if you're using Dreamweaver's site-management tools. Or simply make a list or open the Windows Explorer to the folder that contains your page files. Figure 5.3 shows a folder of HTML files; each file is a page within the site in progress. You will enter these file names into the Properties Inspector as the linked pages connected to selected text and graphics.

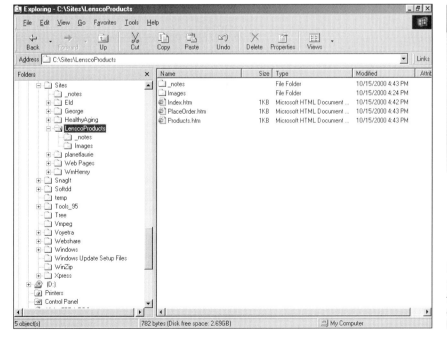

What's in a Name?

If you know what you'll be calling your pages, you can set up links as you design each page, creating links to pages that don't exist yet. As long as you save the pages with the file names you've specified in your links, the links will work once the pages are created.

Figure 5.3

Using any available display of the file names as a reference, you can set up your links after you have built all your pages.

Working with Text Links

Text links are easy on you, because all you need to do to create them is select the text and establish the link information for that text in the Properties Inspector. Text links are easy on your site visitors, because the text itself indicates what will happen or where they'll end up when they click the link, as shown in Figure 5.4.

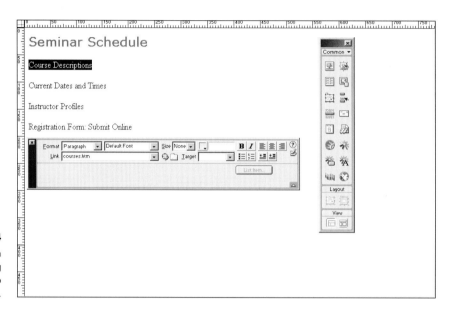

Figure 5.4

Turn any text—a single word, a short phrase by itself, or a string of text within a paragraph—into a hyperlink.

To turn selected text into a hyperlink, follow these steps:

1. If it isn't already displayed, open the Properties Inspector by choosing Properties from the Window menu.

2. Be sure that the selected text is the text you want to serve as a link. Bear in mind that turning the text into a link will cause it to be underlined and, depending on your Page Properties settings, the text might change color.

3. In the Link box in the Properties Inspector, type the exact name of the page to which your selected text will link. If the link is a page within your site, you don't need to type the whole path, because the page to which you're linking and the page you're on will be stored in the same folder on the Web server.

4. If you don't know the file name, or you want to avoid typing it (a good idea if the name is long or is any kind of abbreviation), click the Browse To File button, which opens the Select File dialog box (see Figure 5.5).

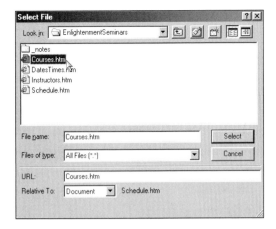

Figure 5.5
Make sure you're selecting an HTML file for the link, and not an image or some other type of file that might have the same name as the desired Web page. I will discuss links to documents and graphics later in this chapter.

5. Double-click the file to which you want the text to link, and the dialog box closes, establishing the link (the link will appear in the box, as shown in Figure 5.6).

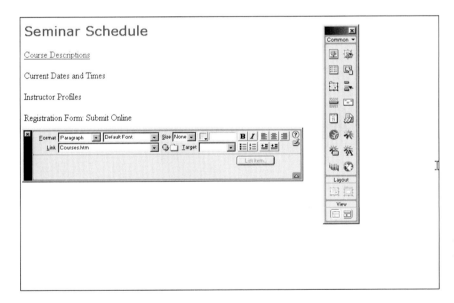

Figure 5.6
The full name of the selected (or typed) file appears in the Link box whenever the hyperlink text is selected.

As I said before, after you've turned your text into a link, the text becomes underlined. The color of the text will change, as well, to the default link color established by your default browser (Internet Explorer or Netscape). If you want to set up a different color for your link text, follow these steps:

1. Choose Page Properties from the Modify menu. The Page Properties dialog box opens, as shown in Figure 5.7.

2. Click the color well for the Links option, and choose a color from the resulting palette. Be sure to choose a color that's compatible with your other page colors, but that still lets your link text stand out. Figure 5.8 shows the process of selecting a color from the palette.

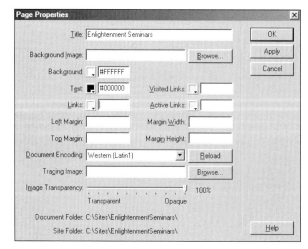

Figure 5.7
When a gray color-well button and no color number appear in the dialog box, you know the link colors are defaulting to your browser link-color settings.

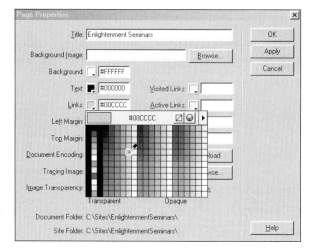

Figure 5.8
If you know the color of existing text in your page, enter that color, or browse for it by dragging the eyedropper through the palette.

I Feel Like I've Been Here Before

Don't make your Visited Links color the same as the Links color—visitors won't know which links they've clicked. If you want people to visit all your subpages, don't hide the trail from them. Choose a color that's compatible with your Links color but that will help your visitors know which pages they've visited. If people find themselves returning to the same page again and again (a likely outcome if you have many text links), they'll get fed up and simply stop following your links.

3. To set colors for visited and active links, repeat Step 2 for those color wells.

4. Click OK to close the dialog box and put your changes into effect.

If you want to choose a color not in the color palette, drag the eyedropper out of the palette, beyond the Properties Inspector, and onto your page. Click on existing text or graphic to select its color, and choose that color as your link color. Figure 5.9 shows color being selected from an existing sample on the page.

Setting Up Graphic Links

You know the old saying: "A picture's worth a thousand words." That saying's never been truer than in the case of Web pages. You can speak volumes with a single image—and if that image also serves as a door to another page within your site (or to another site), so much the better. As Figure 5.10 shows, a picture can tell visitors what to expect on the page they're about to visit (via the link). The picture also serves as an informative, tone-setting image on the page that contains it.

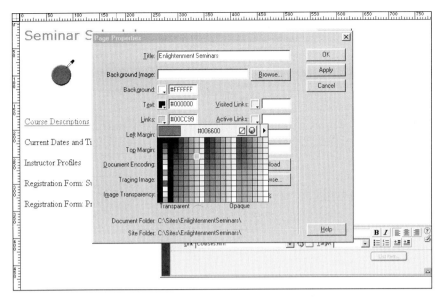

Figure 5.9

You can use the eyedropper that appears when you're selecting a color to "sip up" color from anywhere on your screen—the page content, the menu bar, or even the Windows title bar or a button on the taskbar.

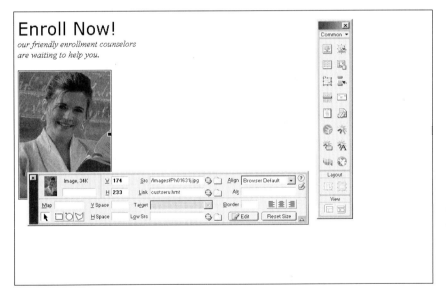

Figure 5.10

Tell your visitors that you have a friendly, professional customer service department, and use a picture of a friendly, professional representative as a link to that department's page.

If there's any doubt about what's going to happen when a visitor clicks a link, you can provide more information. When a graphic is selected, notice that not only a Link box but also a box labeled *Alt* appears in the Properties Inspector. In this Alt box, shown in Figure 5.11, you type the text that will pop up when someone moves the mouse over the graphic link.

Figure 5.11

The Alt box accepts long strings of text, but keeping your Alt text short—say, eight words or less—is a good idea. Longer strings can be hard to read in the small type in which they appear through a browser.

Until you view your page online or via the File|Preview In Browser command (viewing your page locally), you can see the text only in the Alt box itself. When you type the text, picture it on screen—be careful to use proper spelling and capitalization, and make your text clear and concise. Figure 5.12 shows the Alt text as it appears on a page viewed through a browser.

Figure 5.12
Give the visitors instructions or tell them what they'll find once they click the link to which they're pointing.

Like a Trail of Breadcrumbs . . .

If you ever need to change the link or Alt text for a graphic, simply click on the graphic and then edit the settings displayed in the Properties Inspector. If you'd rather change this information through the HTML window, you can use the Edit|Find And Replace command to search the source code. Using the Find dialog box, enter the image file name to help you locate the code that pertains to that image within your HTML document.

Establishing Graphic Hotspots

Most graphical links consist of a single image that points to a single Web page, site, file, or email address. If you have a large image—a map, a photo, a drawing—you can turn specific areas of the image into links by selecting sections of it and linking those individual sections to any page, site, file, or email address you want. The designated sections are called *hotspots*, and you create them using the Rectangular, Oval, and Polygon Hotspot tools on the Properties Inspector. Figure 5.13 shows a map with sections turned into hotspots.

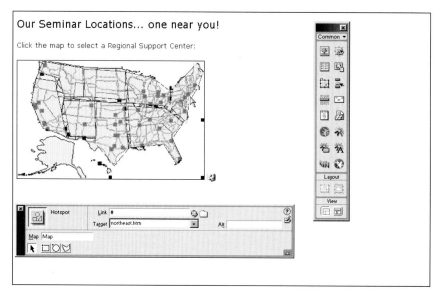

Figure 5.13
Draw a shape on the surface of your graphic and enter the link information for that hotspot.

Using a large image and chopping it into several linked hotspots has obvious design benefits—you don't have to create or obtain individual images and go to the trouble of arranging them on the page. You also can use a large image that is best seen in one piece, yet you can link its parts to relevant pages, files, or email addresses. Some ideas for using large images and hotspots are:

- Use a group photo of your staff, and link each person's face to his or her email address. When someone clicks the person's face, an email window already addressed to that person pops up.

- If your organization has locations in different cities or your sales staff covers different areas of the country, use a map graphic and create polygon hotspots (free-form geometric shapes) for the cities or regions. When someone clicks the individual areas, he or she is taken to a page that pertains to that city's office or to the sales contact information for the representatives who cover that area.

- Turn an office complex, a large shopping mall, or a housing development into an interactive tool for obtaining information about parts thereof. Using an aerial view of the location, turn offices, stores, or streets into hotspots, and link those hotspots to more information about the selected spot.

To create hotspots on any image, follow these steps:

1. Click once on the image to select it. The Properties Inspector displays image-related tools, including the three Hotspot tools: Rectangular, Oval, and Polygon, as shown in Figure 5.14.

> **Don't Keep Them Waiting**
>
> Of course, you want to keep the file size small enough so that the image doesn't take too long to load—try to keep the size below 50KB, and when you save the file as a JPEG file, choose a Progressive format. If you save the file as a GIF file, use the Interlaced option. These options will make the image appear immediately and compose slowly. Because the image appears immediately, visitors will know "something's coming" and will (hopefully) wait for the image to compose completely.

Figure 5.14
You can create any shape of hotspot you need, in any size you want.

2. Click once on the Hotspot tool you want to use first. Your mouse turns to a crosshair.

3. To draw a shape, drag on the surface of the image. A light-blue filled shape appears on the image (see Figure 5.15), with at least four

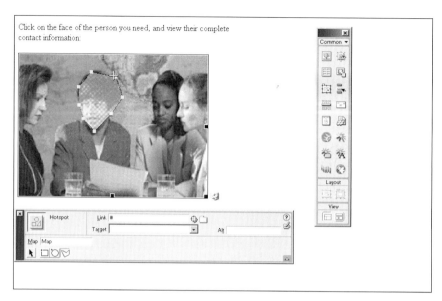

Figure 5.15
The hotspot area is slightly transparent, so you can still see your image even if you've placed hotspots all over it.

handles around it (more handles might appear for complex polygon hotspots).

4. While the Hotspot is active, click in the Link box, and type the name of the site, page, file, or email address to which the spot should link. You can also use the Browse To File button if you want to select the file by name rather than type the name. Figure 5.16 shows the link information for a hotspot.

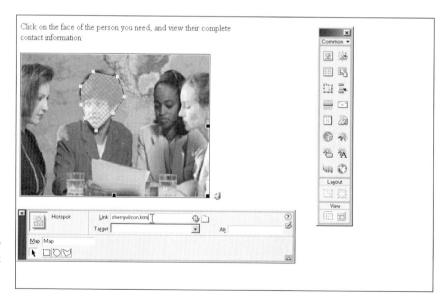

Figure 5.16
If you're not sure of the exact Web page name, use the Browse To File button to locate it.

5. Type any Alt text that you want to appear when people move a mouse over the spot.

6. Click away from the image to deselect it, or click a Hotspot tool to draw another hotspot on the image (see Figure 5.17). Repeat Steps 3 through 5 until you've created all the desired links for the selected image.

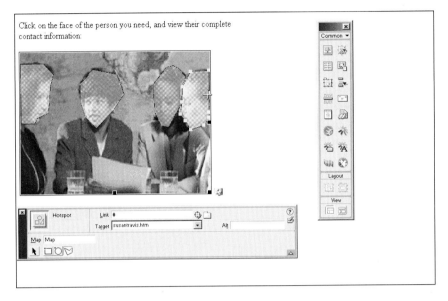

Figure 5.17
You can place as many hotspots as you want on an image. Be careful not to let the hotspots overlap, because you can't link the overlapped area to two different places, files, or email addresses.

You can use the handles to resize the hotspot, making it larger, smaller, wider, or taller, as shown in Figure 5.18. You can also move the hotspot by pointing to it with your mouse and dragging it to another location on the image.

Figure 5.18
Point to a handle and drag your mouse outward to increase the size, or inward to make the spot smaller.

Testing Links within Your Site

Setting up links can be a huge waste of time if they don't work. Typos in the Web page file names, or in the path to and file name of downloadable files, can result in nonfunctioning links—as can correct addresses and names for places or files that no longer exist. Before you post your site to the Web, test the site to make sure the links work. You can use the File|Preview In Browser command or open the file through an existing browser window.

Testing your pages in both of the popular browsers—Internet Explorer and Netscape—is a good idea, to make sure your pages look the same through both applications. In terms of links, though, they either work or they don't, without regard for the browser you're using for the test. Figure 5.19 shows the error message you'll see if the page you've linked to can't be found.

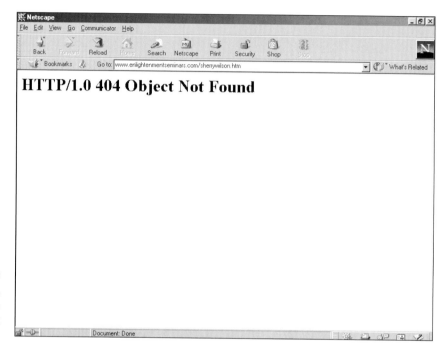

Figure 5.19
"Object Not Found" are the three little words no one wants to see when he or she clicks a link at your site.

Link to Other Sites

The purpose of links between the pages in your site is obvious—links make it possible for visitors to easily and quickly navigate, and get from page to page, without having to type new addresses for each page in your site. The purpose of links to other sites is less obvious and varies for each person or organization. Of course, links to sites outside your own are a convenience for your visitors, assuming they're interested in the content the other sites offer. Providing a link to someone else's site also lets you take advantage of the information that site offers and eliminates the need to provide that same information at your own site. Linking to another site is also a way to associate yourself (conceptually, at the very least) with someone else's site—its content, purpose, and even its status on the Web.

How can a link to another Web site connect you or your visitors to that site's status? In the same way that being seen in public with an important person, or at a place that's "in," can potentially elevate your social or professional standing. If your organization belongs to a larger organization, such as a professional society or association, a link to that larger entity's site makes clear that you have that group's approval. If, for example, you're a board-certified surgeon, a link to that board's site, where patients can see you listed as a member in good standing, will help patients know you have the requisite skills and education to maintain your board certification. You can see this relationship between a smaller entity and a larger one in virtually any industry—from plumbers to scientists, members can usually use a membership or association to their advantage by not only being a member but also by linking their Web site to that organization's Web site.

The information other sites provide is also important and, as I said, saves you repeating that same information at your site. If, for example, your visitors are also visitors to another site where they can search for important information, creating a link to that site from yours gives them another way to get at that data. Linking to the site also associates yourself with that data—and with the convenience to your visitors of finding the other site and its important information through your site. As you choose the sites to which your site will link, think about your visitors' needs. While your site doesn't have to become a clearinghouse for hundreds of other sites, it will enjoy increased traffic if people know you provide convenient links to things they might not otherwise have found by themselves.

Inserting URL Links

When you know which sites you want to link to, you're ready to set up the links. You can link to other sites via text or graphics at your site, and, of course, you can link to Web addresses any hotspots you create on graphic images. The only difference between a link to a page within your site and a link to another site is that, for the link to another site, you need to include the **http://www.domain.com** information in the Properties Inspector's Link text box (see Figure 5.20). Other than that, the process is the same as the one you use for setting up links among your site's pages—simply select the text or graphic that will serve as the link, and type the complete URL for the target site in the Link box.

Loftier Motivations

Beyond cashing in on the reputation or status of another Web site, you can benefit from links to other sites by letting your visitors know what you're interested in, what you believe, or what political/social causes you support. If you're creating a personal Web site (e.g., posting your resume with the hope of finding a job or adding to your client list) or a site for a nonprofit organization (e.g., to help find donors and volunteers), links to related sites and to sites that reveal more about you and your personal beliefs can be an easy and effective way to tell your visitors more about you. In the case of a nonprofit organization, a link to such an organization can be an act of charity unto itself. Helping people find sites whereby they can make donations or volunteer their services is a great way to use the Web for a higher purpose.

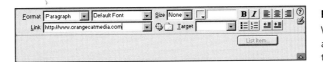

Figure 5.20
When you are creating a link to another Web site, be sure to type the entire URL in the Link box.

Testing URL Links

Making sure you have the correct URL (Web address) is also important, so that the link actually goes where you want it to. With the millions of Web addresses out there, it's easy to accidentally link a graphic or text on your site to the wrong Web site—and leave your visitors confused. Testing the addresses you type into the Properties Inspector's Link box is a good idea—*before* you post pages with links to the Web. You're better off finding out that the address is wrong or that the one you wanted has a .net rather than a .com extension *before* you've made the links available to everyone online.

Mailto: Email Links

One of the most convenient links for your visitors to use is an email link. Email links help your visitors make contact with you, with your staff—or with anyone else, for that matter—without having to type or look up an email address. By creating the email link, you've made it possible for your site's visitors to simply click the link and have a message window pop up, already addressed to the intended recipient (see Figure 5.21). At that point, your visitors only have to type in a subject and body for the message and click the Send button as they normally would. The email link will automatically invoke the default email program on the visitors' computers—whether they use Outlook or Netscape, or even if they subscribe to an online community such as America Online (AOL) or The Microsoft Network (MSN).

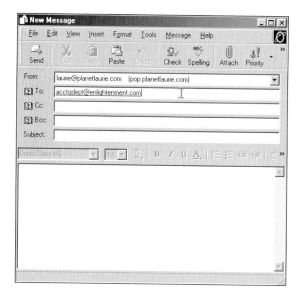

Figure 5.21

Provide your visitors with an email link so they can easily reach your Web master or customer service.

To build an email link into your page, follow these steps:

1. Select text (typically, "Contact Us" or "Send Us an Email") or a graphic on your page. You can also turn a hotspot into an email link—just click on the hotspot itself to select it.

2. Click inside the Link box in the Properties Inspector.

3. Type "mailto:" then immediately (no space) type the full email address to which messages should be sent, as Figure 5.22 shows.

4. Press Enter, or click outside the Properties Inspector.

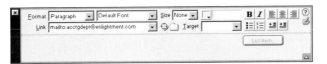

Figure 5.22
The mailto: addition to the link tells the visitor's computer that the link should open an email message window.

Making clear that the link in question is an email link is helpful to your visitors. If you're using text as the link, make sure the text itself makes the link's purpose clear. If you're using a graphic, pick one that communicates the idea of an email message—a picture of a mailbox or an envelope, for example—so that the visitor isn't surprised when a message window pops up. To make doubly sure that visitors know which link will open an email message window, use the Alt text box and insert a quick warning or instructions that will appear when someone moves the mouse over the link. Use a message that is short and to the point, as shown in Figure 5.23.

Figure 5.23
Insert Alt text to make clear that your link is an email link.

OBJECT Set Up Site Navigation Links

As shown in Figure 5.24, a Web site with more than one page needs links to help people get to the site's subpages and, once they're on those subpages, links to take them to the other pages and back to the home page, as desired. Those links can be text or graphics, and many Web sites employ both—prominently displayed graphics to link to all the site's pages and then text links in a less prominent position. In this project, you'll create the navigational links for an existing home page and two of its subpages. You'll also create text links for people who can't—or won't—display graphics.

Open a Web Page

You will find the pages you'll use to complete this project on the CD-ROM that accompanies this book. To open the pages in Dreamweaver, insert the CD-ROM; using Dreamweaver's Open dialog box, navigate to the CD's Project 5A folder, and open the following files:

- index5a.htm

- contact5a.htm

- associations5a.htm

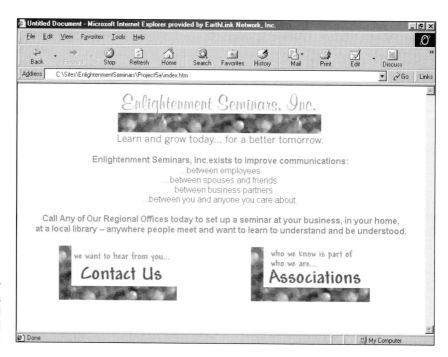

Select Text to Be Linked

All three of the pages have a list of text entries that list the other pages in the site. Select these list items individually, and create links to the appropriate pages. For example, select the word "Home" at the bottom of the contact5a.htm page, and turn that word into a link to the index5a.htm page. Do this on all three pages, using the green Arial text at the bottom of the pages.

Set Up Graphic Links

Using graphics already on the three Web pages, perform these tasks:

1. Each page has a copy of the company logo on it. The logo appears centered and large on the home page and in the upper-left corner of the other two pages. On the two subpages, select the logo graphic and set it up to be a link to the home page.

2. On the home page, turn the Contact Us graphic into a link to the contact5a.htm page and the Who We Are graphic into a link to the associations5a.htm page.

3. On the contact5a.htm page, set up the Who We Are graphic to link to the associations5a.htm page.

4. On the associations5a.htm page, set up the Contact Us graphic so it links to the contact5a.htm page.

After you set up the links, perform these tasks:

1. For all links to the home page, insert as Alt text: "Return to the Home Page."

2. For the links to the contact5a.htm page, insert as Alt text: "Tell us what you think!"

3. For the links to the associations5a.htm page, insert as Alt text: "We are proud members of several great organizations."

Create Map Hotspots

The contact5a.htm page contains a map of the United States with four cities labeled. Using the Hotspot tools on the Properties inspector, create email links on this map for the following addresses:

- nycsales@company.com

- philasales@company.com

- seattlesales@company.com

- sanfransales@company.com

Test Text, Graphic, and Hotspot Links

Using the File|Preview In Browser command, check the links between pages and to email addresses, and make sure the links work.

Links to Files for Download

Just about everyone who has used the Web has used it to download a file—a picture, a document, a database, or a program. If you've ever purchased software, graphics, screensavers, or any other file online that you can display or run on your computer, chances are that you downloaded that material from the vendor's Web site, copying the file(s) to your local computer after you clicked a "Download" (or similarly worded) link.

Creating links on your Web page that will let visitors download files is easy. In addition to creating the link, all you have to do is make sure the file to be downloaded is stored on the Web server, along with the Web page itself. When a visitor clicks your link, a File Download dialog box opens, as shown in Figure 5.25.

The dialog box offers visitors the choice to save the file to their local drive or open it from the source, but saving the file is best—you might even consider adding instructions to your link (using Alt text), or placing instructions nearby, telling people to save the file to their local drive and then open it on their own

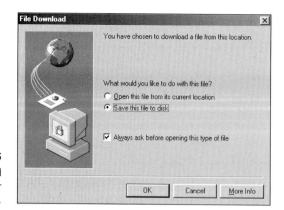

Figure 5.25

Offer documents, graphics, sound files, movies, or programs for download from your Web site.

computer. Why? Because larger files will (hopefully) be stored as zipped (compressed) files to allow for a speedier download, and zipped files should be opened and unzipped only on the drive where the unzipped files will be used. Another reason to save files to disk is the possibility that they contain a virus (though you'd never intentionally post an infected file) or, in the case of programs, the possibility that the program could be somehow incompatible with the visitor's operating system or system settings and consequently create problems.

Creating Links to Documents and Application Files

If you have a document, graphic, sound file, movie, spreadsheet, database, or presentation file (to name just a few types) that you want to make available to your site's visitors, you can create a link to that file on your page, just as you would create a link to another Web page or Web site. The difference? In this case, instead of entering the name of a Web page or the URL of a site, you'll be entering the path to and file name of the file you're offering for download.

To create a file link, follow these steps:

1. Select the text or graphic that will serve as a link to the file.

2. Using the Properties Inspector, click in the Link box and type the file name. If the file will be stored anywhere other than in the same folder as the Web page itself, type the full path to the file—for example, /files/ article1.doc. If the file will be stored in the same folder as the page that contains its link, just type the file name by itself.

3. If you don't know the exact file name, or you don't want to risk a typo, use the Browse To File button and navigate to the file on your local drive. Hopefully, you've done the proper preparation for site building, and the file is stored in the folder together with your Web pages and images, per the instructions in Chapter 2. Figure 5.26 shows a file link in the Properties Inspector.

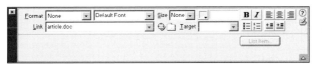

Figure 5.26
Avoid typos and the wrong files being linked to your page by using the Browse To File button, which lets you select, rather than type, the name of the linked file.

4. Click on the page, or press Enter, to complete your entry into the Properties Inspector and save your Web page.

Creating Links to Download Programs

The process for creating a link to *allow* the download of a program you want to share is the same as that for creating a link to download documents, graphics, or other files. The only difference is in the potential size of the program file—if the file is very big (more than 500KB), the download time might be prohibitive for many of your visitors, especially those using a dial-up (modem) connection to the Internet.

To make the download go faster, compress the program file, using a program such as WinZip. You can compress several files—the program might consist of more than one file—into one zipped file and then create a link to that file rather than to the uncompressed file(s) (see Figure 5.27). When visitors download the zipped file, they'll unzip the file to access the file or files it contains. They can then install the program per instructions you'll have provided at the Web site.

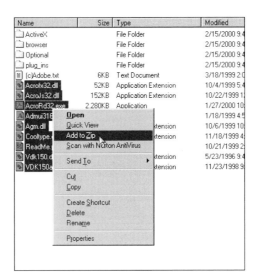

Figure 5.27
Compress one or more files into a smaller, single, zipped file so visitors can more easily download large or multiple files.

To help people use or install the program you've given them, you might even include in the zipped file a readme.doc file that explains how to install the program. Of course, if the program is a single, small, executable file (a file that ends in .exe), you can simply link to that file, and visitors can run it as soon as they've downloaded it, by double-clicking the program through their My Computer or Windows Explorer window.

Text Link Display Options

By default, linked text follows the color scheme established in your default Web browser for linked text. In Internet Explorer, for example, linked text is blue, and visited links are a deep shade of red. You can reset the colors through your browser if you don't like those defaults. When you do reset the colors through your browser, your Web pages (designed in Dreamweaver) will follow the new settings when you view them through your default browser.

If you want to customize your link colors for a Web page (and you probably will, unless all of your Web pages are designed in colors that look good with your browser defaults), use the Page Properties dialog box, and follow these instructions:

1. Choose Modify|Page Properties. The Page Properties dialog box opens, as Figure 5.28 shows.

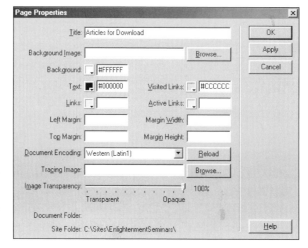

Figure 5.28

The Page Properties dialog box shows you your page title, background color or image, and the color of your text and text links under new, visited, and active conditions.

2. Observe the Links, Visited Links, and Active Links options and accompanying color wells—apparently, some shade of gray has been chosen, but, in fact, no color is present—which is Dreamweaver's way of telling you that it's following a default set elsewhere.

3. To change one or all of these color settings, click the color well for the color to be changed (see Figure 5.29), or type a color number in the text box to the right of the color well.

4. When you've set the colors you want to use for all your links, click OK to close the dialog box.

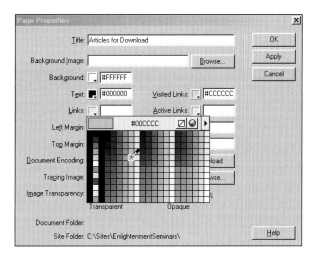

Figure 5.29
Select a color that will both stand out and complement your page colors. Hyperlink text will also be underlined, so you can rely on the underlining to differentiate regular text and link text if you want to set your links to the same color as your body text.

Links in HTML

If you're not already familiar with HTML, you can learn how to use the language by observing the way your actions within the Dreamweaver Design view turn into HTML code in the Code view. By using the Code and Design views button (which splits your screen into two panes—one for your WYSIWYG environment, one for your HTML code), you can see both what you've typed, formatted, inserted, moved, resized, and so on, and the HTML code that implements those actions when you view the results through a Web browser.

With regard to links, the HTML tag you want to look for is **<a href="_____">** (with a closing **</a>** tag following). The blank shown here represents the name of the Web page, the URL, the file name, or the email address to which the text or graphic is linked. Figure 5.30 shows the HTML code for text that's linked to a Web site.

If your link is a graphic, the **<a href="_____">** tag will be accompanied by an **<img src="_____">** tag, in which the blank link represents the path to and file name of the graphic that appears on the page. Figure 5.31 shows a graphic link and the accompanying HTML code.

Of course, editing links through the Design view, using the Properties Inspector, is much easier than making changes in HTML code. So why tell you about the underlying HTML code? Because you might find yourself working on a computer that doesn't have Dreamweaver installed, so you'll be forced to edit a Web page through some text-editing program, such as Notepad, which comes with Windows in its Accessories group. If you can find the references to your links and any graphics that serve as links, you can edit those references as needed.

Color See, Color Do

If you want to use a color that's already in use somewhere on screen—within your Web page or anywhere in the visible areas of the computer screen—move the eyedropper mouse pointer (which appears when you click the color well) out of the Page Properties dialog box, and click the pointer on the color you want to use.

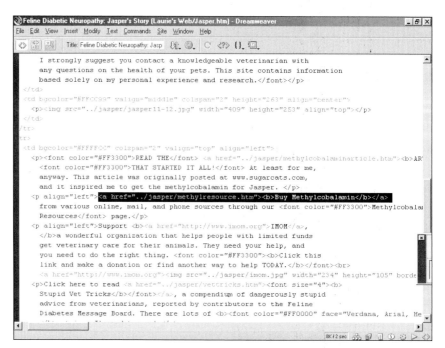

Figure 5.30

If you need to edit a link, you can do so via the HTML code, by changing the path and/or file name to which a link points.

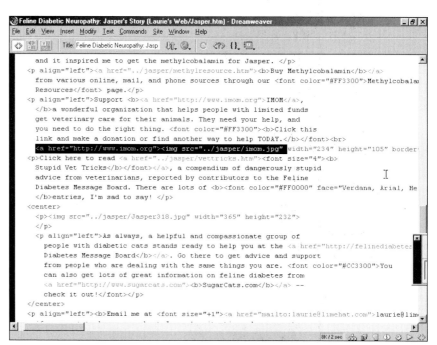

Figure 5.31

You can change the image that serves as a link by changing the **<img src= "_____">** reference.

PROJECT Create Links to Other Sites

For this project, you'll use the associations5b.htm file you'll find in the Project 5B folder on the CD-ROM. This file is the same as the associations5a.htm file, but the associations5b.htm file is a clean copy, in case you made changes to the 5a version.

On the associations5b.htm page, you'll be creating links to the imaginary professional organizations that the imaginary company belongs to.

Open the Web Page

The page will consist of several logo graphics for professional organizations. You will turn each logo into a link to that organization's Web site, using addresses provided in the next step.

In the Project 5B folder on the CD-ROM, find and open associations5b.htm.

Create the Site Links

Click on each of the logo graphics and create site links to the following Web sites:

- www.planetlaurie.com/aboutlaurie.htm
- www.elephants.com
- www.imom.org

For each link, insert this Alt text: "Click here to access this organization's Web site."

Test the Links Online

Using the File|Preview In Browser command, preview the saved associations5b.htm Web page and test the links—each one should take you to an actual Web page. The sites don't have anything to do with the imaginary associations, but you can test your links to see that you wind up at actual Web sites.

Send an Email Message to a Mailto: Link

On the **www.planetlaurie.com/aboutlaurie.htm** site, you'll see a link that tells you to click it to send an email requesting a resume. Ignore the link instructions and type "Dreamweaver Reader" in the subject line. You'll be sending email to me, the author, which will test the email link on the associations5b.htm page.

Receive Your Subscription Confirmation via Email

After receiving your subscription email, I'll respond to you.

Moving On

Now that you know how to insert, format, and create hyperlinks using your workbook text and graphic content, you're ready to master tools that give you more freedom to position that content and create effective page layouts. Chapter 6 will show you how to insert and format tables and control the position of content placed within the tables' cells.

Chapter 6

Structuring a Web Page with Tables

One of the major challenges for any Web designer is page layout. Without the use of tables, putting things where you want them can be difficult or impossible. Frames and layers are useful alternatives, but they have limitations that tables do not. Chapter 6 will show you how to build and use tables to achieve the page layout you have in mind.

Build a Table

Building a table with Dreamweaver is a simple process. You can use the Insert|Table command, or click the Insert Table button on the Objects palette. Either approach results in the appearance of the Insert Table dialog box (see Figure 6.1), through which you can specify the dimensions of your table, how much space will appear between table cells, the distance between the cell walls and cell content, and how big the overall table will be in relation to your Web page. You can also choose whether or not to have a visible border on your table and, if you want one, how thick that border will be.

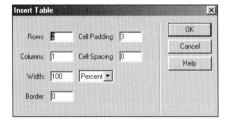

Figure 6.1
Use the Insert Table dialog box to set up a table on your Web page.

Once you've built the table, you have a variety of options for changing table dimensions; the size of individual cells, columns, and rows within the table; and the position of the table. As you continue reading this chapter, you'll learn all you need to know to customize your tables to meet virtually any Web page layout requirement.

Establishing Table Location

Your cursor location on the page when you issue the Insert Table command dictates table location. Just as you would click to place your cursor where an image would go, or before you type any text, you should click on the page (in Design view, of course) to position your cursor, and then choose Insert|Table, or click the Insert Table button.

Once your table is positioned, you can move it by cutting and pasting it to a new location, or by dragging it. As Figure 6.2 shows, if you hover over the upper-left corner of your table, a four-headed arrow appears. Once that mouse pointer is displayed, click and drag your table to another spot on the page.

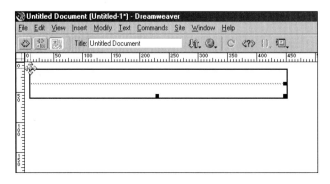

Figure 6.2
Drag your table to move it in relation to other content on the page.

Setting Table Dimensions

When you open the Insert Table dialog box, you'll see text boxes into which you can enter the number of rows and columns. By default, the dialog box displays the dimensions of the last table you created. You can type new dimensions by selecting the existing number and typing a new one in its place.

How do you know how many rows or columns your table should have? Think about the page layout you want to create. If, for example, you want a vertical series of graphics with text next to each one (as shown in Figure 6.3), you would create a two-column table with as many rows as you'll have graphics and paired paragraph text. Knowing the number of rows you'll need isn't as important as entering the right number of columns—if you set up the table to have three rows, for example, and you really needed four, simply pressing the Tab key in the last cell of the table will create a new row.

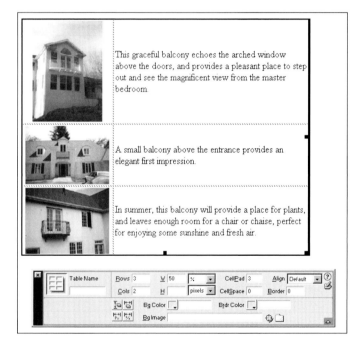

Figure 6.3
When setting table dimensions, think of your page layout and how many separate elements you need to position.

Table View Options

When working with tables, you have two view choices: Standard and Layout. Standard view lets you build a table that starts with uniformly sized and distributed columns and rows. You're essentially building a grid, the cells of which you will use to position text and images. Layout view lets you draw a table that isn't necessarily uniform—you can build cells within cells and rows and columns of virtually any size.

Your preference for Standard or Layout view will be dictated by whether you prefer drawing table cells with your mouse or creating a table through a dialog box, and how clearly you've envisioned your goals for page layout. You can switch between the views using the Objects palette, as shown in Figure 6.4.

Figure 6.4

Click the Layout View button, and your mouse turns to a crosshair, ready to help you draw your table cells.

Figure 6.5

Standard view lets you start with a uniform grid of evenly spaced and sized columns and rows.

Working in Standard View

Standard view requires the use of the Insert Table dialog box, which I discussed under "Build a Table" at the beginning of this chapter. Simply click the Insert Table button in the Objects palette, or choose Insert|Table. The dialog box lets you establish every aspect of the table, except for any changes to the size of individual columns and rows. You can resize later, though—you're not stuck with a uniform grid just because that's the type of table you get by default. As Figure 6.5 shows, using Standard view to create a table results in a table with evenly spaced columns and rows.

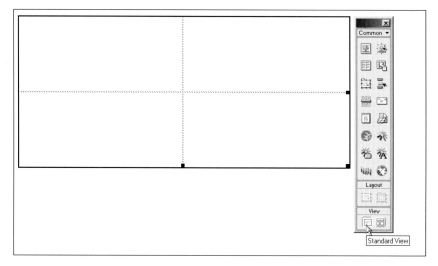

Working in Layout View

Layout view provides a more free-form environment and process for building tables. Rather than using a dialog box to enter the number of columns and rows (and, therefore, cells) in your table, you can draw individual cells and, through the process of doing so, create a customized table with random-width columns and rows. As Figure 6.6 shows, you can create the layout you have in mind in Layout view by drawing cells—and cells within cells—of any size you need.

Whichever view you work in, you'll be able to resize your table cells later and add and remove cells as necessary. Nothing about the table is carved in stone and, through the normal Web-design process, which typically includes changing your mind and design goals, you can change your table to meet the needs of your evolving page design.

Resize Columns and Rows

If you employ the Insert Table dialog box to create your table, you're presented with a uniform grid of equal-sized cells, based on columns of equal width and rows of equal height. You can change the width of any particular column or

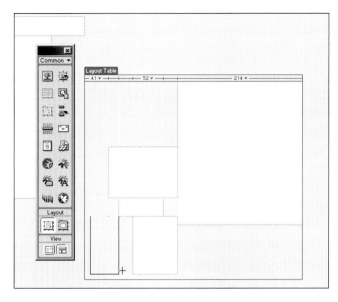

Figure 6.6

Take a more creative approach to building a table in Layout view.

the height of any particular row quite easily by dragging the column or row wall with your mouse, as shown in Figure 6.7. You'll want to do this to make room for a graphic that's larger or smaller than the cell in which you've placed it, and to affect the flow of paragraph text within a table cell. Because you can also use table cells, columns, and rows as visual dividers between sections of a page, you might need to resize those dividers to be wider or taller, or thinner or shorter, so that they take up either more or less space on the page.

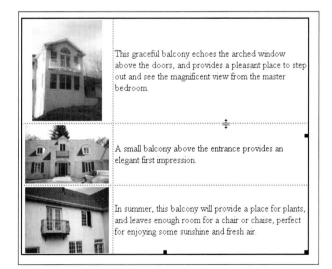

Figure 6.7

Point to a seam between columns or rows, and drag it to resize that portion of the table.

There are some limitations on the potential width of columns and the height of rows as you drag to resize them. For example, you can't make a column narrower than the content of that column—if you have an image in any cell in that column that is 150 pixels wide, you can't make that column narrower than 150 pixels, assuming your cell padding is set to 0 (no pixels) (similar to a margin, *cell padding* inserts one or more pixels of space to keep your text from running into the walls of the cell). If your cell padding is set to 5 pixels, the narrowest you can make the hypothetical column is 155 pixels.

Further, if you've set dimensions for your overall table, you can't resize an individual column or row to a size that will cause the table itself to exceed specified dimensions. If, for example, you want to have three 200-pixel-wide columns, your table must be at least 600 pixels wide. If you've set the table to 500 pixels, you won't be able to have three 200-pixel columns inside the table without resetting its width to 600 or more pixels.

Resizing Tables with the Properties Inspector

You can set the size of your table when you first build it, and reset the size through the Properties Inspector or via your HTML code. To use the Properties Inspector, you must first select the table and then adjust the width and height of the table. Follow these steps:

1. Click in any cell in the table, and choose Modify|Table|Select Table. A solid border appears around the entire table, as shown in Figure 6.8.

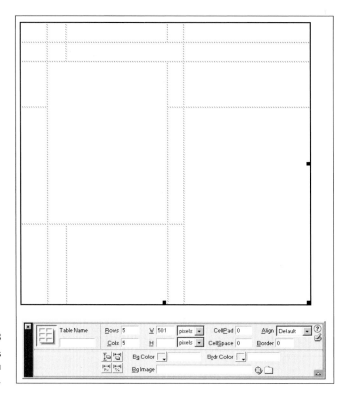

Figure 6.8

To display the Properties Inspector's table options, you must select the entire table.

2. With the Properties Inspector displayed, adjust the width by entering a number in the W box. If you follow the number with a percent sign (%), the table width will be adjusted to a percentage of the entire page.

3. Click in the H box, and type the pixel height of the table. If you want your table's height to be a percentage of the page height, enter that percentage, including the percent sign. Figure 6.9 shows a table set to be 700 pixels wide and 100 percent of the page height.

Figure 6.9

Enter table dimensions in pixels, or as a percentage of the size of the page.

Resizing Table Dimensions with Your Mouse

While the table is selected, you'll notice handles (black boxes) in the corners and in the center of each side of the table. You can drag these handles to reduce or expand the size of the entire table. You can use a corner handle to adjust the width and height at the same time, as shown in Figure 6.10.

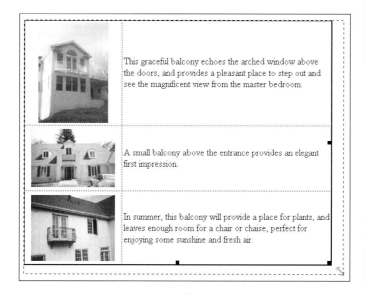

Four Marks the Spot

You can select the entire table by hovering your mouse over the top of the table. When the pointer turns to a gray four-headed arrow, click. The entire table is selected, and the Properties Inspector displays table settings rather than settings for an individual cell.

Figure 6.10

Resize a table as you would resize a graphic—by dragging its handles out to make it bigger, and in to make it smaller.

When you resize a table this way, the table's cells will resize proportionately. This means that if you have four columns that are each 150 pixels wide, and you reduce the width of the entire table by 20 pixels, each column will be reduced by 5 pixels. The same rule applies to an increase in table size. And, if you resize the table both horizontally and vertically, column widths and row heights will be affected.

Split and Merge Cells

A great technique for redesigning a table is to split and/or merge cells. Imagine that you set up your table to be two columns wide and four rows tall, with graphics in the first column and paragraphs in the second column, each paragraph paired with an image. After you enter some text and insert a few graphics, you realize that one of the paragraphs needs to be paired with two images instead of just one. Therefore, you need to place two images next to a single paragraph; with the layout of your table as it is, that placement will be impossible. By splitting a cell in the first column and adding a row within the cell, you can position two graphics paired with a single paragraph. Figure 6.11 shows the table before the split, and Figure 6.12 shows the table after the split.

Figure 6.11

Who knew? You thought you had your table set up to meet your needs, but now you realize you need a single, extra cell.

Figure 6.12

Rather than inserting an entire new row that spans both columns, just break a single cell into two cells.

Splitting Cells

To split a cell, simply click inside it, and then use the Split Cells button on the Properties Inspector. A dialog box appears (as shown in Figure 6.13), and you can specify how you want the cell split—into columns or rows—and how many new cells the split should create.

You can split a single cell into as many columns and rows as you need to. The only limitations are the size of the page and the size of the content to be placed in the cells created by the splits.

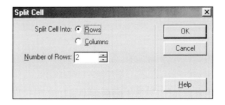

Figure 6.13
If you want to split a cell vertically, add columns. To split a cell horizontally, add rows.

Merging Cells

When you have more cells than you need, you can often solve the problem by merging those cells into a single cell. This doesn't mean that you can eliminate an unwanted column or row by merging, but if you have a row that spans three columns, and you want only two cells in the row, merge two of the three cells into a single cell, which will leave you with just two cells.

Merging cells is even easier than splitting them. Simply select the contiguous cells to be merged (see Figure 6.14), and click the Merge Cells button on the Properties Inspector. A single cell is created, as shown in Figure 6.15.

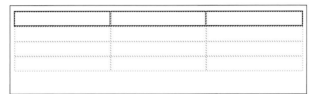

Figure 6.14
Do you need a single cell where you now have two or more? Merge the cells.

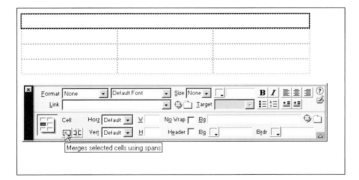

Figure 6.15
Once cells are merged, you can format and resize the single cell as you would any other cell.

Using Nested Tables

Very similar to the results of splitting a cell into two or more new cells is the process of *nesting* a table. A nested table is a table that lives inside another table, within a single cell of the original table. Nesting is easy to accomplish, using either Standard view and the Insert Table dialog box, or using Layout view and drawing a group of cells within an existing cell.

Creating a Nested Table

To create a nested table, follow these steps:

1. Click inside a cell in the existing table.

2. Choose Insert|Table, or click the Insert Table button on the Object palette.

3. In the resulting Insert Table dialog box, enter the number of columns and rows the nested table should have, and establish the cell padding and spacing as needed.

4. Click OK. The table is created inside the cell (see Figure 6.16), and you can resize and populate the table with text and graphics just like you would any other table.

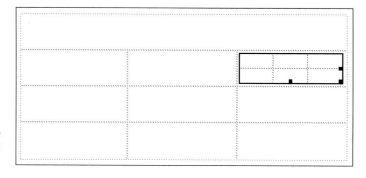

Figure 6.16
A table within another table's cell is a nested table.

Nested Table Pros and Cons

Old versions of browsers cannot deal with nested tables. If you and your assumed site visitors are using versions of Netscape later than version 2, however, you're safe. Nested tables also can present problems for sizing table cells and adjusting the overall layout of a table: They not only act as a solid object filling a cell within the original table (just as a graphic would affect the size that the cell could be), but they also bring their own table attributes into the picture. The nested table cannot be any larger than the cell in which it resides, and it can't be made smaller than the space any of its own content requires.

Drawing Nested Tables

If you're working in Layout view and are drawing your table cells, you can create a nested table by drawing within an existing cell. As Figure 6.17 shows, you can draw a table within a cell using the Draw Layout Table button.

When You Can't See the Table for the Cells

Not sure what you've accomplished in Layout view? Switch back to Standard view, and a clearer picture of the tables you've created will appear.

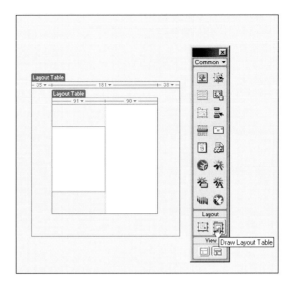

Figure 6.17
Click the Draw Layout button, and draw a table within an existing table cell.

PROJECT Lay Out an Online Newsletter

In this project, you'll create a table layout to house the contents of a newsletter. This table includes a cell to contain the newsletter title and date, cells to contain images and paragraph text, and cells that exist solely to create visual space between newsletter sections.

Set Up the Newsletter with Tables

On a new, blank Dreamweaver page, create a two-column, four-row table that has the following settings:

- Cell padding: 3
- Cell spacing: 1
- Table Width: 100%
- Border: 0

Resize the cells within the table so that, in an 800×600-pixel display, the top row is 50 pixels high and the full width of the page. Merge the two cells in the top row, so that the row consists of a single cell.

With regard to the rest of the table, the first column should be 30 percent of the table's width, and the second column 70 percent of the width. Make the remaining three rows of the table the same height.

Insert Picture and Article Placeholders

Type and center the newsletter title "The Online News" in the top row. Make the title font size 6. You can choose any font you like.

On the CD-ROM, you'll find a folder called Project 6A. In this folder are several images, each called Holder plus a number. Insert the images in order into the table cells, moving left to right in the table, starting in the first row beneath the row that contains the newsletter title. These placeholders will tell future users of the newsletter where to place their content; the placeholders also let you preview your layout in a browser.

Format Table Cells for Alignment of Content

Format the cells that will contain the articles so that their content is left-aligned. Format cells that will contain pictures for centered content.

Insert Text Content

Replace the article placeholders by typing text into the columns, or paste text from the document called newslettertext you found in folder Project 6A on the CD-ROM. The document contains simple text that you can paste repeatedly into the cells to fill them with "articles."

Preview the Newsletter in a Browser

To see how your layout looks, press F12 to preview the page in your default browser. As necessary, adjust any column widths and row heights to achieve an attractive layout for your newsletter in general, the individual "articles," and the images themselves.

Create a Site and Save the Page

Create a site folder called Newsletter on your local hard drive, and set it up as a site folder for your newsletter. Save the page and images to the site. Call the Web page Newsletter Sample, and copy the images from the CD-ROM to the Images folder in your new site folder.

Position and Format Table Text

Typing in table cells is easy. Simply click inside the cell and start typing. You can also paste text copied (with an Edit|Copy command) from another document into the cells by clicking to position your cursor and choosing Edit|Paste. After you've inserted the text, you can format it as you would any other text—select it and apply fonts, sizes, alignment, and color settings through the Properties Inspector. Figure 6.18 shows paragraph text in a table cell.

Setting Cell Padding and Spacing

If you want more or less space between the walls of the cell and the cell content, you must adjust the cell padding. As I mentioned earlier, the cell padding inserts one or more pixels of space to keep your text from running into the walls of the cell.

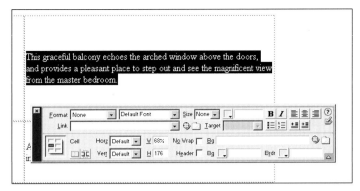

Figure 6.18
The size of the cell dictates the flow of paragraph text.

To adjust cell padding, follow these steps:

1. Click in any cell in the table.

2. Choose Modify|Table|Select Table, or right-click the table and choose Table|Select Table from the shortcut menu.

3. With the table selected, the Properties Inspector displays table settings. Enter a number in the CellPad box, as shown in Figure 6.19.

4. Click inside the table, or press Enter, to see the results. Figure 6.20 shows a 3-pixel cell padding and a paragraph within a table cell.

Figure 6.19
Enter "3" into the CellPad box for an effective buffer between the cell's walls and your text.

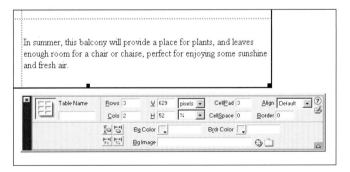

Figure 6.20
You don't want too much cell space for paragraph text—you want just enough to keep contiguous cells and their text content from looking as though they run together.

Aligning Text in a Table Cell

By default, text you type into a cell is aligned to the left horizontally, and centered vertically, as Figure 6.21 shows. You can adjust these settings by selecting the content to adjust its horizontal alignment and by selecting the cell to adjust the vertical alignment of any content in the cell.

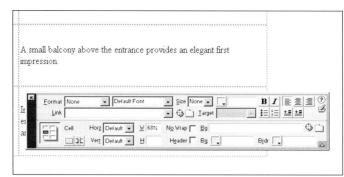

Figure 6.21

By default, text adheres to the left side of the cell.

Figure 6.22

From the Properties Inspector, you can apply Center, Left, and Right alignment, using the buttons in the upper right of the Inspector.

Cell Padding: One for All

Cell padding is set for an entire table, not for individual cells. Therefore, you cannot have different cell padding in different cells in the same table. If you want to have varied cell-padding settings throughout a series of cells, create nested, single-cell tables within other cells, and set the cell padding for each nested table/cell to meet your needs.

The Properties Inspector provides all the help you need to adjust text alignment in a table cell. Figure 6.22 shows text and the buttons you'll need to adjust the horizontal alignment. Select the text you want to align, and then click the button. You can apply multiple alignments within a single cell, provided each selection is in its own distinct paragraph within the cell.

If you want your text to start at the top or bottom of the cell instead of the middle, adjust the vertical alignment. Use the Vert drop list (see Figure 6.23) to adjust the vertical alignment for an individual cell. Obviously, you can apply only one vertical alignment per cell, regardless of how many distinct paragraphs the cell contains.

Figure 6.23

Make your text flow from the top down by changing the vertical alignment.

You might think that you could use the Horz (horizontal) drop list interchangeably with the Left, Center, and Right text alignment tools, but you can't. The Horz drop list pertains to the alignment of *all* cell content—not just text—and will, therefore, not let you create different alignment for separate paragraphs within the cell.

Crossing the Line

When your cursor is among text in a table cell, the Properties Inspector is divided into two horizontal sections. The top half of the palette offers text-formatting options, and the bottom half offers tools for adjusting settings for the cell. Keeping this partitioning in mind will help you choose the right tools for the job at hand.

Position Graphics in a Table

As you know, when a graphic is selected on the page, tools pertaining to the placement, formatting, and size of graphics appear in the Properties Inspector. You'll find two different sets of tools for positioning the graphic—one set, in the top half of the Properties Inspector (above the horizontal line), lets you change the alignment of the image itself (see Figure 6.24).

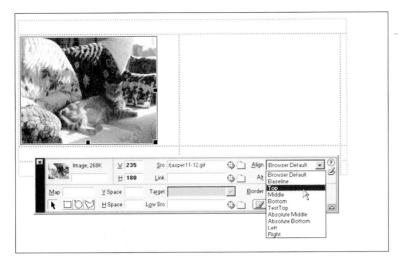

Figure 6.24

Change the alignment of the graphic by choosing from a variety of options in the Align drop list.

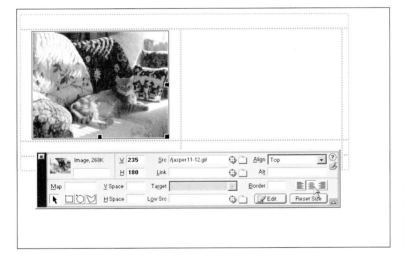

Figure 6.25

Do you want everything in the cell to be aligned the same way? If so, click the Left, Center, or Right Align button.

The other alignment tools—the collection of Left, Center, and Right alignment buttons on the bottom half of the Inspector (see Figure 6.25)—let you change the alignment of the cell. What's the difference between these two toolsets? If you change the *cell's* alignment setting, all content will adhere to that setting. If you change the *image* alignment setting, only the selected image will be realigned; conceivably, other content, such as text or a second graphic, could be aligned differently.

Apply Table Colors

By default, table cells are transparent, which means that the color of your page, or any background image you've applied to the page, will show through the table cells. Only a graphic image inside a table cell will block the view of your page color or background image, as Figure 6.26 shows. You can, however, apply color to individual table cells or to the entire table.

V Space and H Space

The V Space and H Space settings let you place a certain number of pixels above and below (V Space) and to the left and right (H Space) of the graphic. While these options sound convenient, you might regret using this feature later when you go to adjust column widths or row heights. If, for example, you've applied 50 pixels above and below an image that's 100 pixels high, the cell cannot be made smaller than 200 pixels (the combined height of the image and the inserted V Space).

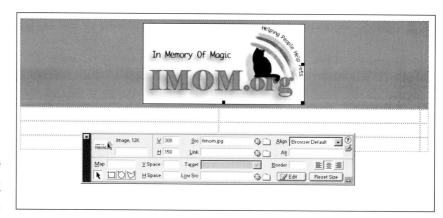

Figure 6.26
A table is see-through by default, providing a transparent grid for your text and graphics.

Applying Cell Color

To color an individual cell, click in the cell and click the Bg color button on the Properties Inspector. You can use the eyedropper to select a color from the resulting palette, or you can click on anything in the window to select its color as your cell's fill color. Figure 6.27 shows individual cells that have had background color applied.

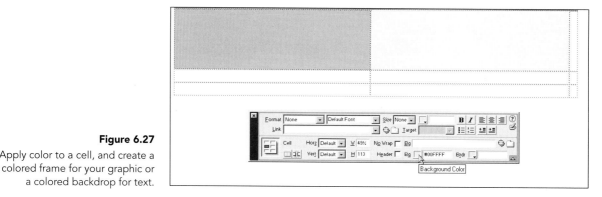

Figure 6.27
Apply color to a cell, and create a colored frame for your graphic or a colored backdrop for text.

You can apply different colors to every cell in your table, or to only certain cells, leaving the others transparent. Of course, if you apply a dark color to a cell, you'll want to apply a light color to any text you type into that cell so that the text can be read. Conversely, if you have a light-colored background, you'll want dark-colored text.

Applying Color to a Table

If you want to apply a colored background to the entire table, select the table first, and then use the Bg color button in the Properties Inspector. Because the entire table is selected, the color will be applied to every cell in the table—and to cells that you add by splitting cells or by inserting rows and columns. Figure 6.28 shows a table with a uniformly colored background.

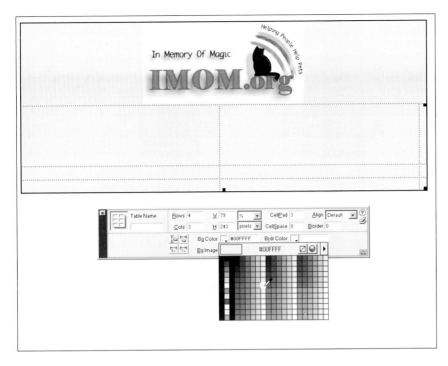

Figure 6.28
Make your whole table stand out as a unit by applying a single color to the table and all its cells.

Format Table and Cell Borders

A table border is just that—a border applied to an entire table. You cannot apply a table border to individual cells unless the table consists of only one cell. You establish the border thickness when you create the table through the Insert Table dialog box, and the thickness is measured in pixels. If you've already created a table with or without a border, you can adjust the border thickness through the Properties Inspector, as shown in Figure 6.29.

Most tables exist purely to provide a structure for the placement of text and graphics on the Web page and, therefore, don't need a border. When a table has a border, however, the table becomes a graphical feature unto itself, and its role as a grid in which to place objects is expanded to include horizontal and vertical lines. A border can help people visually separate content within the table, or to read across a row or down a column without accidentally reading content from adjoining cells. Borders can be especially useful if the table contains information that must be read accurately, such as a transit or event schedule, as shown in Figure 6.30.

A Cool Effect

You can create a flat, colored border around your table by placing a nested, white-background table inside a cell filled with another color. By shrinking the nested table so that the colored background of the cell that contains the nested table shows, you create a colored frame around the nested table.

Figure 6.29
Enter the pixel thickness of the border.

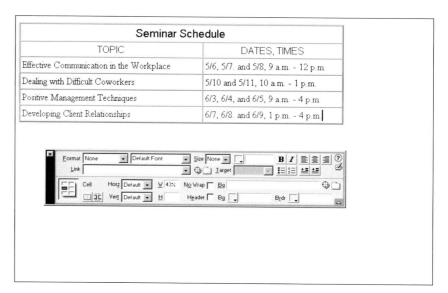

Figure 6.30

Help your site's visitors read complex information by providing a table border to guide their eyes across a row or down a column.

Choosing a Border Color

By default, borders are gray. A 1-pixel border appears as a black hairline and, as the thickness of the border increases, a gray, 3-D effect is achieved, as Figure 6.31 shows. You can apply other colors to the border, but be forewarned that many browsers (and versions thereof) don't support the border color tag in the HTML code that is created when you apply a border color. In these cases, the colored border will appear as you desire in the Dreamweaver window, but when it's viewed through the non-supporting browser, the border will be gray.

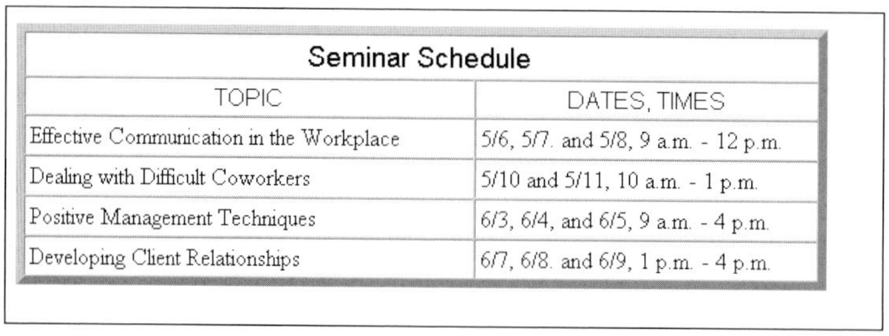

Figure 6.31

A 6-pixel border appears as a thick, 3-D frame around the table cells.

Zero, Zip, Nada

If you don't want any border, change the border thickness to 0 (zero) pixels. Any color set will be ignored, because no visible border exists to which the color can be applied.

To apply a border color, select the table (Modify|Table|Select Table) and, in the Properties Inspector, click the Brdr color well, and select a color. As always, you can select a color from anywhere on the screen by clicking the color with the eyedropper that results from your clicking the color well. Figure 6.32 shows a border color being selected from an object already on the page.

Applying Color to an Individual Cell Border

Although you can't apply a border to an individual cell in a multiple-cell table, you can apply a color to a single cell or range of cells. To apply a color to a cell or range of cells, select the cell(s) and click the Brdr color well in the

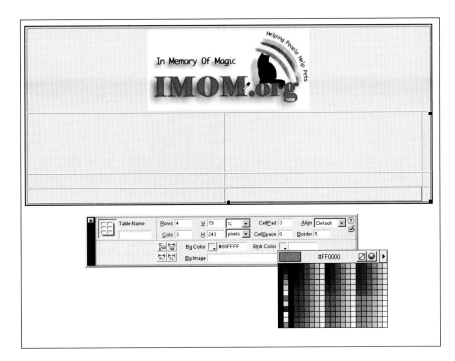

Figure 6.32
Matching borders to other page elements is easy by sipping colors with the Brdr Color eyedropper.

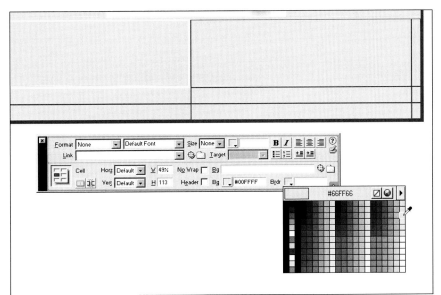

Figure 6.33
Make one cell stand out by applying a different color to its border.

Properties Inspector. If the table that contains the selected cells has a border of 1 pixel or greater, the color will be applied to the selected cell(s) border, as Figure 6.33 shows.

Controlling Tables with HTML

Building a table in HTML is a complex process in terms of the number of tags the code requires. Even if you're a fan of HTML coding, you might find that creating the table in Dreamweaver's Design view is easier than typing

```
<table width="50%" border="2" cellspacing="0" cellpadding="3">
  <tr>
    <td> </td>
    <td> </td>
  </tr>
  <tr>
    <td> </td>
    <td> </td>
  </tr>
  <tr>
    <td> </td>
    <td> </td>
  </tr>
</table>
```

Figure 6.34
You must enter and correctly position table, row, and column tags for the HTML code to successfully result in the creation of a table.

the multiple tags required for even the simplest of tables. Figure 6.34 shows the HTML code required to create a two-column, three-row table with a 2-pixel border.

Creating and Editing Tables in Code View

If you decide to build a table in Design view, you can watch the code being generated by switching to Design and Code views, in which a split screen shows both the code and WYSIWYG views of your Web page. After you build the basic table in Design view, you can tweak the HTML code to adjust the border, color, and size of the table as you want, as shown in Figure 6.35.

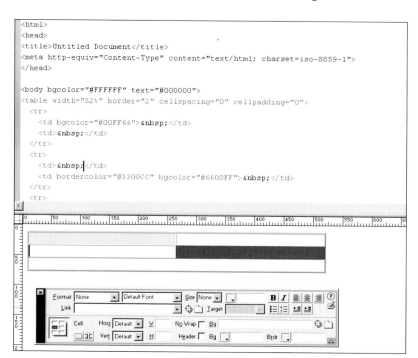

Figure 6.35
Build a simple table, and then add the attributes you need to customize it.

If you do decide to build a table in Code view, you'll need to insert the following tags, in the following order:

- A starting <**table**> tag
- A <**td**> tag for each column
- A <**tr**> tag for each row
- A closing </**td**> and </**tr**> for each column and row
- A closing </**table**> tag at the end of the table

After you've inserted these basic tags, you can go back and add attributes, such as table height and width, border thickness, border color, and code to position the table relative to the page, as shown in Figure 6.36.

A <table> is a Table

Remember that the attributes you apply within the **<table>** tag will apply to the entire table.

```
<table width="50%" border="2" cellspacing="0" cellpadding="3" bgcolor="#9900FF" bordercolor="#996699">
  <tr>
    <td> </td>
    <td bgcolor="#99CCCC" bordercolor="#9966FF"> </td>
  </tr>
  <tr>
    <td> </td>
    <td> </td>
  </tr>
  <tr>
    <td> </td>
    <td> </td>
  </tr>
</table>
```

Figure 6.36
Add table attributes within the opening <table> tag.

Nesting Tables in HTML

If you wish to create a nested table, you need an entire set of <**table**>, <**td**>, and <**tr**> tags (along with their closing tags) for the nested table, and this set of tags must be placed within the cell that will contain the nested table. Figure 6.37 shows the code for a nested table within a table cell.

```
<table width="50%" border="2" cellspacing="0" cellpadding="3" bgcolor="#9900FF" bordercolor="#996699">
  <tr>
    <td>
      <table width="50%" border="2" cellspacing="0" cellpadding="3">
        <tr>
          <td> </td>
          <td> </td>
        </tr>
        <tr>
          <td> </td>
          <td> </td>
        </tr>
        <tr>
          <td> </td>
          <td> </td>
        </tr>
      </table>
    </td>
    <td bgcolor="#99CCCC" bordercolor="#9966FF"> </td>
  </tr>
  <tr>
    <td> </td>
    <td> </td>
  </tr>
  <tr>
    <td> </td>
    <td> </td>
  </tr>
</table>
```

Figure 6.37
Tuck a set of table, column, and row tags inside an existing table cell's tags to create a nested table.

Create an Online Gallery with Tables

In this project, you'll create a Web page to house artwork. The art images will appear in table cells that you set up to create a pleasing composition.

Set Up the Table

The table will have three types of artwork, and each group of images will appear in a nested table. To make the main table, you'll need one column and three rows. Make the table the width of the page (the entire page filling an 800×600-pixel maximized window), and let the image sizes determine the height of individual cells (within the nested tables—therefore, automatically adjusting the height of the original table's rows).

Apply a Background Color to the Page

The images will look best on a black background. Apply black as the background color for the entire page.

Create Image Groups with Nested Tables

Now create the nested tables.

1. In the top row, which should consist of a single cell, create a three-column, three-row table. This table will house six images plus a group title.

2. In the second row of the original table, create a table that consists of two rows and three columns. The top row of this nested table will contain the title for this grouping, and the second row of the nested table will contain three images.

3. In the third row of the original table, create a nested table that consists of two rows and two columns. The top row will contain the group title, and the second row will contain two images.

Group Titles

Type and format the group titles.

1. To make the titles stand out, apply a white background color to the cells that contain the titles.

2. In the top row of the first nested table, type "OIL PAINTINGS". Center the text, and apply any size or font you think is appropriate.

3. In the top row of the second nested table, type "WATERCOLORS". Format the text as you did the title for the first nested table.

4. In the top row of the third nested table, type "DRAWINGS". Format this title to match the previous two.

Insert the Graphics

On the CD-ROM, in the Project 6B folder, you'll find three subfolders: Oils, Watercolors, and Drawings. The images you need to fill the nested tables are in each of these subfolders. Place one image in each cell of the nested tables, grouping the images logically—oils in the oil paintings table, watercolors in the watercolors table, and so on. Center all of the images in their cells.

Resize the Table Cells for Maximum Visibility

As necessary, increase or decrease the size of table cells so that a greater or lesser amount of space appears around the images. This spacing is an aesthetic choice, and it's entirely up to you.

Create the Picture Captions

Click to the right of each picture, press Shift+Enter to insert a line break, and type the name of the image. This name should be the same as the file name, without the .jpg extension.

Preview the Page

Press F12 to preview the page in your default browser. To make sure the page will look right to people using any browser, check it in an alternate browser, such as Netscape, if your default is Internet Explorer, or vice versa.

Save the Page and Create a New Site

Save the Web page as Gallery, and store it in a new site folder called Gallery Site. Copy the images from the CD-ROM folders to the Images folder in the gallery site.

Moving On

A table is an effective tool to use in setting up page layout. Another way to create sections within your page and position text and graphics across the page is through the use of frames. In Chapter 7, you'll learn to create a *frameset* and create, position, and customize frames to give you and your site's visitors great tools for viewing site content.

Chapter 7

Controlling a Page
with Frames

*Some people love frames, and other people . . . well, they
don't love them as much. You may not know yet which
group you fall into, and you might end up liking and using
frames in some circumstances and disliking them in others.
This chapter will show you when and where frames can be
a great tool for structuring and controlling access to your
pages, and how to build frames successfully.*

Understanding Frames

Frames are panes within your Web page, and each pane, or frame, acts as a distinct document. A Web page with frames is called a *frameset*, and each frame in the set has its own file name and operates as an independent window within the Web page. The page that contains the frames (the frameset) is also a distinct file with its own name.

What do frames do? They let you create rectangular areas in your Web page where text, graphics, and multimedia objects are stored and displayed. Figure 7.1 shows a page that consists of three frames—one across the top of the page, one down the left side of the page, and a large frame that makes up the center and right-lower side of the page.

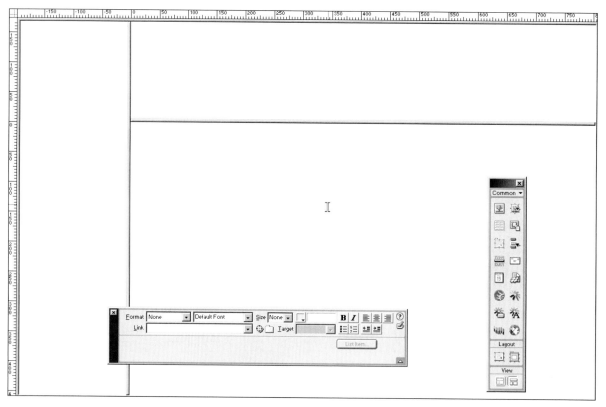

Figure 7.1

Display three Web pages at once with three frames in your page frameset.

Frames also let you arrange content on the page in virtually any combination of rectangular shapes you can imagine. Your page can have as many frames in it as you want, and you can size the frames quickly and easily with your mouse. You can also prevent site users from resizing your frames, so that anyone visiting the site does not alter your frame arrangement.

What don't frames do? Frames don't allow browsers to find your page, because none of the page content within frames is indexed, so search engines (such as **www.yahoo.com**, **www.hotbot.com**, or **www.google.com**) cannot find keywords on your site. For this reason alone, many Web designers avoid using frames, even when the design benefits would seemingly outweigh this drawback. If it's important that people find your site when they're searching the Web, you might want to use tables, rather than frames, to structure your page.

Ways exist to overcome this significant objection, however—including a home page without frames that contains the keywords you want search engines to find. You can then have that home page link to your main page that consists of frames.

Frames can also be hard for users to navigate and to print. If users follow a link from a non-frames Web page to another page on your site (or to another site), they can click the Back button on the browser toolbar to go back to your page, where they started. If your page is made up of frames, the Back button won't take them back to the original page, and this unexpected response is confusing to many users.

If your page includes content that you know people will want to print (and you want them to be able to), you might want to avoid using frames. With frames, when visitors issue the File|Print command through their browsers, they must decide whether they want to print each frame separately, print one particular frame, or print all of the frames in their current onscreen configuration. Because many users aren't aware that they need to specify what to print, they click the Print button without taking advantage of these options and end up frustrated if the printout isn't what they wanted.

In short, frames are a great design tool that provides a lot of power and freedom for the designer—which makes frames popular with many designers. An equal number of designers, however, find that frames' navigating, printing, and searching limitations are significant drawbacks, and they will strive to make tables and layers do the page-layout job they need done. With the exception of being able to scroll through one frame while the rest of the page remains static, you can achieve everything with tables and/or layers that you can with frames.

Building a Frameset

Creating frames on a Web page is simple, and you can approach the process in any of three ways. The method you prefer will have a lot to do with how you intend to use the frames, what sort of control you want over the formatting of your frames, and whether or not you like to work directly with HTML code.

It's a Long Story

Do you have a long article you want people to be able to read on one Web page? Normally, a long article must span several pages, like an article in a printed magazine does, with continuations that lead you from page to page to finish the article. If you don't want people leaving your single Web page to read the entire article, place the article in a frame. That way, readers can scroll through the frame and read the entire article, while the rest of the page remains static.

Hey—Where Are You?

Web search engines look at the first 100 or so words in a Web page and compare those words to the keywords a user has typed into the search criteria. If, for example, your site sells "widgets," you'll want the word "widget"—as well as any other words people might use in searching for a quality provider of widgets—to appear in the first 150 words on your home page. If your page is made up of frames, the search engine won't see the word "widget" on the page, no matter how many times it appears.

Viewing and Manipulating Frame Borders

A quick way to build a series of frames in your Web page is to turn on Frame Borders and then drag the borders from the perimeter into the inner area of the page. This method divides your page into blocks, and each block is a frame. You can drag and re-drag from one or more of the four sides of the window until you've created the frame configuration you need.

To turn on Frame Borders, choose View|Visual Aids|Frame Borders. A thick frame appears around the edge of the page, as Figure 7.2 shows. Point to the edge of the window, and your mouse turns to a two-headed arrow. When this happens, click and drag to create a frame, releasing the mouse when the frame is the size and in the spot you want it to be. The change to the look of the page is subtle, and you might not notice the frame immediately.

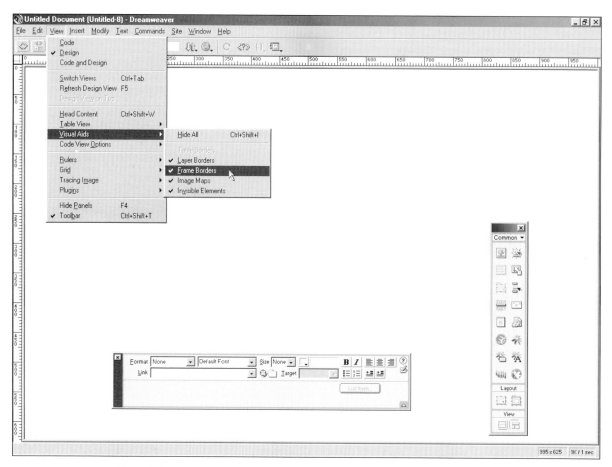

Figure 7.2

With Frame Borders turned on, you've created a single frame that can become many frames.

Inserting Predesigned Frames

If you use the Insert menu's Frame command, a submenu of frames appears: Left, Right, Top, Bottom, and so on, as Figure 7.3 shows. Each command in the submenu inserts a frame relative to the position of your cursor when you make the selection. For example, if you already have two vertical frames, choosing

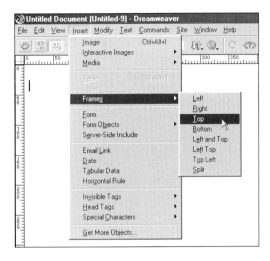

Figure 7.3
Choose from eight different
frame types and positions in the
Insert|Frames submenu.

Top from the submenu will place a frame across the top of the frame that contains your blinking cursor, and the other frame will remain intact.

You can also insert predesigned frames from the Objects panel. Click the Common button at the top of the Objects panel, and choose Frames. The panel changes to display a series of eight buttons, each a different kind of frame. Click the button for the frame you want, and the frame is created on the page. Figure 7.4 shows the Frames version of the Object panel, and a frame created with one of the Frame buttons.

Positioning Frames

Your choices for where to place your frames are limited to eight points on the page: Left, Right, Top, Bottom, Left and Top, Left Top, Top Left, and Split. The results of your choice from these eight locations depend on where your cursor is when you make the choice—on an empty, frameless page, or within an existing frame.

Once the frames are positioned, you can move them by resizing them. You can create a virtually unlimited combination of frames by creating frames and then inserting frames within them, or by splitting frames into two or more new frames. The potential hazard, of course, is that your page is broken into so many frames that, within the size of the visitor's screen, no frame would be large enough to display any content in its entirety, as Figure 7.5 demonstrates. Placing text that exceeds the length of a frame to be inserted is fine, because the visitor can scroll to read the extra text. When it comes to graphics, however, you want the entire image to be visible within the frame, with no scrolling required.

Removing Frames

If you need to remove a frame, you can drag the frame border to the edge of the page, or onto another frame border. As Figure 7.6 shows, if the frame you want to get rid of shares a wall with another frame, removing that border or wall will remove two frames.

Figure 7.4
Build frames quickly with the
Frames Object panel.

**Frames inside Frames
inside Frames**

If you create a predesigned frame within an existing frame, the existing frame becomes a new frameset. Nesting frames is similar to nesting tables—you choose where to nest the new frame, and then you select the frame type you want. Once created, the nested frames can be formatted just as you would format any other frame, and you can drag to resize the nested frames within the frame that contains them.

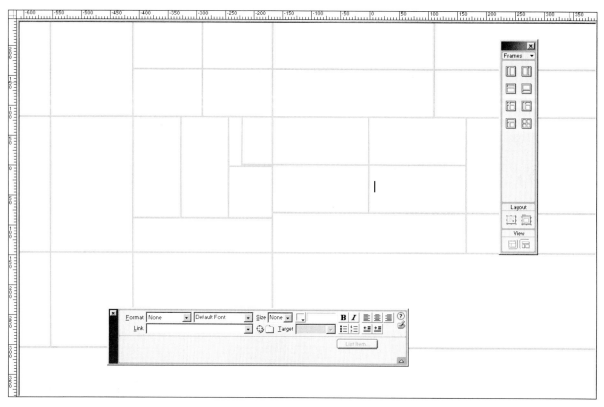

Figure 7.5

Although you can create as many frames as you want, create only as many as you need to house your content effectively.

Applying Frame Colors

As with tables and table cells, you can apply a background color to any individual frame. Unlike the process with tables and cells, however, the process of applying a frame color requires use of the Page Properties dialog box—remember that each frame is actually a separate page within the frameset.

To apply a color to an individual frame, follow these steps:

1. Click to place your cursor inside the frame you want to color.

2. Choose Modify|Page Properties.

3. In the Page Properties dialog box, click the Background color well, as shown in Figure 7.7. Click the eyedropper on a color in the resulting palette.

4. Click OK to apply the color and close the dialog box.

You can also apply a background image to an individual frame. Using the Page Properties dialog box, click the Browse button at the end of the Background Image text box, and navigate to the graphic file you want to use as the image for the frame. The image, like an image placed in the background on a regular Web page, will fall behind any text or other graphic content you add to the frame, as shown in Figure 7.8.

Just Taking Up Space

You can use a frame with a graphic or color background to create visual space between two other frames. The spacing frame need not have any actual content of its own—its role is simply to create a visual break between two frames that contain a lot of text, or perhaps images, that shouldn't be viewed right next to each other.

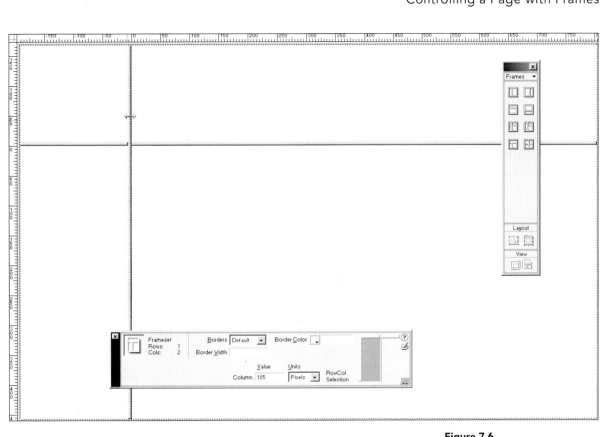

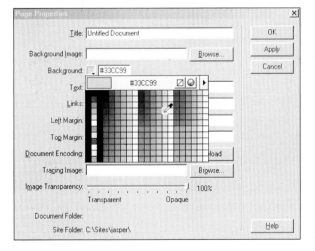

Figure 7.6
In this four-frame configuration, removing one frame actually results in the removal of two frames, one of which will have to be recreated.

Figure 7.7
Select a Web-safe color for your frame background, keeping eventual graphic and text content in mind.

Adding Text and Graphics to Frames

Frames present no special problems for inserting text and graphics. But, because your site's visitors can resize frames (unless you have applied sizing controls), you must think about whether or not the entire graphic or all of the text can be viewed effectively within the frame if someone were to change the width and/or height.

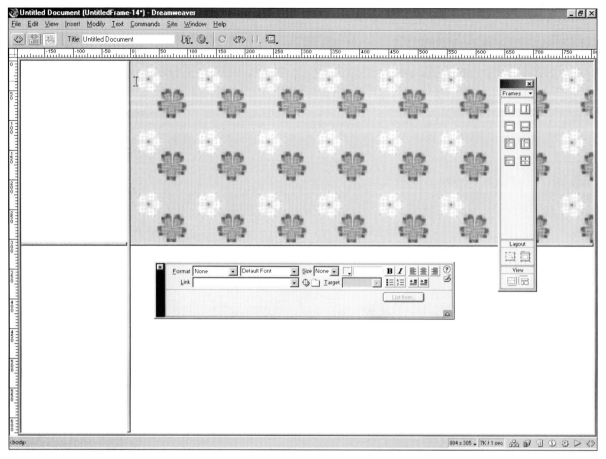

Figure 7.8

Choose a background image that won't interfere with any text typed into the frame or overwhelm any graphics you insert.

When you add text or graphics to a frame, you have many of the same options as you do when you're adding text or graphics to a table cell or layer—you can adjust the alignment and the size; add and remove line or paragraph breaks above, below, and within (in the case of text); and play with colors to achieve the effects you want. The Properties Inspector appears as it does on any Web page when your cursor is active in the frame.

Inserting Frame Text

To add text to a frame, simply type or paste the text from another existing document. As you type, if the text reaches the right side of the frame, it will wrap to the next line. If you reduce the width of the frame, the word-wrap effect becomes more pronounced. When you're typing paragraphs in any restricted space, be sure not to press Shift+Enter (for a line break) within a paragraph—if you do so, unpleasant results can occur if the frame width is changed after the text has been typed. As Figure 7.9 shows, odd breaks will occur when resizing the frame moves the right margin.

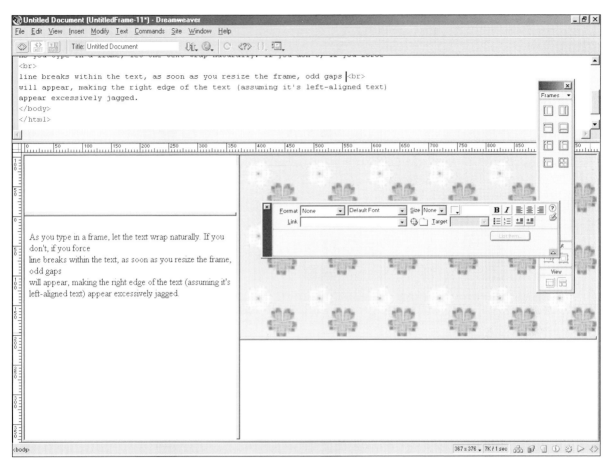

Figure 7.9
You can tell when someone didn't let the text wrap naturally—gaps within and at the end of lines can result.

Sizing Frames for Text and Graphic Content

To resize a frame, drag its borders. When you point to the border of the frame, your mouse turns into a two-headed arrow, which indicates that you can drag the border to resize the frame. As Figure 7.10 shows, you can use the ruler to make adjustments if you need to make a frame a specific number of pixels wide or tall.

When you click on a frame border, the Properties Inspector changes to show frame options, as you see in Figure 7.11. You can use these options to adjust the row position, the frame-border thickness, and the border color.

Establishing Frame Sizing Controls

Once you've taken the trouble to size a frame to a specific width and height, you probably don't want site visitors to resize the frames when they view your pages online. Although, by default, frames are resizable on the page, you can remove this capability, thus protecting the layout you've painstakingly set up.

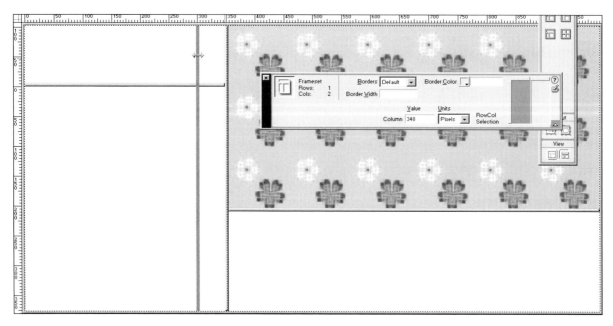

Figure 7.10

If you want your frame to have certain dimensions, watch the ruler as you drag the frame's borders with your mouse.

To prevent visitors from resizing your pages online, use the No Resize checkbox in the Properties Inspector. Pressing the Alt key and clicking inside the frame in question displays this particular version of the Properties Inspector, which you can see in Figure 7.12.

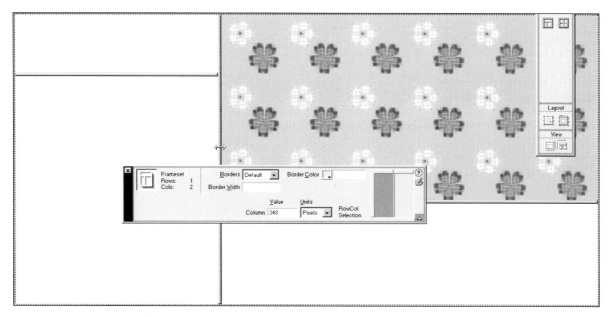

Figure 7.11

View the Properties Inspector's options for a selected frame.

Bear in mind that, if you set a frame to No Resize and that frame shares borders with other frames, those frames will also be protected from resizing, whether you want them to be or not. Although you can Alt+click in the surrounding

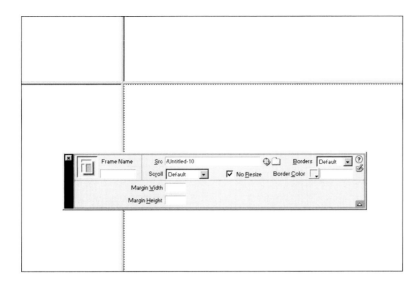

Figure 7.12

Place a check next to the No Resize attribute to prevent changes in the size of your frame.

frames and turn off the No Resize option, because of the shared borders, those frames still won't be resizable when they're previewed in a browser or viewed online. If you need visitors to have the capability to resize a frame, make sure the frame has no sides in common with any frame for which the No Resize option is turned on.

Setting Frame Scrolling Options

Another frame customization you can apply is the capability to scroll within the frame. By default, if the frame's content exceeds the size of the frame, a scrollbar will appear across the bottom and down the right side of the frame. If you don't want a scrollbar to appear, you can turn off the scrolling for an individual frame. (You also can turn the scrolling on, so that even if the content fits entirely within the frame, a scrollbar appears.)

To access the controls for frame scrolling, press the Alt key and click inside the frame you want to customize. The Properties Inspector changes to display frame settings, which include the list of scrolling options you see in Figure 7.13.

Testing 1, 2, 3

Always test your frame settings before you post content to the Web. Choose File|Preview In Browser to test your page and its frames. This action will help you make sure your resizing controls and other frame options are as you want them to be before you let the world see your Web site.

Figure 7.13

Choose whether or not your frame will include a scrollbar to assist visitors in viewing all of the frame's content.

The options for scrolling are as follows:

- *Yes*—means that a scrollbar will appear whether or not the frame's content requires it. This option is good if you're allowing the visitor to resize the frame, because the visitor might make the frame too small to show everything in it. This option is not good if the appearance of a scrollbar will have a negative effect on your layout or design.

- *No*—means that even if the content is more than will fit inside the frame, the visitor cannot scroll through it. Obviously, this is not a good option for frames that contain text, but it is a good option for frames that contain a graphic that is intended to serve as a background or filler image for the frame—the image might be larger than the frame, but viewers don't need to scroll around to see the graphic in its entirety.

- *Auto*—means that the scrollbar will appear only if needed. As long as the frame is larger than the content, no scrollbar will be added. This option is really the same as the Default option.

- *Default*—is the same as Auto—no scrollbar will appear unless the frame is resized to obscure some of the content (or in the case of frames that cannot be resized, if the frame has more in it—long paragraphs of text, for example—than are visible all at once in the frame).

Controlling Frame Links and Effects

Frames, like table cells or pages that contain no special structural devices, often contain links. These links can be in the form of text or graphics, and when a site visitor clicks them, you can control what happens. That control begins, of course, with the link target you establish through the Properties Inspector—you type the exact page name or URL for the site to which the link points. With frames, however, your control doesn't end there. You can control how the linked page or site is displayed—within the frame that contains the link, in a new window, and how the target is displayed. Figure 7.14 shows the Target drop list and your choices for the display of linked content.

Figure 7.14
Choose how your linked page or site will appear when a visitor's mouse-click activates the target.

Your choices for the display of linked pages and content are the following:

- _blank

- _parent

- _self

- _top

The _blank option opens the target in a new, blank browser window. The new window is on top of the window that contains the link, and you can close the new window if you want to return to the frame. This option is a good choice if you want visitors to explore another page or site but not really leave your site—an effective technique if the target site has no reciprocal link, or if you're not sure whether your visitors are familiar enough with the browser interface to know to click the Back button to return to your page (or to use the History feature to go back to where they left off at your site).

The _parent option causes the linked page or site to open in the parent frame, a *parent* being a frame that contains a nested frame. Imagine, for example, a three-frame frameset within another frame that fills half the page. The _parent option will cause the target to be displayed in the half-page frame, replacing the three-frame frameset. This is a good choice if you want to keep visitors on your page but show them external content. If the frame that contains the link is too small to contain that linked content, having the target appear in a larger frame will help visitors see more of the content all at once.

If you want the linked page or site to appear in the same frame that contained the link, choose the _self option. This is a good choice if the linked content is the same size as the original frame content, or if scrolling won't be a nuisance—should the targeted content be a long article, for example.

You'll like the _top option if you want the target page or site to replace the current window entirely. This choice isn't good if the target is an entirely different site with no clear, simple way back to your site from within it. It's a good choice if the target is within your site and includes navigation buttons back to the starting page.

Naming Frames

As I discussed earlier in this chapter, you must save each frame on a page as a distinct file, and a collection of frames on a single page is a frameset. This step isn't the end of the frame-naming process, and it's not all you need to do to establish the identity of the individual frames in the frameset. If your frames will contain targets, the frames need names. Applying these names is not the same as naming the frame files when you save them—rather, it's a process

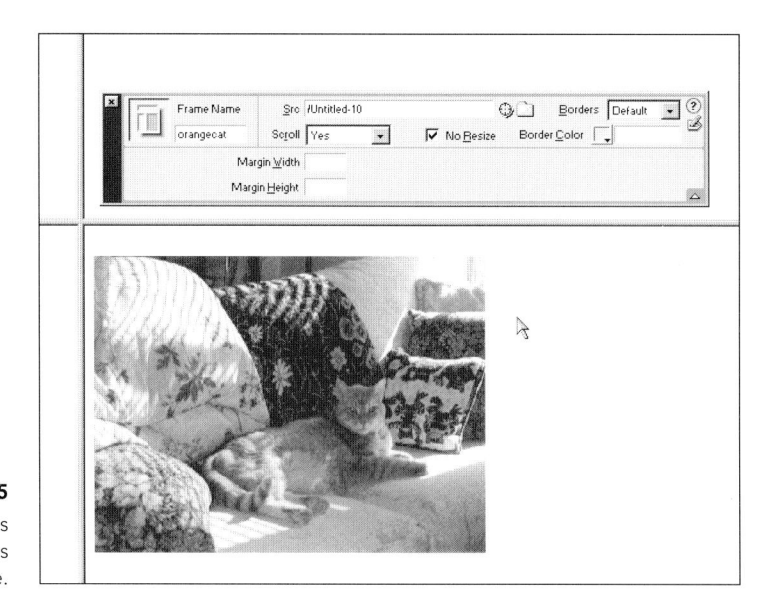

Figure 7.15
Frame names can't have spaces or hyphens, though underscores are fine.

you perform in the frames version of the Properties Inspector, as shown in Figure 7.15. You'll want to go through each frame (pressing the Alt key as you click inside each frame), to display the proper set of Properties Inspector options for each frame, and give each frame a name.

When you're naming frames, try to use simple, yet relevant, names. The names can be indicative of the frame content, or they can indicate the location of the frame on the page. For example, the name "mainstory" for a frame that contains the main news story on a news page would be useful, and the name "across_top" would be good for the frame that spans the top of the page.

PROJECT Create Frames for a Company Intranet Directory

In this project, you'll create a Web page for a hypothetical company. The frames will contain lists of employees and their phone extensions, a list of contact numbers for emergencies, and a list of forms available on the company's network. One of the frames will be linked to another page within the company's intranet and, when clicked, will open a new window.

Build the Frameset

Create a frameset on a blank new page. The frameset will have a total of four frames, as Figure 7.16 shows.

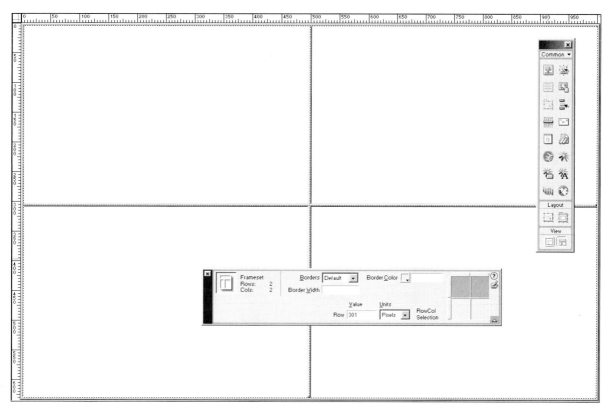

Size the Frames

Size the four frames so that the top frame (spanning the top of the page) is 100 percent of the width of the page, and 100 pixels tall. The remaining three frames should appear as in Figure 7.17:

1. The two frames on the left will be of equal size, their combined height equaling the height of the single frame on the right side of the page.

2. The column (two frames) on the left should be one-third the width of the page width.

3. The largest frame should be two-thirds the width of the page.

Format the Individual Frames

Format frames as follows:

1. Apply colored backgrounds to each of the frames, employing your own choice of colors.

2. Set all the frames to No Resize, and turn Scrolling to Yes for the largest frame. The top frame should have no scrollbar.

Figure 7.16
Drag the frame borders onto the page to create four frames.

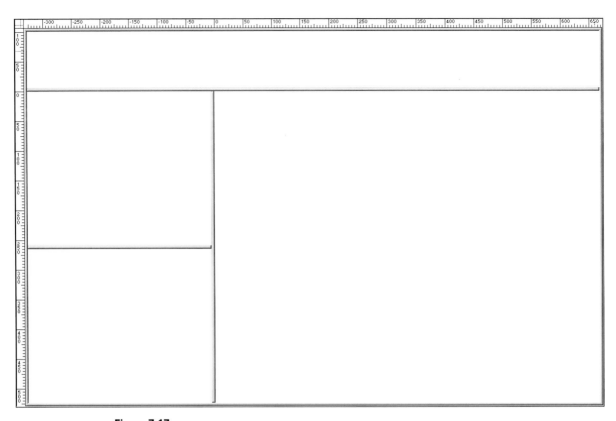

Figure 7.17

Configure your four frames as shown.

3. Set the two smaller frames on the left to Auto so that the amount of content in the frame dictates whether a scrollbar appears.

Insert Frame Content

You'll find the content for the frames on the CD-ROM in the form of text files—one file for each of the three lower frames.

1. Type "EMPLOYEE CONTACT INFO and FORMS" into the top frame (the frame spanning the top of the page).

2. Format this page heading, as you desire.

3. Open the text files, one at a time, and copy the text from each file to the Clipboard.

4. Switch back to Dreamweaver, click in the frame that will contain the text, and use the Paste command to insert the text. The files and their associated frames are as follows:

   • In the largest frame insert the content of the file called names&numbers.txt.

- In the top of the two frames on the left insert the content of the file named emergency.txt.

- In the bottom of the two frames on the left insert the text from the file called forms.txt.

You do not need to format the text in any of the frames, although you can apply fonts and font colors, as you desire, so that the text remains legible on your colored backgrounds.

Save and Name the Frames

Save the frameset, naming each frame numerically, clockwise from the top— Frame1, Frame2, and so on. Name the frameset employeeinfo.htm.

Using the Properties Inspector, name each frame as follows:

- topframe

- employees

- emergency

- forms

Build the Frame Link and Link Settings

The Forms frame will have links to documents that users can print or save to their own computers. Set the links to _blank so that the documents open in a new window. The three links are as follows:

- *Vacation Requests*—should link to vacationrequest.htm.

- *Leave of Absence*—should link to leave.htm.

- *Expense Reimbursement*—should link to expenses.htm.

The three HTM files are on the CD-ROM, in the folder called Project 7A.

Preview and Test the Frames

Press the F12 key to use your default browser to preview the page. As soon as the page opens, test the frames' links to make sure they work as you intended.

Understanding HTML Frame Codes

The HTML you'll see created as you build and populate frames is similar to the code created when you build tables. Instead of **<table>** tags, and **<td>** and **<tr>** tags for columns and rows, you'll see a **<frameset>** tag, with numbers representing the dimensions (in pixels) of the frame. What's really different from tables is that you'll see the **<frameset>** and related tags only when the frame is selected. If your cursor is simply in the frame, you'll see only the code

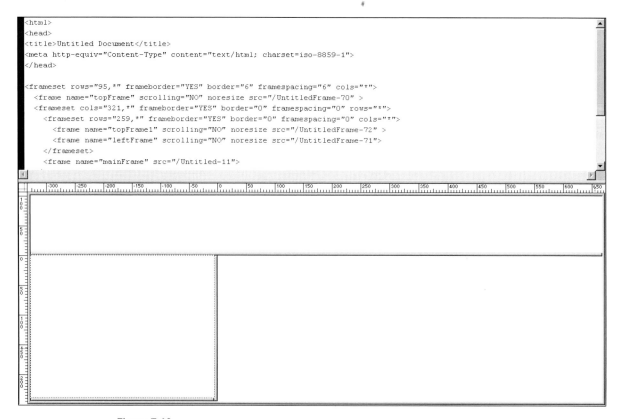

```
<html>
<head>
<title>Untitled Document</title>
<meta http-equiv="Content-Type" content="text/html; charset=iso-8859-1">
</head>

<frameset rows="95,*" frameborder="YES" border="6" framespacing="6" cols="*">
  <frame name="topFrame" scrolling="NO" noresize src="/UntitledFrame-70" >
    <frameset cols="321,*" frameborder="YES" border="0" framespacing="0" rows="*">
      <frameset rows="259,*" frameborder="YES" border="0" framespacing="0" cols="*">
        <frame name="topFrame1" scrolling="NO" noresize src="/UntitledFrame-72" >
        <frame name="leftFrame" scrolling="NO" noresize src="/UntitledFrame-71">
      </frameset>
      <frame name="mainFrame" src="/Untitled-11">
```

Figure 7.18

The active frameset's dimensions, and the settings for all of its frames, appear in a simple set of tags and attributes.

for the frame's content, as though the frame were a page unto itself—which it really is, despite the fact that we think of the frame as being part of a page. Figure 7.18 shows the combined Code and Design views, with the code displayed when a frame is active, and Figure 7.19 shows that same frame, with the cursor inside it.

Building a Frameset in HTML

Even more so than tables, frames are much easier to create in a WYSIWYG environment than through direct HTML coding. Unless you already know the exact layout of your frameset, the dimensions of each frame, and all the options you want to employ for each frame, it's much easier to draw your frames by dragging frame borders on the page, and then using the Properties Inspector to assign the frames' colors, border width, scrolling, and resizing options.

If you want to try your hand at coding a frameset from scratch, be sure to map the frame setup on paper first—or at least have a clear picture of the layout of the frameset and the size of each frame before you get started. As Figure 7.20 shows, the tags include references to untitled (unsaved) frame files, as well as the pixel dimensions of each frame.

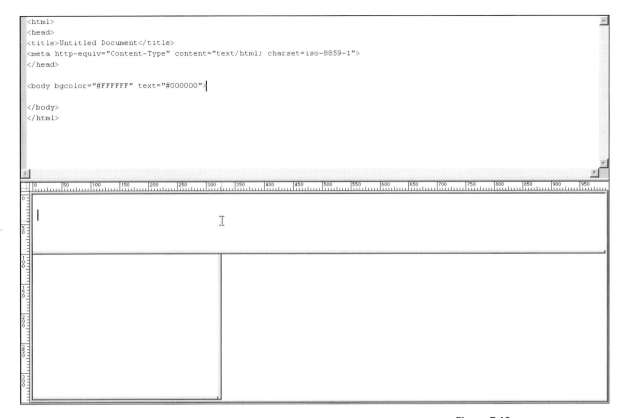

```
<html>
<head>
<title>Untitled Document</title>
<meta http-equiv="Content-Type" content="text/html; charset=iso-8859-1">
</head>

<body bgcolor="#FFFFFF" text="#000000">

</body>
</html>
```

Figure 7.19
The code for the frame's content gives no indication that the content is in a frame.

```
<frameset rows="95,*" frameborder="YES" border="6" framespacing="6" cols="*">
  <frame name="topFrame" scrolling="NO" noresize src="/UntitledFrame-70" >
  <frameset cols="321,*" frameborder="YES" border="0" framespacing="0" rows="*">
    <frameset rows="259,*" frameborder="YES" border="0" framespacing="0" cols="*">
      <frame name="topFrame1" scrolling="NO" noresize src="/UntitledFrame-72" >
      <frame name="leftFrame" scrolling="NO" noresize src="/UntitledFrame-71">
    </frameset>
    <frame name="mainFrame" src="/Untitled-11">
  </frameset>
</frameset>
<noframes><body bgcolor="#FFFFFF" text="#000000">

</body></noframes>
</html>
```

Figure 7.20
The rows and cols dimensions within the **<frameset>** tag indicate the size of the frameset.

Moving On

Now that you know about frames, we'll move on to the third feature that helps you control the structure of your Web page and the placement of page elements: layers. In Chapter 8, you'll learn to create and format layers in a creative and effective configuration, and you'll discover when to use (and not to use) layers in your Web-page development. You'll also learn to animate layers—yet another way to add visual interest to your Web page.

Chapter 8

Positioning Page Content with Layers

Layers give you the freedom to position Web content virtually anywhere on the page, without the constraints that tables and frames impose. This chapter shows you how to build and populate layers with graphics, text, and color— and how to animate layers so you can add visually interesting motion to your Web designs.

Working with Layers

Probably the best way to describe how layers work on a Web page is to ask you to imagine a sheet of paper covered with sticky notes. You can write anything you want on the notes—even draw pictures on them, and then move them anywhere on the paper. Layers work much the same way on your Web page. You can create the layers (in virtually any size you want) anywhere on your Web page—you can even make layers overlap other layers. You can draw layers on top of a table or inside a frame. The free-form way in which you can draw, resize, and move layers around on the page makes them an effective design tool—with one major drawback.

Layers would be perfect except that only the latest versions of the major browsers recognize them. I don't mean the layer might not display properly for a visitor using an old browser—I mean that visitor won't even see the layer or anything in it. Browsers that existed before Netscape 4 and Internet Explorer 4 don't acknowledge layers at all.

Does this mean you can't use layers? Well, if you don't know which browser your visitors will be using, putting important information in a layer, or using layers if your design hinges on their visibility, is not a good idea. Because most of us don't know which browser our visitors are using, many designers avoid using layers entirely. One exception is intranets. If you're designing for a company's intranet, and all the employees in the company have browsers that are version 4 or later, you can safely use layers because you know that the only visitors to the site will be using a browser that can see the layers.

Creating Layers

One of the best things about layers is how easy they are to create. To add a layer to your page, you can let Dreamweaver place a predesigned layer on your page (predesigned in terms of its size), or you can draw a layer by hand to your sizing specifications. The two methods are as follows:

- *Choose Insert|Layer.* A 125-pixel-high by 200-pixel-wide layer appears on your page, at the cursor, as shown in Figure 8.1. Once you've inserted the layer, you can move and resize it as needed. If you continue to add layers with this method without repositioning your cursor, the layers will stack up, and you'll have to move them around on the page to place them where you want them.

- *Use the Draw Layer button on the Objects palette.* This method gives you more control over your layers from the beginning. As soon as you click this button, your mouse turns to a crosshair, and you can draw a layer anywhere on your page, of any size you need, as shown in Figure 8.2. Once you've drawn the layer, you can move and resize it to meet your needs.

Backward Compatibility?

You can make layers compatible with browsers (either Netscape or Internet Explorer) prior to version 4, but doing so requires you to convert your layers to a table (I discuss the technique later in this chapter). For most designers, the point of using layers is that they allow a more free-form arrangement of page content, and converting layers to tables might defeat that purpose. If you want to make your layers-laden page backward compatible—a reasonable idea if you know that the majority of your audience will be using older software—choose File|Convert|3.0 Browser Compatible. In the resulting dialog box, choose to convert your layers to tables, and click OK.

But I Really Want to Use Layers

If you're not in a position to control the browser visitors to your site use, yet you really want to use layers in your page design, make two versions of your page—one version with layers, and one version without. On the version with layers, add a link (not inside a layer, of course) that takes people to the non-layers version. That link might say something like, "If you don't see any page content, click this link." You don't need to tell visitors why they aren't seeing your content, but you're giving them a quick way to get to a page they can see properly.

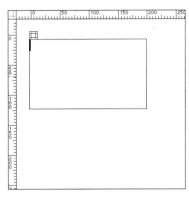

Figure 8.1
Create a 125x200-pixel layer quickly with the Insert|Layer command.

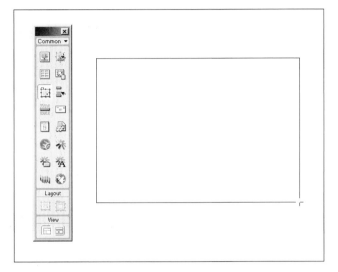

Figure 8.2
Click the Layer button, then draw a layer in the exact spot you want it, in the exact size you need.

Converting Tables to Layers

If you've already created a page layout, or organized a portion of your page with a table, you can convert that table to a series of layers, retaining their size, placement, and content. This approach is obviously preferable to creating layers from scratch, copying content from the table to the layers, and then deleting the table. Note that when you're converting a table to layers, only the table cells that have content—text or graphics—will be converted to layers. The thinking behind this caveat is that, presumably, if the cell doesn't have anything in it, you don't need a layer to replace it.

To convert a table to layers, follow these simple steps:

1. Select the table to be converted, as shown in Figure 8.3. You can click in any cell of the table and press Ctrl+A until the entire table is selected— this step might require two or more presses of the keyboard shortcut.

2. Choose Modify|Convert|Table To Layers. The Convert Table To Layers dialog box opens, as shown in Figure 8.4.

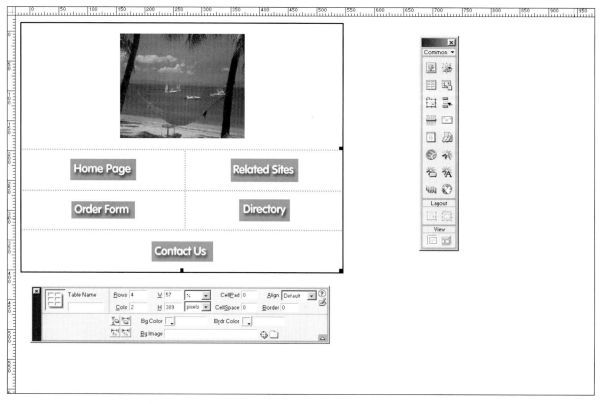

Figure 8.3

While it's ok to simply position your cursor in a cell of the table to be converted, selecting the entire table avoids confusion if you have more than one table on the page.

3. Using the checkboxes next to the four conversion options, turn options on and off as desired. Your options (all of which are on by default) are as follows:

- *Prevent Layer Overlaps*—This option does what it implies—it keeps the table cells from overlapping once they're converted to layers. If your table cells currently have spacing set to 0 pixels, this option is a good one to turn on if you don't want the layers to run into and over each other. Bear in mind, however, that using this option will also prevent future changes in size or position of the layers in question—you won't be able to move the layers or change their size in any way that would result in overlapping within the layers created through the conversion process.

- *Show Layer Palette*—This option turns on the Layers palette, through which you can name and change the stacking order of layers. You can also turn layers on and off through this palette, which makes it

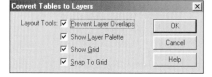

Figure 8.4

Choose how your table-to-layer conversion will be performed.

easier to edit a layer that is partially obscured by another, or to create some visual simplicity for yourself during the design process by turning off distracting surrounding layers and their content. Turning the layers off affects their visibility in Dreamweaver only—it doesn't delete them or remove them from view when the page is seen in a browser window locally or online.

- *Show Grid*—This is another easily deciphered option. If you want a page grid to appear to assist you in placing the layers you create through the conversion process, leave this option on.

- *Snap To Grid*—This option takes viewing the grid to another level by forcing your layers to adhere to the vertical and horizontal lines that make up the grid. You'll feel the layers pulled toward those lines as you move layers around on the page, and you will be unable to place layers other than along the lines in the grid. Of course, the grid is for design use only—it doesn't show when the page is viewed through the browser.

4. Click OK to convert the table's cells to layers. As Figure 8.5 shows, the layers are sized to match the original table cells.

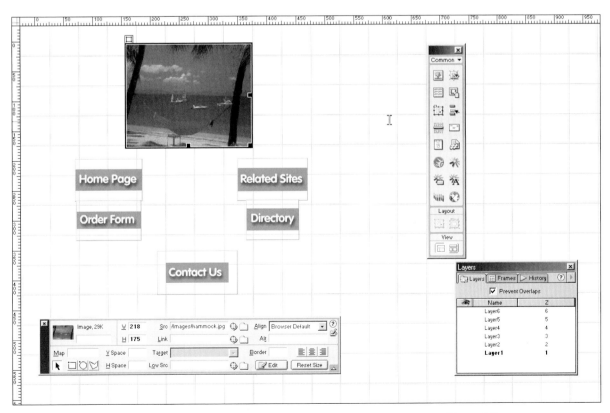

Figure 8.5

A six-cell table has become a group of six layers.

Moving and Resizing Layers

Anyone who has drawn a shape in a graphics or illustration application, or even in a current version of a word processor, has the skills required to move and resize a layer. Just like a drawn shape, when a layer is selected, it has handles you can drag to resize it, as shown in Figure 8.6.

When you're resizing a layer, drag the corner handles to maintain the layer's current *aspect ratio*, or proportion of the layer's height and width (see Figure 8.7). Of course, dragging the side handles will adjust the layer's dimensions in only one direction at a time. Dragging the top, or bottom, center handles will affect the layer's height, and dragging from a side, center handle (left or right sides) will affect the layer's width.

To move a layer, click its selection handle (which looks like a folder tab, as shown in Figure 8.8). When your mouse is over that handle, the mouse will appear as a four-headed arrow. While that mouse pointer is displayed, you can move the layer in any direction you want, dragging it with your mouse to any spot on the page. As soon as you release the mouse, the layer is repositioned.

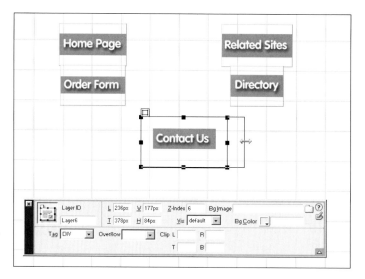

Figure 8.6

Point to a layer's handles, and drag outward to make the layer larger; drag inward to make the layer smaller.

Using the Layers Panel

Although the Layers panel (or palette) is not essential to your use of layers on a Web page, it is a great tool for keeping track of the layers on your page. Through this floating box on your Dreamweaver window, you can name your layers (to help you identify them by their content or intended position), turn them on and off (to control which ones are visible on screen as you develop your page), and change their stacking order (which is especially useful if your layers overlap). As Figure 8.9 shows, the Layers panel contains the key information about each of your layers on the active page.

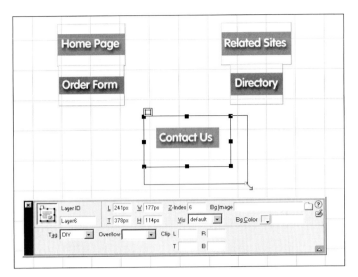

Figure 8.7
Use the corner handles if you don't want to change the layer's proportions.

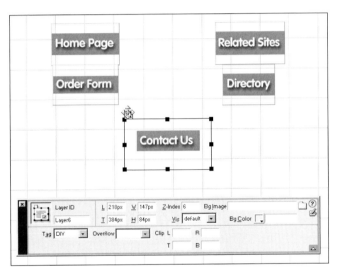

Figure 8.8
Point to the layer's selection tab to select and then drag the layer to a new location on the page.

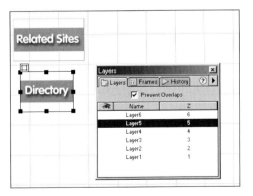

Figure 8.9
In the Layers panel, view and edit the names and stacking order of your layers.

Moving without a Mouse

You can reposition a selected layer without using your mouse to drag it. Simply click once on the layer to select it, and then use your keyboard's arrow keys to move the layer, one pixel at a time. This method is especially helpful if you want to move the layer in only one direction. Moving the layer with your mouse won't assure you of a single-direction move—as a human, you're not capable of that level of precision, and certainly not with a standard mouse or trackball. However, if you use the arrow keys, the layer is moved precisely in one direction at a time, one pixel at a time.

Until You Say So

Once displayed, the Layers panel will appear on screen each time you open Dreamweaver, and with each new and reopened Web-page document—that is, until you turn the panel off. To turn it off, click the X (Close) button in the upper-right corner of the panel; right-click the panel's title bar, and choose Close from the pop-up menu; or select Layers from the Window menu to toggle the displayed panel off. This on-until-you-turn-it-off status applies to all panels and palettes after you've turned them on. In addition, when the panel/palette appears, it will be right where you left it the last time you used Dreamweaver.

Figure 8.10

Double-click the layer name and type a replacement.

Displaying the Layers Panel

Simply creating a layer on your page doesn't automatically cause the Layers panel to appear. If the panel isn't already visible, you must choose to display it, which you can do in one of two ways:

- Choose Window|Layers

- Press F2

After you display the panel, you can click on any layer on your page and see that layer become selected on the panel.

Naming Layers

If your page has only one or two layers, you probably don't need to name them—keeping track of such a small number of layers won't be too difficult, even if they have names such as Layer 1 or Layer 2. However, if you have several (or many) layers, you'll probably want to name them, if only to help you keep track of them and select them quickly.

That's right—I said, "Select them." That's another use for the Layers panel. You can click on a layer by name in the panel, and that layer is selected on the page. This feature is handy if you have overlapping layers, and getting at an edge of a layer without selecting something nearby, or selecting content within the layer itself, is difficult.

To make this selection method more effective, name your layers by double-clicking the generic name the layer was assigned when you created it. When you double-click the layer name, a box forms around the layer name (as Figure 8.10 shows), and you can type a new name in the box for the layer. Obviously, keeping the name short is a good idea, as in "Logo" or "Warehouse" for a layer that will contain a photo of your company's warehouse. Why keep names short? So you don't have to make the Layers panel wider to be able to see the entire name. A name such as "List of Departments" is a little long (and it contains spaces, which are forbidden); the more succinct "Departments" does the job quite nicely.

After you've typed the new name for your layer, click outside the panel or press Enter to complete the naming process. You can rename layers as often as you'd like, but the names can contain only letters and numbers (no punctuation or spaces), and the names must start with a letter.

Changing the Order of Overlapping Layers

As you create layers, Dreamweaver places them in stacking order. If, for example, you draw a layer and then draw a second layer, the second layer will automatically overlay the first layer—even if you drag Layer 1 (the first one drawn) onto Layer 2 (the second one). In short, the most recently drawn layer will rise to the top of any stack, as Figure 8.11 shows. In this figure, you see the Layers panel and three numbered layers (the numbers you see within the layers were typed for illustrative purposes).

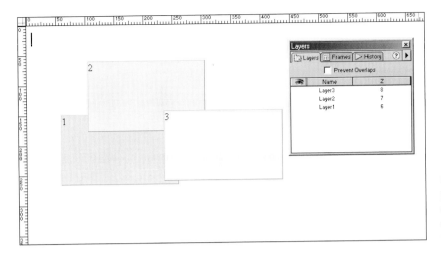

Figure 8.11
Even if you drag an earlier layer on top of another, more recent one, the layer you created most recently will stay on top.

Of course, this situation is the default and, like most defaults, you can change it. You don't have to live with the stacking order as Dreamweaver assigns it, based on the order in which you draw your layers. If you want Layer 3 to be under Layer 1, you can use the Layers panel to change the order of the layers. Just drag the layer (by name, within the panel) you want to restack, and deposit that layer name after (below) the name of the layer in the list that should be on top of it. Conversely, if you have a layer that sticks to the bottom of the stack by default, drag the name of that layer up in the list of layers and drop it in above the name of the layer that should be under it in the stack. Figure 8.12 shows a restacking in progress.

Turning Layers On and Off

Sometimes, as you're designing a Web page, you feel overwhelmed by all the stuff on the page. You wish you could just put things away—shove them aside—until you've completed the work on a particular area of the page. For example, having a background image on screen while you're typing text onto the page, or having a graphic very near another graphic as you work to position one of them or to draw hotspots on top of an image, can be annoying. The same phenomenon certainly occurs when you're working on a page with multiple layers, especially when those layers are close together or actually overlapping.

Figure 8.12
The thick horizontal line shows the current stacking position of the layer in transit.

Normally, if you're feeling visually overwhelmed, no relief exists (short of using the Edit|Cut command to delete something, and be able to replace it quickly using the Paste command) to get something out of the way; you're generally stuck with a visually busy page. If, however, your content is on one or more layers, you can turn off the layer(s) to more easily work undistracted on a specific area of the page. Because layers can overlap, being able to turn off one or more of them is important—working in one layer would be nearly impossible if another layer were on top of or overlapping it. Be aware that although the active layer always moves to the top of any stack of layers, having the other layers in view risks your accidentally clicking in one of them, which will bring that layer to the top and obscure the layer you wanted to work on.

To turn a layer on or off, click in the "eye" column in the Layers panel, directly next to the layer you want to turn on or off. By default, no eye appears in the column. If you click in the column, however, a closed eye appears (see Figure 8.13), and the corresponding layer disappears. If you want that layer to come back, click the closed eye, and an open eye appears, as does the previously hidden layer.

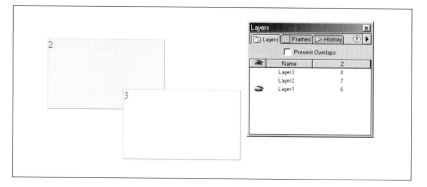

Figure 8.13
A closed eye means the layer is hidden.

Using a Tracing Image to Lay Out a Page

So, layers are easy to create, move, and resize—and to restack and select by name using the handy Layers panel. Layers free you to create a virtually unlimited structure for your Web page. But what if all that freedom makes designing a page more difficult? What if you can't quite picture the layout you want, and having all that freedom to place any layer anywhere on the page is keeping you from developing a layout in your mind, and then making it happen on the page? With layers, that situation is common. You have an idea for a page layout in mind, but you can't quite imagine how it would translate to the actual page. You start drawing layers and moving them around, but the size and placement of the layers don't work once you start adding content. And the overall composition of the page isn't what you had pictured in your mind's eye.

What do you do? Apply a blueprint to the page, in the form of a *tracing image*. A tracing image is a picture, normally the size of an entire page (or a good portion thereof), which Dreamweaver places on the page background (hiding your actual background image, if you have one applied). The tracing image gives you a map to work with as you place and size layers to house your page

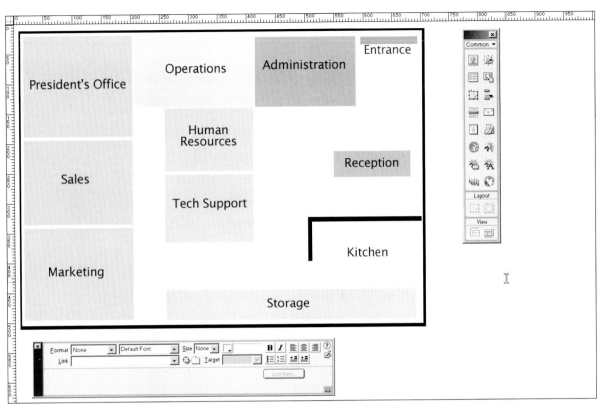

Figure 8.14

Use a tracing image to help you position your layers on the page.

content. Figure 8.14 shows a tracing image that helps the designer lay out a page to match a company's office floor plan. By using a schematic of the floor plan as the tracing image, the designer can draw layers the size of each office, and various common areas and hallways, and then insert the office-specific content into each layer.

Once you've placed and resized all your layers, you can get rid of the tracing image, and any background image you'd applied will reappear. Remember that the tracing image won't appear when the page is viewed through a browser, whether you're previewing it locally or viewing the page online.

Choosing an Image

You will normally create tracing images in a graphics or illustration application such as Photoshop, CorelDRAW, or Fireworks. The application you choose will depend on the complexity and content of the image. Often, an image (such as a photograph or schematic) already exists for another purpose (think of the office floor plan in Figure 8.15—that floor plan was created to assist builders in setting up walls where they were needed, but it also works well as a tracing image for a page that needs a layout that matches the configuration of an actual office space).

Only with Layers?

Of course, you can use a tracing image even if you aren't working with layers. If you're setting up a table or a frame, or you're simply entering content on a page that contains no other structural devices, the tracing image can help you position your content. A tracing image is so effective with layers because, with the freedom to place layers anywhere on the page, the tracing image helps you choose the right spots for the layers and make them the right size. Placing a table randomly on a page isn't possible, so the tracing image won't help much with that. It can help, however, in terms of sizing the table and its cells.

If you're going to use an image that already exists, you'll probably need to resize it to the full size of the page you're designing, or to the portion of that page that requires the use of the tracing image. If, for example, your page is designed for an 800×600-pixel display, the page itself will be in the neighborhood of 700×500 pixels. Your tracing image, therefore, should be that same size. Forget all the rules about using small images on a Web page—your tracing image won't ever be loaded by a browser, so a big image that's several hundred kilobytes in size won't slow down the display of your page. You don't even need to load the image on your Web server, because it outlives its usefulness the minute you've finished setting up your page layers and other content.

Applying a Tracing Image

After you choose and resize the image you want to use, you need to display the image on the page. To apply a tracing image to your page-in-progress, follow these steps:

1. In the Web-page document to which you want to apply a tracing image, choose View|Tracing Image|Load. The Select Image Source dialog box opens, as shown in Figure 8.15.

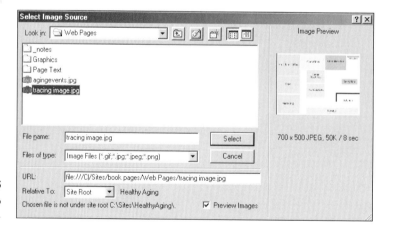

Figure 8.15
Choose the graphic you want to use for your tracing image.

2. As necessary, navigate to the drive and/or folder that contains the image you want to use. You're restricted to using GIF-, JPEG-, and PNG-format images, even though the images won't be displayed online or through a browser.

3. Double-click the image you want to load, and the dialog box closes. Immediately, the Page Properties dialog box opens, with the cursor blinking in the Tracing Image text box, as shown in Figure 8.16.

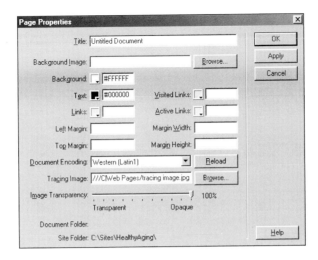

4. Click OK to accept the image as it appears in this dialog box, and the image appears on the page, behind any existing content. Figure 8.17 shows a tracing image in place on a partially filled page.

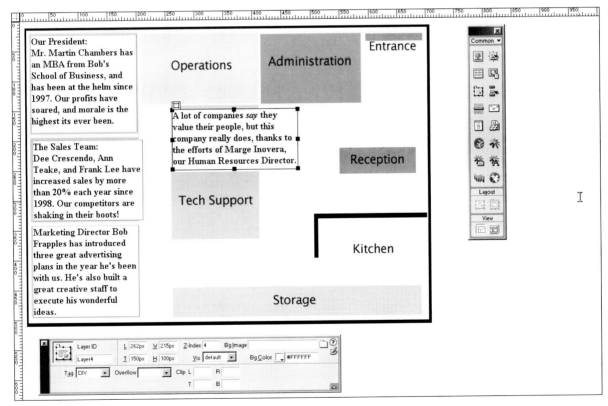

Moving a Tracing Image

Unless your tracing image is exactly the same size as your Web page, you'll probably need to reposition the tracing image on the page to make it work as a design tool. As Figure 8.18 shows, the tracing image appears in the upper left

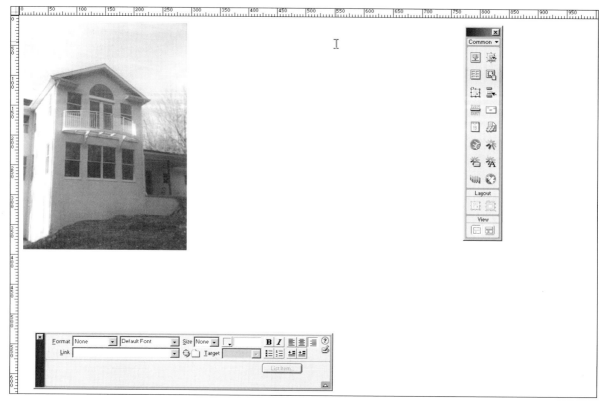

Figure 8.18

The tracing image rarely appears in exactly the right position from the start, but moving the image is easy.

of the page by default. To serve as a blueprint for a page that will be centered within the window (or that will take up the entire allocated space), the image must be moved to the right and down a little bit.

Positioning the Image

To reposition your tracing image, choose View|Tracing Image|Adjust Position. The Adjust Tracing Image Position dialog box appears, as Figure 8.19 shows.

Figure 8.19

The X- and Y-coordinates represent the horizontal and vertical position of your image.

Referring to your rulers for help, enter new X and/or Y positions for your image. If you're entering both X (horizontal) and Y (vertical) position changes, press Tab to move from the X text box to the Y text box. Note that, as soon as you press Tab to move from X to Y, the image moves to the new position you entered in the X text box.

After you enter the pixel settings for the location where your image should be, click OK. The image is repositioned and, assuming it is now in the right spot, you can proceed to build your page layers with the help of the tracing image.

If the image still needs to be moved, simply repeat the Adjust Position process as many times as you need to until the image is exactly where you want it.

Aligning an Image to Existing Content

If you already have content on your page, you can use that content to help you position the tracing image. Select the content to which your image should be aligned, and choose View|Tracing Image|Align With Selection. The image will snap to the selected content, be it text, a graphic, a table, or a layer on the page, as shown in Figure 8.20. If you move the content later, you'll have to reposition the tracing image—no connection exists between the content you used to align the image and the image itself, so the image won't follow the content if you move that content somewhere else on the page.

Where Are the Rulers When You Need 'Em?

If your rulers aren't displayed, now is probably a good time to turn them on—choose View| Rulers|Show. Without rulers across the top and down the left side of the Dreamweaver workspace, you'll have a hard time expressing (in pixels) how far to the left, right, up, or down your image needs to be moved.

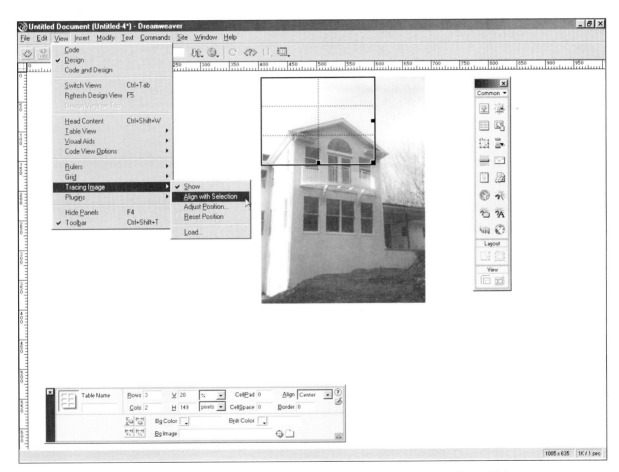

Figure 8.20

Do you need your image to line up with something already on the page? That's no problem with the Align With Selection command.

Hiding or Removing a Tracing Image

Of course, once a tracing image has outlived its usefulness, you might want to remove it from the page. You can always bring the image back as necessary. But, after you've positioned and sized your layers, entered and formatted

Back Where You Started

If, after repositioning or aligning a tracing image, you want to put the image back where it was when it was first loaded, choose View|Tracing Image| Reset Position. The image will snap back to the spot where it appeared originally, regardless of any content to which it was aligned or any other adjustments you made to its vertical or horizontal position on the page.

content, and adjusted other page elements to work within the blueprint provided by the image, the tracing image becomes more of a distraction than a help. To remove the image entirely, choose Modify|Page Properties and, in the Tracing Image text box, highlight and delete the path and file name that appear there. Click OK to confirm your change, and close the dialog box.

If you might need to use the image again, and you merely want to hide it for a while as you continue to design and develop your page, choose View|Tracing Image|Show. The image, which was displayed, will be hidden until and unless you again choose View|Tracing Image|Show.

Create a Web Page from a Tracing-Image Blueprint

In this project, you'll apply a tracing image to a new Web page and use the image as a guide to help you design your page with several layers.

Start a New Blank Web Page

Open a blank new page by choosing File|New in the Dreamweaver window.

Apply the Tracing Image from the CD-ROM

Using either the Page Properties dialog box or the View|Tracing Image|Load command, select the file called tracing.jpg from the Project 8A folder on the CD-ROM. The image is already sized to completely fill a 700×500-pixel space on a Web page viewed at 800×600-pixel resolution.

As necessary, especially if your page is not at the recommended 800×600-pixel resolution, you might need to adjust the position of the image. Make sure it fills the working area (700×500 pixels) of the page.

Insert Layers on the Tracing Image

Using the tracing image, position layers on the page. The image represents a map of a city. Each section of the city should have its own layer, on which information about that city, such as links to merchant Web sites, municipal sites, and emergency phone numbers (fire, police, commissioners) can be found.

Save the Web-Page File

Once the layers are drawn and positioned on the tracing image, save the file as citypage.htm.

Animating Layers

Because layers are free-floating objects on your page—not locked into a grid like a table cell, not bound by borders like a frame—they can be moved. Yes, you can drag layers around the page to change your design, but the layers can also move by themselves. By animating your layers, you create visual interest on your page, and you can draw attention to important information—the site visitor is sure to read, or more closely observe, the layer that moves.

Although you can create animation through Macromedia Fireworks (generating animated GIF files, as described in Appendix C), you can also create animation right within Dreamweaver by selecting a layer and plotting its movement along a prescribed path. Dreamweaver does the work for you in terms of setting up all the interim steps the layer must take to get from point A (where the layer starts) to point B (where the layer ends up)—all you have to do is choose which layer to animate, and then tell Dreamweaver what path you'd like the layer to follow.

Selecting Layers to Be Animated

The first step in animating layers is to choose the first (or, perhaps, only) layer you want to animate. This step begins with your clicking inside the layer, then when the layer is activated, clicking the selection handle above the top-left corner of the layer so that the layer, and not something inside it, is selected.

If your layer is already positioned where it should begin its journey across, up, down, or on some path around your page, leave it where it is. If not, move the layer to where you want it to be at the beginning of the animation, and leave it there, selected and ready for the next step in the animation process.

Establishing the Animation Effect

With the layer selected and placed in its starting position, choose Modify| Timeline|Record Path Of Layer. The Timelines panel will appear on the workspace. Dreamweaver will begin to track the positions of the selected layer, and all you need to do is drag the layer on the exact path you want it to follow when the animation plays on the page. Figure 8.21 shows a layer being dragged from a spot on the right side of the page to a location on the left.

As you drag the layer, a series of dots is created, like footprints, showing the path the layer has taken. When you release the mouse, that path turns from a series of dots to a solid line. Another thing happens as soon as you stop dragging your layer and release the mouse—Dreamweaver stops recording the layer's path, and the Timelines panel appears on the workspace, as shown in Figure 8.22. You can use the Timelines panel to rewind and play your animation, to copy timelines and apply them to other layers, and to customize an animation's path and speed.

Before you begin working with the Timelines panel, identifying its parts and understanding the components of an animation as they're represented in the panel are important. The panel's parts are as follows:

- *The Playback head*—shows which frame of the timeline is currently displayed on the page.

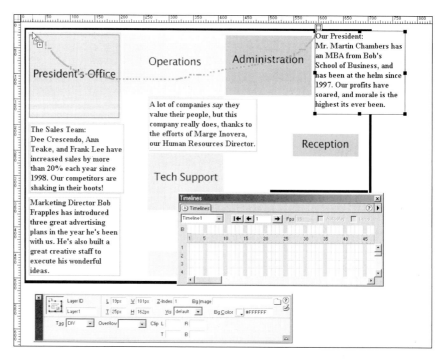

Figure 8.21

Drag your layer around on the page—Dreamweaver will record the movements and store them as the animated path your layer should follow.

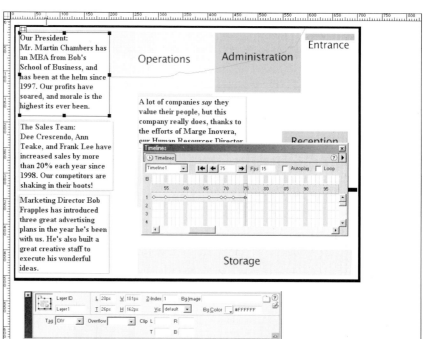

Figure 8.22

The Timelines panel appears as soon as you release the mouse after you've taken your layer on its animated journey.

- *The Timelines menu*—(see Figure 8.23) lets you choose which of the document's timelines is currently displayed in the Timelines panel. If you've animated more than one layer, the panel will contain more than one timeline.

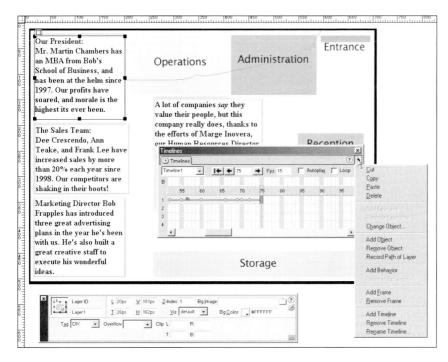

Figure 8.23

Choose from a series of timeline-related commands in the Timelines menu.

- *Frames*—are the segments of the timeline. Each block along the timeline is a frame.

- *Keyframes*—are frames in the timeline that have a white dot in them, which indicates that the frame contains content. Keyframes in a layer animation represent changes in direction along the path. Figure 8.24 shows both frames and keyframes.

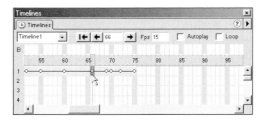

Figure 8.24

A timeline consists of many frames, some of which are keyframes.

- *The Behaviors channel*—(with a B to the left of it) is the channel for behaviors that should be executed at a particular frame in the timeline. Figure 8.25 shows a behavior that appeared when Loop was turned on. You can drag your mouse through this strip to run the animation.

- *The Rewind button*—(left-pointing arrow with a vertical line at the arrow point) moves the Playback head to the first frame in the timeline.

- *The Back button*—moves the Playback head one frame to the left. If you want to run your timeline in reverse, click Back, and hold down the mouse button at the same time.

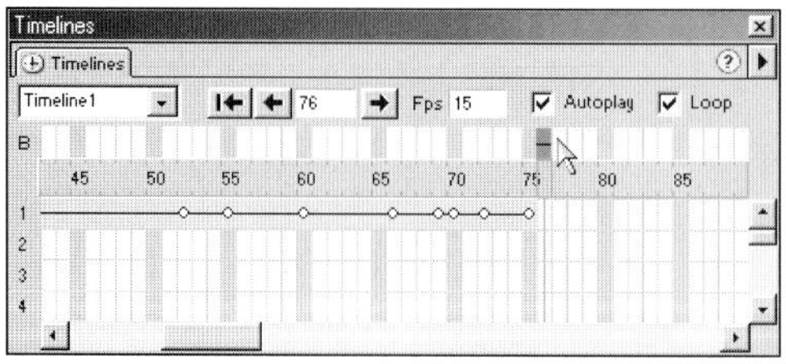

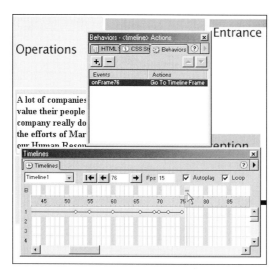

Figure 8.25
Turn on Loop, and see a behavior added to the Behaviors channel.

- *The Play button*—moves the Playback head one frame to the right. Click Play, and hold down the mouse button at the same time to run the animation forward.

- *The Autoplay option*—will force the animation to play automatically when the page loads in a browser.

- *The Loop option*—forces the animation to play repeatedly, without stopping. If you want to have the animation loop a certain number of times and then stop, double-click the Go To Timeline entry (a blue frame with a minus sign in it, in the Behaviors channel, as shown in Figure 8.26) and, in the resulting dialog box (see Figure 8.27), enter the number of times you want the animation to loop.

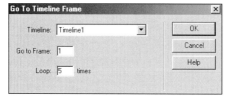

Figure 8.26
If you have Loop turned on, a behavior is added to the timeline, and an entry appears in the Behaviors channel. Double-click the entry to display the Behaviors panel.

Figure 8.27
Rather than having the timeline loop indefinitely, you can set it to loop once, or as many times as you'd like.

Testing the Animation

After you've created your timeline, you can test your layer animation. Click the Rewind button in the Timelines panel, moving the layer back to the beginning of its path. You can then drag the Playback head (the red tab above the timeline) by pointing just above the head and dragging through the frame boxes in the B timeline. The animated layer will move along its path at the speed at which you drag your mouse. Figure 8.28 shows the timeline for an animated layer.

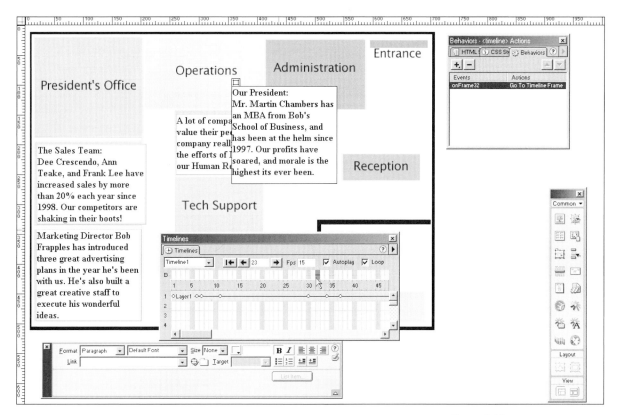

Figure 8.28

The animated layer follows its path as you drag the Playback head through the timeline.

To see how the animation will look when it's viewed online, press F12 to preview the Web page in your default browser.

If, upon previewing the layer's movement, you decide to make any changes, you can go back to your page and tinker with the timeline (through the Timelines panel), or delete the animation and start over.

Customizing the Animation Timeline

Only after you see an animation through a browser will you know whether the animation has the desired effect. If you decide that you don't like something about the animation—perhaps it goes too slowly, the layer wanders a bit, or it doesn't begin and/or end where it should—you can adjust the timeline accordingly. Of course, if the animation is completely incorrect, you can delete the timeline and re-record.

Adjusting Animation Speed

The speed of your animation depends on the number of frames per second (fps). Of course, when site visitors view the animation online, the speed at which the visitors see it will be dependent on their connections to the Internet, at least on the speed of their first viewing of the page. To speed up (or slow down) the animation within Dreamweaver, change the fps in the Fps box in the Timelines panel, as shown in Figure 8.29.

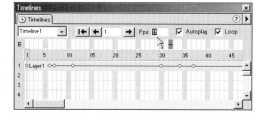

Figure 8.29
By default, all animated layers move at 15 frames per second (fps).

Of course, increasing the frames per second will increase the speed of your animation. You don't want to increase it substantially, however, because some browsers, especially older versions, won't be able to display the animation much faster than 15 fps, anyway. The browser (assuming it displays layers in the first place) will play every frame of the animation, and it will play the frames at the animation's fps rate, or at the fastest rate the browser can handle, whichever is lower.

Removing Frames

Another way to speed up the animation (and also to potentially alter the path the layer follows) is to remove frames and keyframes from the timeline. If you remove frames, you shorten the distance between keyframes and tighten the path that the layer follows. If you delete keyframes, you alter the path that the layer takes by removing pivotal steps in the path, such as directional changes.

- *To delete a frame*—right-click the frame you want to delete, and choose Remove Frame from the resulting shortcut menu.

- *To delete a keyframe*—right-click the keyframe you want to delete, and choose Delete or Remove Keyframe from the resulting shortcut menu.

Deleting a Timeline

To remove a timeline, click anywhere on the timeline, and press the Delete key. You can also right-click the timeline and choose Delete or Remove Timeline from the shortcut menu. If you delete the timeline and then regret your action, choose Edit|Undo, or press Ctrl+Z. If you want to get rid of the timeline and be able to bring it back, right-click the timeline, and choose Cut from the shortcut menu. At any time until—and unless—you cut or copy something else, or exit Dreamweaver, you can right-click the Timelines panel and choose Paste to bring back the timeline you cut.

 ## Create an Employee Directory with Layers

In this project, you'll create a Web page that contains several layers—one layer for each department in a company. Each department's layer will contain a list of the employees in that department, along with their extension numbers. To make the employee directory more interesting to look at, and to allow different departments to take on a "personality" of their own on the page, the departmental layers will be animated.

Start a New Web Page

Choose File|New to start with a blank Web page.

Insert Layers for Each Department

Insert four layers on the page, and arrange the layers as shown in Figure 8.30. The layers should be 200 pixels wide and 300 pixels tall, and they should overlap each other in the upper-left corner of the page.

Name the Layers

Use the Layers panel to name the four layers as follows: Marketing, Accounting, Operations, and Sales.

Insert Content

Insert content on each of the department layers.

1. Type the department name, and using the Properties Inspector, format the name in Heading 2 style.

2. Press Enter, then type a series of names, each followed by a three-digit number (for example, "Mary Smith, 234").

3. Enter at least three names on each department layer.

As you enter content onto each layer, you'll probably want to hide the other three layers. You can also move the other layers out of the way, but be sure to return them to the configuration you saw in Figure 8.30.

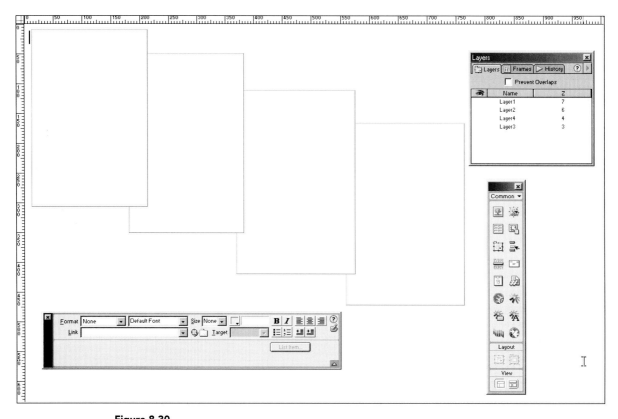

Figure 8.30

Draw three 200x300-pixel layers, and place the layers in the upper-left corner of the page, as shown.

Apply Background Colors to the Layers

So that each department's layer stands out visually, apply a different color to the background of each layer. Choose colors that will allow the text to be legible. If you want to use a dark background color, be sure to apply a light color to the text.

Animate the Layers

For each layer, create a timeline by using the Modify|Timeline|Record Path Of Layer command. When you're recording each layer's path, give each department a different "personality": a slow, straight path for Accounting; a rapid, upward path for Sales; perhaps a wandering, circular path for Marketing; and a path that resembles a staircase (sort of a diagonal zig-zag) for Operations. When you are finished, the Timelines panel should contain four timelines.

Preview Your Animation

Press F12 to preview the animation in a browser. If you want to alter the speed or path of any particular department layer's animation, go back to the page and use the Timelines panel to make your changes.

Save the File

Save the file as departmentstaff.htm.

Moving On

Now that you've mastered Dreamweaver's tools for establishing an effective page layout, you're ready to learn all you need to know about choosing and applying colors to your page, your tables, layers, frames, and text content. Chapter 9 will explain the concepts of Web-safe colors, how to approximate printed colors with colors any browser can display, and how to make effective choices when creating a color scheme for your Web page.

Chapter 9

Using Color Effectively

In print, using color is expensive—which explains why many printed advertisements and marketing materials use only one or two colors. On the Web, however, using many colors in personal and business Web pages is easy and inexpensive. This chapter will help you understand how the Web looks at and displays color, and how to make good choices when you're applying color to your pages.

Using Web-Safe Colors

Web-safe colors are colors that Web browsers can display accurately. Web-safe colors consist of 256 choices. That number might sound limited if you're coming from a background in graphic design for print media (and are, therefore, used to an unlimited palette of available colors). But 256 colors are more than enough for any Web designer when you consider the hardware limitations (i.e., end users' computers), and the fact that Web browsers must play to the lowest common denominator—someone with an 8-bit video card, which is capable of displaying only 256 colors. Figure 9.1 shows the entire Web-safe palette as you will see it in a Dreamweaver color well. The palette is accessible through the Properties Inspector and a variety of dialog boxes.

Figure 9.1

The number 256 might sound like too few—or maybe too many—colors for your Web-design needs, but that's the limit of Web-safe colors.

If you're still feeling limited by this range of colors, the good news is that the 256 Web-safe colors cover the entire color spectrum, and you'll be able to find light and dark shades of every color on the color wheel (see Figure 9.2). As you'll discover later in this chapter, you'll also be able to closely match the print colors you need—even shades from within the seemingly limitless Pantone™ palette—so your Web pages can match your brochures and business cards. The addition of Web-based marketing need not force a change in your marketing materials' color scheme.

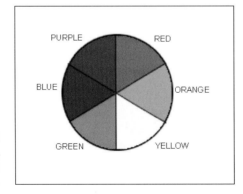

Figure 9.2

The color wheel shows the entire spectrum of primary and secondary colors.

Color Names and Numbers

You apply Web-safe colors to your Web page elements in Dreamweaver through the Properties Inspector and various dialog boxes (depending on the element to which you're applying color). As a result of your actions, HTML code is created, and the code includes a color number. The numbers for each color are hexadecimal numbers, such as #336633 for a deep shade of green. Figure 9.3 shows some HTML code for a Web page and the color attributes for a table cell.

```
<html>
<head>
<title>Untitled Document</title>
<meta http-equiv="Content-Type" content="text/html; charset=iso-8859-1">
</head>

<body bgcolor="#000000" text="#CCFFFF" link="#FFFF66" vlink="#FFFF66" alink="#FFFF66">
<table width="50%" border="0" cellspacing="0" cellpadding="0" align="center">
  <tr bgcolor="#FFFFFF">
    <td bgcolor="#FF0000" width="50%"> </td>
    <td bgcolor="#993399" width="50%"> </td>
  </tr>
  <tr bgcolor="#FFFFFF">
    <td bgcolor="#FF9900" width="50%"> </td>
    <td bgcolor="#6666FF" width="50%"> </td>
  </tr>
  <tr bgcolor="#FFFFFF">
    <td bgcolor="#FFFF00" width="50%"> </td>
    <td width="50%" bgcolor="#66CC00"> </td>
  </tr>
</table>
<h1 align="center">Adventures in Color</h1>
<h1 align="center"><a href="http://www.macromedia.com"><img src="/spinningwheel.gif" width="150" height="150" border="0"></a></h1>
</body>
</html>
```

Figure 9.3

Have you filled your table cell with red? That color is really #FF0000, as far as your computer is concerned.

Another number model associated with Web-safe colors (or with any color, for that matter) uses *RGB levels*. RGB stands for red, green, and blue—which, in a Web-safe palette, is the color model used to determine how a color is "built." For example, white, which is the presence of all color, is 255 red, 255 blue, and 255 green. Black, which is the absence of all color, is 0 (zero) for red, green, and blue. Varying levels of these three colors represent all colors between the polar opposites of white and black. The aforementioned color, #336633, is 51 red, 102 green, and 51 blue. A color's RGB levels are expressed as a hexadecimal number so that your computer can interpret the number as it displays the HTML document (your Web page) on screen.

Testing Color Display

When you apply color to text, page backgrounds, table cells, frames, or layers, testing the display before you post the page to the Web is a good idea. If possible, if the color's displayed value is key to the success or failure of your design, test the display on a few different computers. Why? Because, for example, deep red on one computer can look like purple on another; and other shades, such as those of blue-green and orange, can look very different on different monitors.

If you don't have access to several different monitors to test your page, try changing your own monitor's color-display settings. In the Windows Control Panel, choose Display, and on the Settings tab (as shown in Figure 9.4), adjust the Color setting. On older monitors, your choices might be somewhat limited; —on newer monitors, you can choose from extremes ranging from 16 colors to True Color.

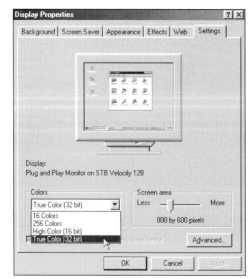

Sea Green or Pea Green?

When you're choosing colors for a Web page, another good idea is to get an objective opinion of any color selections you're unsure of. What looks like a lovely, soothing shade of sea green to you might look bilious to someone else. When color is essential to the success of your design, leave no stone unturned in choosing and applying the right colors.

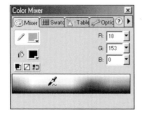

Figure 9.5

Pick a color and view its levels in Fireworks.

Testing your page on different monitors will help you fine-tune your color choices. You might decide to use a lighter or brighter shade of red to avoid the possibility of your deep red being seen as purple, or you might choose an entirely different color for something on the page once you've seen how it looks on one of the test computers.

Understanding Color Models

Color models are systems that break colors down into levels. As I discussed in the previous section, the RGB model expresses colors in terms of their amounts of red, green, and blue. Other color models include *CMYK*, which breaks colors into cyan, magenta, yellow, and black. Remember: These models are taking the same colors and breaking them into different levels—the famous shade of green (#336633) is, as stated, 51 red, 102 green, and 51 blue. In the CMYK model, that green shade is 70 cyan, 24 magenta, 85 yellow, and 38 black. Whether you express the color in terms of RGB levels or CMYK, the color is the same. Figure 9.5 shows the Fireworks color palette and the RGB levels of a Web-safe color. If you click the triangle at the top-right corner of this palette, you can switch to other models, including CMYK and Grayscale (which converts colors to shades of black and white).

The other major color model is Pantone. Pantone colors are process colors, and thousands of them exist, each expressed as a number—such as 197 (which is a deep shade of blue). Figure 9.6 shows the Pantone colors and numbers as they appear through Adobe Photoshop—a program you might use to create, capture, or retouch a graphic for Web use. Pantone colors are used for print work, but—in response to the fact that most designers who were creating work for print are now also creating Web designs, or graphics that will be used on

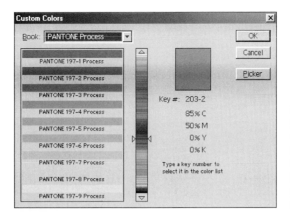

Figure 9.6
Because it's also used for print work, Adobe Photoshop provides tools for applying Pantone colors to your images. Fireworks is intended for use on Web-bound graphics only and, therefore, doesn't offer the Pantone palette.

the Web—Pantone has a Web site (**www.pantone.com**) that helps you find Web-safe matches for Pantone colors.

Matching Pantone and Other Non-Web Colors

For many Web designers, whether they're developing sites for themselves or for clients, the need to match existing printed materials—brochures, business cards, letterhead, and other stationery—is significant. Don't despair if you're using process colors (or if your client used them) for the printed materials, or if you used a color you're not finding among the Web-safe colors you've seen in the Dreamweaver palette, or in various printed and online resources on Web color. A nearly perfect match is just a few keystrokes away.

To match a print color, the first thing you need to do is find the RGB levels for that color. If you're using a Pantone color, open Adobe Photoshop or CorelDRAW or some other application that supports the Pantone palettes. You can also go to the Pantone Web site (**www.pantone.com**) and find the color your printed materials use. In any of the dialog boxes that let you view a palette (for the purpose of applying that color to a graphic in progress), you'll also see the RGB levels for that color. Make a note of those levels.

Back in Dreamweaver, to find and apply the closest-matching, Web-safe color to your Web content (text, borders, backgrounds), click on a color-well button in the Page Properties dialog box or the Properties Inspector (as shown in Figure 9.7), and click the System Color Picker button. The Color dialog box opens (this is a Windows feature, not a Dreamweaver dialog box) and displays tools for creating custom color combinations. Figure 9.8 shows this dialog box.

Hue! I'm Saturated with Color

Other levels you might see displayed (not in Dreamweaver, but in products such as Macromedia Fireworks and Adobe Photoshop) that express color values are *HSB* (hue, saturation, and brightness). You might also see *L levels*, in which the *L* stands for luminosity. Rather than expressing the color-level recipe for a particular color, the HSB and L levels express the *quality* of the color—the location of the color on the color wheel or spectrum (hue), the intensity of the color (saturation), and the amount of white the color includes (brightness).

Figure 9.7
Click the System Color Picker button to display a color-creation dialog box.

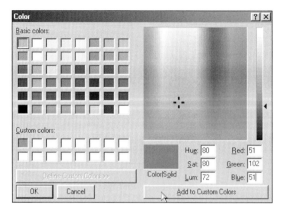

Figure 9.8

Using the Color dialog box, enter the RGB levels for the color you want to use, and click Add To Custom Colors.

In the Color dialog box, enter your color's RGB levels. The color will appear in the dialog box. Click the Add To Custom Colors button, and then click OK. You'll find the closest match from the Web-safe palette of 256 colors displayed in the color well, and that color's hexadecimal number displayed next to it, as shown in Figure 9.9.

Figure 9.9

The Properties Inspector shows the color and color number resulting from the entry of the RGB levels in Figure 9.8.

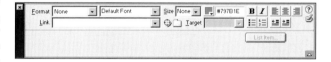

Surviving Color Scrutiny

What if the color that's closest to what you need is just that—closest—and not a perfect match? People who have your business card or a sheet of your letterhead are not going to go to your Web site and hold the paper up to the screen to check for an absolute match. The idea is to find a color that's the closest match within the Web-safe palette, so that you know your color will appear reliably on any site visitor's monitor. A slight red-, green-, and/or blue-level difference between colors is rarely noticeable to the human eye, so don't worry about it—your time is better spent concentrating on making sure the colors you use within the Web page work together.

Selecting Compatible Colors

Compatibility is a subjective concept. Think of couples you know and whether or not they seem compatible. Who gets along with whom is often surprising, and the same is true about colors. Some rules do exist, however, and although you don't need to follow them strictly, the rules are a useful set of guidelines you can rely on when you don't trust your own instincts. Or, if a client asks for a color combination you can't stand, use the color wheel and its rules for pairing colors as an excuse to nix the client's unpleasant selection.

Primary and Secondary Colors

Primary colors are colors that you cannot make by mixing any other two colors. The three primary colors are red, blue, and yellow. You use primary colors to make secondary colors (see Table 9.1) and, by mixing secondary

Table 9.1   Using primary colors to create secondary colors.

Primary Colors	Secondary Colors
Red	Orange (Red and Yellow)
Blue	Purple (Red and Blue)
Yellow	Green (Yellow and Blue)

and primary colors, you get tertiary colors. You don't need to memorize this little fact (although it might come in handy if you're ever on a game show), but the concepts are useful.

A good example of a tertiary color is brown—you can't create brown by mixing any two primary colors, but you can produce it by mixing three primary colors, or a primary and a secondary color. Of course, the color we refer to as *brown* can be any one of many different shades. No two people will agree on what constitutes a "real" brown. That's the beauty (and challenge) of color— it's subjective once you get past the basic six primary and secondary colors. And even within those colors are so many varieties—shades of red, blue, yellow, green, orange, and purple—many of which have descriptive and universally used names, such as *fire-engine red* and *canary yellow*.

Color Compatibility

How do you know which colors work well together? Look at the color wheel. The color wheel is your best guide for picking colors that work when they're placed near or immediately next to each other. When you're picking colors, stick to the color next to the color you have, or the color's opposite—the color directly opposite from it on the wheel (see Figure 9.10). For example, if you know you have to use blue on the page, pick an opposite color (orange) or the color on either side of blue (purple or green).

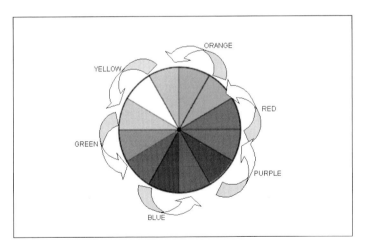

Figure 9.10

Find your starting color (the one you know you want to use) on the wheel, and then look next to that color, or right across from it, for the colors that will work well together.

Of course, these are rules, and you know what they say about rules: They're meant to be broken. Certainly, I'm not suggesting you mix colors that make people seasick or force them to shield their eyes. Go with what looks good to you, to your client, and to people whose opinion you trust.

> ### Roy G. Who?
>
> A trick for remembering the spectrum of colors is to remember the name that the first letters of the colors in the spectrum create. Viewed from left to right, the colors are red, orange, yellow, green, blue, indigo, violet. The first letters or each color spell Roy G. Biv. And, if you remember Roy, you'll be able to conjure up a mental image of the spectrum, which is really just the linear version of the color wheel with one extra color: indigo.

Applying Page Colors

Now that you know more about the nature of colors—how the Web and your computer see them, and which ones look right together—you can apply colors to content in your Web pages with more confidence. With Dreamweaver, you can easily and quickly take your color choices and turn them into reality—applying them to your page, table cells, frames, layers, and the borders that separate these elements.

Applying a Page Background Color

The background color of your page is white by default and, for many Web pages, white's a great choice. Sticking with white isn't chickening out; white isn't boring, and it doesn't show a lack of imagination. A white background can be the foundation of a clean, crisp page. A white background might mean some limitations in terms of text colors, but the same is true for any color you might apply to your background. With a white background, the only colors you should avoid for text are yellow and very light shades of any other color. As Figure 9.11 shows, a white background looks great with dark text, and graphics pop out with no interference or visual competition from behind.

Figure 9.11

A white background gives all but the lightest colors a clean, crisp foundation.

Using colored backgrounds can make your page more interesting—assuming, of course, that the color you choose works with the color of your text, any filled tables or layers, and the graphics you use. For example, if your page will contain many portraits that include a blue background in the picture, you might not want to use a blue background for the page—the portraits will blend in too much and won't stand out on their own. You might, however, want to apply a shade of blue from one of the pictures to the background, so that an effective blending in occurs.

To apply a color to your page background, choose Modify|Page Properties. In the Page Properties dialog box, click the Background color well, and choose a color from the palette. You can also type a color number into the box to the right of the well, as Figure 9.12 shows.

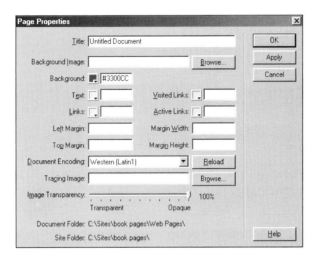

Figure 9.12

Choose one of the 256 Web-safe colors for your page background.

Applying Table Colors

Tables are clear by default, so that any page or frame background color or image is visible through them. For most tables, because they're generally used to give structure to your Web-page content, the fact that the table is transparent is a good thing—transparency lets the table serve its structural purpose without imposing anything else on the appearance of the page.

At times, however, you'll want some color in your table. Pages with white backgrounds often use table color, as do pages with black backgrounds. Tables on these stark backgrounds might need some color of their own to enhance their structural purpose, especially if the table contains text that must be read across the page, with the visitor's eye moving from the left side of the table to the right, one cell at a time. A schedule, and a list of people and their phone numbers, are good examples of the kind of table content that might benefit from the use of color in the table—either with the entire table being one color, or with color applied to individual cells or groups of cells, as shown in Figure 9.13.

Pick a Color, Any Color

Remember that you can click the color eyedropper on anything on your page to select a color. To apply a color from one of your graphic images to the background of your page, choose Modify|Page Properties, and move the resulting dialog box aside so that you can see the image from which you'd like to pick up a color. Click the Background color well, take the eyedropper out onto the page, and click the eyedropper on the color you want to use for your background. Click OK to apply your changes, and close the dialog box.

Event Schedule	
Event	DATES, TIMES
Community Car Wash	Saturday, August 18th, 10 - 4 pm
Craft Bazaar	Saturday, November 17th, 9 - 5 pm
Silent Auction	Wednesday, December 12th, 6 - 9 pm
Antique Show and Sale	Friday, April 13th, 4 - 10 pm

Figure 9.13

Make a schedule easy to read by applying alternating colors to individual rows (which are groups of cells) in the table.

When you apply color to tables and/or table cells, remember this rule: Table *cell* colors supersede *table* colors. Therefore, if you apply a color to an entire table, and then apply a different color to one of the cells, the cell's color will show in that cell, obscuring the table color within the walls of that cell.

Coloring the Entire Table

To apply color to a table, you must first select the table, then in the Properties Inspector (which will be displaying table-related tools), use the Bg color well to apply a color to the table. Figure 9.14 shows tables filled with color, which makes each stand out.

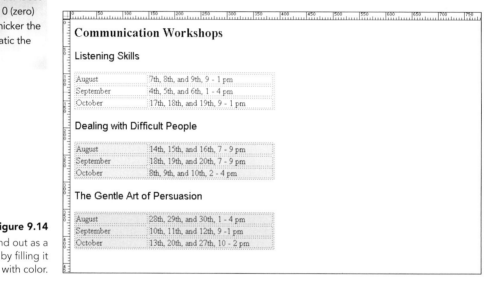

Figure 9.14

Make a table stand out as a single element by filling it with color.

Coloring a Table Cell

You can apply color to a single cell (or to a block of contiguous cells) within a table, whether or not you've applied color to the table that contains the cell. And remember that, if you have applied color to the entire table, the color you apply to the cell(s) will take precedence in those cell(s). Figure 9.15 shows a table with color applied, and a different color applied to a single cell within the table.

Creating Borders with Table and Cell Coloring

As I stated previously, only Internet Explorer displays colored table borders. Although Dreamweaver will let you apply color to a table border, and it will display the border in that color within the Dreamweaver workspace, you can't rely on that color appearing to visitors who come to your site via Netscape—to them, the borders will be gray. So, what should you do? Apply a table color and, using the CellSpace feature (a distance between cells and around the perimeter of the table), you can create the appearance of a border.

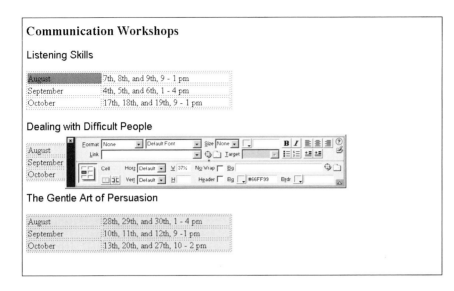

Figure 9.15

Make one cell stand out by applying a different color to that cell.

To create a colored "border" that will show in any browser (because it's not technically a table border), follow these steps:

1. Select the table, and use the Properties Inspector to designate a CellSpace value of 1 pixel or more. The greater the number, the greater the distance between cells and, therefore, the more dramatic the illusion of a colored border will be. Figure 9.16 shows a table with a CellSpace setting of 3 pixels.

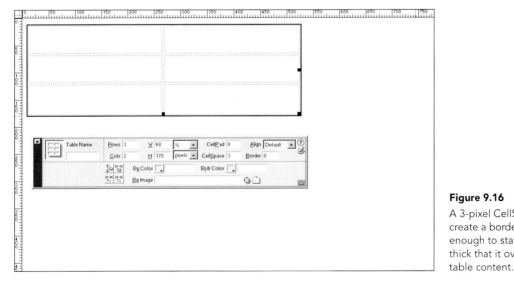

Figure 9.16

A 3-pixel CellSpace setting will create a border that's thick enough to stand out, but not so thick that it overwhelms the table content.

2. With the table still selected, use the Properties Inspector again—this time, to apply a Bg color to the table. Pick the color you want to use for the border effect.

3. Click in one of the table's corner cells. Clicking there will make it easier to drag through the cells and select all of them.

4. Drag to select all of the cells in the table without selecting the table itself. The Properties Inspector will change to offer tools for the cells instead of the entire table.

5. Use the Bg color well to choose a color for the cells. If your page background is white, and you want the "border" to look like the only part of the table that's colored, choose white (#FFFFFF) for the cell background color, as Figure 9.17 shows.

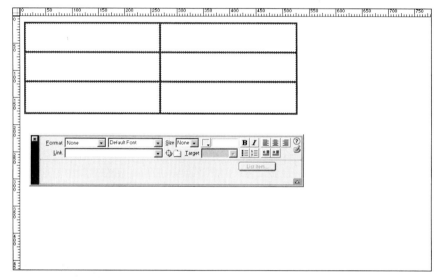

Figure 9.17
A dark-colored table with white cells creates a tidy and visually effective grid on the white Web page.

Nesting a Table within a Colored Cell

Any table—and any cell within any table—can have a background color, and this includes nested tables. Just as you can create the illusion of a border by coloring a table and then applying a different color to the table's cells, you can apply a different color to the cells in a nested table to make that table stand out within the table that contains it. As Figure 9.18 shows, you can turn the already powerful structural effect of a nested table into an equally powerful visual element by choosing a different color for the nested table and its cells.

Using Color with Frames and Layers

Any structural element on a Web page can have a background color, and that includes layers and frames. The colors you choose for these elements should, of course, work with the color of the text and/or graphics you place within them, and with the overall color scheme for the Web page. You can use color to disguise the existence of layers and frames by applying the same color to the

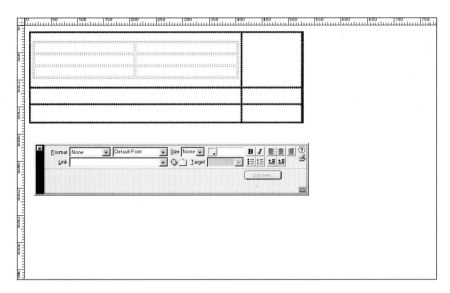

Figure 9.18
Apply color to a nested table and a different color to its cells—the nested table looks like it has a border, and the combination creates an effective grid within the larger table.

frames or layers as you apply to the page background. Or you can make the frames or layers stand out by applying a different color to them.

Coloring Layers

To apply a background color to a layer, select the layer and use the Properties Inspector's Bg color well to choose a color. You can also enter a hexadecimal color number if you know the number. Figure 9.19 shows a selected layer and the resulting Properties Inspector, with the Bg color palette displayed.

Framing a Frame

Frames have a border by default, and that border is gray. You can make the border thicker or thinner, and you can apply color to it. To apply color, click the displayed border itself and, in the resulting version of the Properties Inspector, choose a border color. Unlike with table borders, the color will display in both Internet Explorer and Netscape.

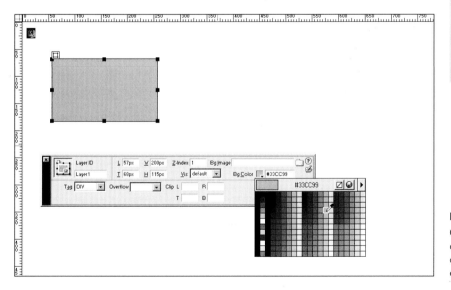

Figure 9.19
Click inside the layer, and then click its handle tab to activate options that will apply to the entire layer.

Selecting a frame and displaying the tools that allow you to fill the frame with color doesn't employ the same process as you use for layers. Layers are objects on a Web page, but frames are pages within the page (frames within a frameset), and frames are filled with color through the Page Properties dialog box. Whether your page has 2 frames or 20, the key is to click inside the frame you want to color, and then choose Modify|Page Properties. The frame that contains your cursor will be the one to which the selected background color will apply. Figure 9.20 shows the Page Properties dialog box for a selected frame.

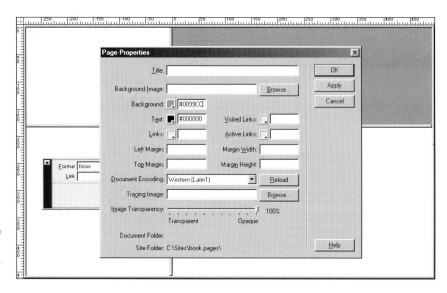

Figure 9.20
Click inside a frame, and apply a background color through the Page Properties dialog box.

Applying Text Colors

The color you choose for text is important on two levels—legibility and aesthetics. Of course, choosing a text color that looks good with the rest of your page colors is important, but more important is that the text be legible. Although the font and size you choose will affect text legibility, color is a significant factor in whether or not visitors can comfortably read your page's text content. Color combinations to avoid include the following:

- Red text on a blue background

- Yellow text on a white background

- Any dark colors on a black or navy background

- Red text on a green background

- Green text on a red background

As I discussed earlier, you need to avoid the last two combinations because red and green are not discernable to the 15 percent of the population that's color-blind. You'll want to avoid the rest of the combinations because they're hard on the eyes.

Create a Colorful Web Page

In this project, you'll build a Web page filled with color—page, table, and frame backgrounds; and text colors—using Dreamweaver's tools and the color-wheel image you'll find on the CD-ROM that accompanies this book.

Open a New Page

Using the File|New command, open a blank new document.

Modify Page Properties

Select colors for your background, links, and text, as follows.

1. Open the Page Properties dialog box, and apply a background color by typing "000000" (six zeros) into the Background text box (to the right of the color well for that option).

2. Using the color wells for each option, set the Links, Visited Links, and Active Links to a bright yellow, such as #FFFF66.

3. Set the Text color to #CCFFFF, a very light blue.

4. Close the dialog box by clicking OK.

The changes will be applied to the page, although the link's settings won't be apparent until you add link text to the page.

Insert a Table

With your cursor at the top of the page, insert a two-column, three-row table. Make the table width 50%, with 0 (zero) pixels for the CellPad and CellSpace settings. Your border should also be set to 0 (zero). Make sure the table is centered on the page.

Apply Table Colors

Using the Properties Inspector, apply the following colors to the cells in the table:

1. First cell, first row: #FF0000

2. First cell, second row: #FF9900

3. First cell, third row: #FFFF00

4. Second cell, first row: #993399

5. Second cell, second row: #6666FF

6. Second cell, third row: #66CC00

Preview the page in a browser. The table should look like a square color wheel.

Insert and Format the Page Heading

Below the table, type and center the heading "Adventures in Color" in the Heading 1 style.

Insert an Animated GIF

Below the heading, insert the graphic spinningwheel.gif from the CD-ROM (you will find the file in the Project 9A folder).

Save the Page

Using the File|Save command, save the Web page as adventure.htm.

Preview the Page in a Browser

Press F12 to preview the page in your default browser. The GIF image you inserted (spinningwheel.gif) should spin in place on the page, and the page should appear as you see in Figure 9.21.

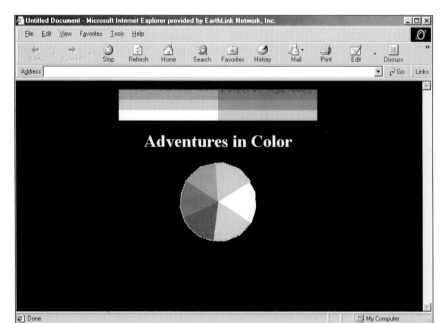

Figure 9.21
Although shown in black and white here, this Web page is very colorful. Creating it should help reinforce your understanding of the relationships between colors—and help you remember the methods of applying color to Web content.

Moving On

Now that you know more about color, you'll be able to make more informed decisions about the colors you choose when you're planning and designing a page, and as you apply colors to your Web-page elements. In the next chapter, you'll be learning about forms—the interactive elements on a page that ask the visitor for information and carry that information back to a database.

Dreamweaver 4 Studio

The Dreamweaver 4 Studio contains a broad cross section of Web-site types, which vary depending upon the nature of the information on, or organization behind, the sites that Dreamweaver will help you create. The studio illustrates how to utilize the most effective and reliable tools for page design given the anticipated audience and challenges presented by current browser software.

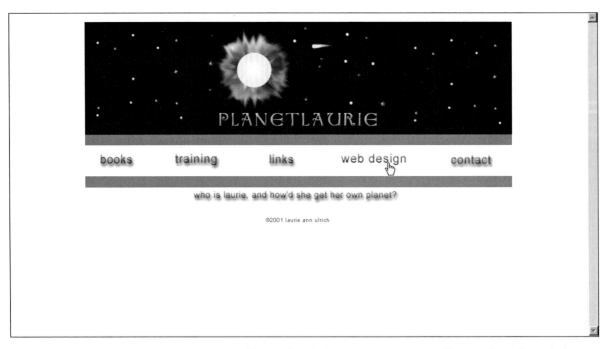

This Web page uses a table. The top row consists of three cells with three graphics, one per cell. Merged rows beneath the top row serve as a colored border. The links are a single row of five cells that each contain a rollover graphic. Below the lower colored row is single rollover graphic. (The drop shadow disappears when someone moves a mouse over the links.) Keywords are hidden in the top colored row (text colored to match the background) so that search engines, which search the first 100 words on a home page, will find the page.

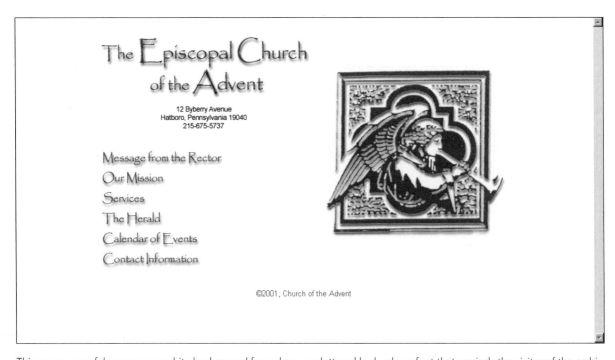

This spare, graceful page uses a white background for a clean, uncluttered look, plus a font that reminds the visitor of the architecture and medieval artwork associated with Anglican churches. The angel graphic was embossed to mimic the carved look of stone. The list of subpages is a single graphic with hotspots. Each subpage's Home button uses a smaller version of the angel graphic to reinforce the visual reference to the home page.

This site's designer also chose to use a table, because tables are more readily found by Web search indexes than frames. Enough text appears on the page to provide keywords needed for the search engines to find the site. Link text in the form of graphics was created in Photoshop and Fireworks.

Local Activities

Help Us Find You Something to Do!

One of the things that prevents most people taking action is not knowing what action to take. Please take the time to fill out the form below, and we'll email you a list of activities and organizations in your area that need your involvement now!

Your Name:	
Your Email Address:	
Your Zip Code:	
Please tell us what interests you most, and the type of activities to which you think you'd make the best contribution of time and effort (check as many as apply):	☐ Rescue Cats & Dogs ☐ Rescue Farm Animals ☐ Public Speaking ☐ Educating Children ☐ Surveillance at Circuses, Zoos, and Laboratories ☐ Contributing articles and info for the Web ☐ Distributing email and printed leaflets ☐ Organizing Demonstrations, Protests, and Boycotts
Are you:	☐ Vegetarian ☐ Vegan ☐ Still eating some animal products, but trying not to
Would you like to receive our newsletter, emailed weekly?	◉ Yes ○ No [Submit] [Reset]

Return to the Home Page

This subpage is reached via the Local Activities link on the home page. The top of this page (the graphic) is in a static frame; the logo remains on screen as the user works through the form. Because you don't know what browser configuration your visitors will have, placing in frames any items that shouldn't move is a good idea. The form is a table, with questions right-aligned in their cells.

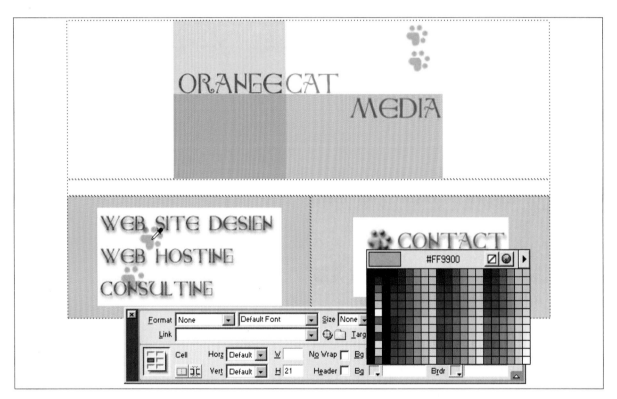

To quickly and accurately match colors from your page images for use in a cell background, border, or even text, use the eye-dropper to "sip" color from a graphic image. Here, I select color from the cat paw print to fill in the empty table row that acts as a break between the top logo and the two navigational graphics.

Jasper, the Big Orange Goodness

DIABETIC NEUROPATHY

Does your diabetic cat have neuropathy? Look for the following symptoms:

- Weak hind legs
- Feet slipping out from under him/her on the floor
- Walking down on the hocks in back and/or on the wrists in front
- Lying down more frequently, especially after short walks

If your diabetic* cat has these symptoms, he or she probably has neuropathy, the result of high glucose (blood sugar) and the damage it does to nerve cells.

THERE IS HELP!

METHYLCOBALAMIN, a form of vitamin B12, has shown great benefit to cats (and people) with diabetic neuropathy and other neuromuscular diseases. Unlike regular B12 (cyanocobalamin), METHYLCOBALAMIN is active in spinal fluid. Because of this, it is able to help heal the damaged nerve cells and restore the signal to your cat's weakened muscles. It is a very safe vitamin (it's water-soluble -- meaning the cat pees out what isn't used -

READ THE ARTICLE THAT STARTED IT ALL! At least for me, anyway. This article was originally posted at www.sugarcats.com, and it inspired me to get the methylcobalamin for Jasper. If you want additional information, try a web search for "methylcobalamin" at any regular search site, such as www.hotbot.com or www.google.com. You'll be surprised how much information is out there, and more becomes available every day. Just a year ago, you couldn't find much information at all, and now there's a great deal of it.

How Do You Get Methylcobalamin?

Buy Methylcobalamin from various online, mail, and phone sources through our Methylcobalamin Resources page. I use Xobaline (in 3 MG tablets) from LifeLink, and am very happy with them.

The informal look of the page, which shares information about a treatment for diabetic neuropathy in cats, is intentional—many of the site's visitors are not familiar with the Web and are likely using it only in a search for information. The text-filled design is essential because the audience for this site wants the information in one place, without fanfare and without having to jump from page to page.

high doses), and even if your vet hasn't heard of it, it's worth a try.** Within a very short time, your cat's legs and overall weakness will improve.

Just 2 weeks after starting on the methylcobalamin, Jasper went from being paralyzed -- from his ribs to his back toes -- to standing and walking. He is now walking long stretches, even jumping on the furniture.

Jasper, who weighs 14 lbs., gets 3 milligrams of methylcobalamin daily. The tablets are "sublingual" (to be dissolved under the tongue), but as cats aren't likely to cooperate with *that*, they can be given like any other pill. If your cat weighs 10 lbs. or more, I'd suggest a 3 MG dose. Smaller cats can have a half of that, or 1.5 MG.

Jasper was totally limp and helpless, and I'm sure a lot of people thought I should have put him to sleep. Thank God I didn't, because the methylcobalamin gave him back his strength and independence.

UPDATE !

People have been writing to ask if Jasper's still doing well. The answer is YES! He's still taking methylcobalamin, and he's jumping and running, and stepping on my keyboard and phone when I'm trying to work (which requires repeated leaps onto my desk -- me putting him back on the floor, him leaping back up), and he continues to do well on the UK PZI insulin. If

Support IMOM, a wonderful organization that helps people with limited funds get veterinary care for their animals. They need your help, and you need to do the right thing. Click this link and make a donation or find another way to help TODAY.

Click here to read **Stupid Vet Tricks,** a compendium of dangerously stupid advice from veterinarians, reported by contributors to the Feline Diabetes Message Board. There are lots of *NEW* entries, I'm sad to say!

As always, a helpful and compassionate group of people with diabetic cats stands ready to help you at the Feline Diabetes Message Board. Go there

Continuation of the diabetic neuropathy page: The variations in font whenever the topic changes help make order out of what could otherwise be chaos. The table cell background colors were chosen to enhance the feeling of hope and encouragement provided by the listed information.

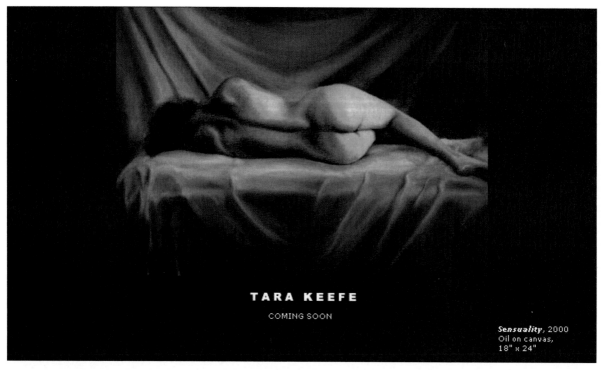

TARA KEEFE

COMING SOON

Sensuality, 2000
Oil on canvas,
18" x 24"

An "under construction" page needn't be boring. This page, designed by Robert Fuller, gives a sense of the online gallery-to-be (**www.tarakeefe.com**). The artist's name serves as an email link, so if a potential client (who wishes either to buy paintings or to show the artist's work) happens upon the site, he or she can make contact even during the site's construction phase.

Robert Fuller's splash page (**www.highstrungproductions.com**) includes Flash animation (the two strips of numbers on the red bar are running back and forth past each other) and sound. Web designers' sites should contain something a little off-the-wall and eye-catching that indicates the designer's talents.

Page design can take on a freeform appearance with layers. The gray text is a background image, and each of the button sets and graphic images is in its own layer. If your target audience is computer users, you can probably assume that most of them will have the latest browsers and therefore will be able to see the layers.

Calendar

February

Sunday	Monday	Tuesday	Wednesday	Thursday	Friday	Saturday
all times are AM except those marked with an *				1 3:00 Maple Village Eucharist*	2	3
4 8:00 Eucharist 9:00 Education Hour 10:00 Eucharist 11:00 Jr/Youth Choir 4:00 Youth Inquirers*	5 8:00 AA Meeting*	6 6:30 Girl Scouts *	7 NO EUCHARIST 7:30 Hand Bell Choir* 8:00 Senior Choir *	8 7:30 Worship Committee*	9	10 10:00 Painting Party at A Women's Place
11 8:00 Eucharist 9:00 Education Hour 10:00 Eucharist 10:00 Godly Play 11:00 Jr/Youth Choir	12 7:30 Committee Night* 8:00 AA Meeting*	13 6:30 Girl Scouts*	14 NO EUCHARIST 7:00 Hand Bell Choir* 8:00 Senior Choir *	15	16	17

A simple table with a 2-pixel border becomes an easy-to-maintain Web calendar. If your client shares in site maintenance duties, this is a page that even an inexperienced Dreamweaver user can update.

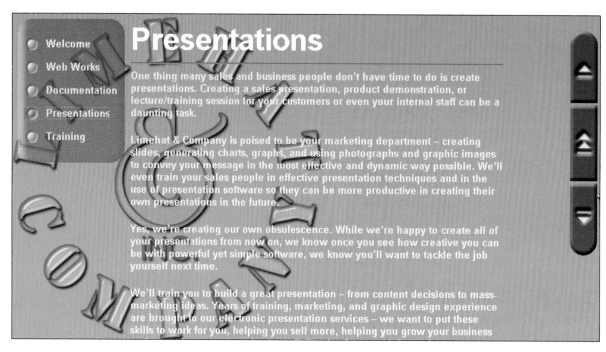

Another site designed by Robert Fuller (**www.limehat.com**) features control buttons that both scroll text down the page and move the translucent background logo from left to right. The navigation buttons are in a see-through box; the color of the buttons indicates which page the user is viewing. The designer used Dynamic HTML, JavaScript, and style sheets to produce this interesting effect.

Keep your background images in line with the tone and topic of the Web page. Here a horticultural theme is maintained between the background, graphics, and text colors.

Pick a color from the graphics or background image to fill a layer or table cell (here, a layer is selected, and the eye-dropper is sipping color from the background). By using colors already in your page, you tie your page elements together. Using color from an image also helps you choose colors that you know work together without consulting a color wheel.

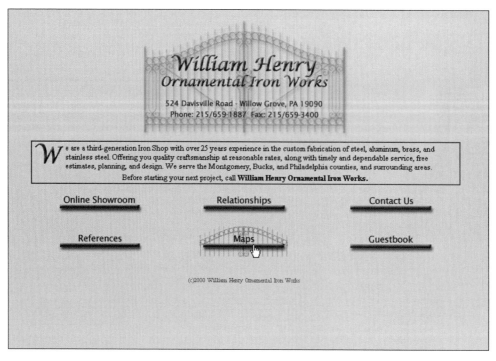

This page incorporates several rollover links and an animated GIF (the large gates at the top). The colors match the client's current marketing materials and the font selections match his literature and his signage. The clean, strong images were created and structured in a linear way to accent the nature of the client's business and the products he creates.

Never make visitors wait for a large image to display unless they've expressed an interest in seeing it. Creating a page of thumbnail images (including instructions for using them), allows the visitor to choose which image to scrutinize.

Ridding your diet of animal products can seem like an insurmountable goal. Even if you stop eating meat (which millions of people have already done to reduce the risk of cancer, heart attack, and stroke), what about eggs, milk, cheese? These foods may not seem like they come at the expense of an animal, but they do. Chickens lead horrible lives, packed thousands to a barn, unable to even flap their wings. Some of them are packed so tight their feet don't touch the floor, which may be a blessing, because the dead bodies of the chickens that didn't survive the ordeal are beneath them, rotting away. Chicks are de-beaked (with a hot, electrified wire) so that when the horribly tight quarters drive them to violence, they can't peck their fellow chickens. These conditions are not the exception, they're the sad, terrible rule.

And what about milk, yogurt, cheese, and all the other dairy goodies we love so much? Eating milk is like drinking meat when it comes to fat, antibiotics, steroids,

One of the things that keeps people from switching to a vegetarian or vegan diet is not knowing what foods are available, what you can eat instead of meat, dairy, and eggs. Here are just some of the things a typical vegan eats:

Vegetables (yeah, big shock there), fruit, pasta, rice, nuts, and beans. Sound boring? It isn't. It's healthy, and you can serve all of these foods in delicious ways. To add more protein, try seitan, a wheat product that tastes like beef. Sauté it in a wok or frying pan with teriyaki sauce or any other marinade you like. Add sautéed onions, mushrooms (portobellos are very meaty-tasting and textured), green onion, and fresh garlic. Serve it over pasta or rice. Filling, good for you, and not a single animal suffered or died to feed you. That feels even better.

Click here for more recipes.

Lunches are easy. Avocado and tomato on toast with soy mayonnaise. Add soy cheese or a soy-based "turkey" or "ham" slice if you want to mimic carnivorous fare. How about an open-faced Garden Burger on pita bread, with a drizzle of some delicious dressing or balsamic vinegar? Make a "sloppy joe" from tomato sauce and browned, crumbled veggie burgers, adding chopped onion and garlic. There are hundreds of tasty and nutritious combinations you can come up with (click below for some ideas) that won't harm a single creature.

Break up the potential monotony of a text-heavy page by emphasizing the first letter of each paragraph. To easily approximate the effect of a drop cap, simply enlarge the first letter in place, change the font, and apply colors found elsewhere on the page or that work well with the background color.

Two versions of the same logo: one that's an effective choice on a page with a background image (top); and one that's better suited to a solid color background (bottom), because the logo itself has a background image within it. Be prepared to tinker with images depending on other page content over which you may not have control.

Layers make it easy to create a freeform structure for your page. Here, an artists' gallery is created on screen, with the paintings (one image per layer) "hung" as they would be on a wall—with some symmetry, but no regimented grid controlling their placement. The image weights and colors are distributed attractively on the page, along with the layer containing text.

This photograph serves as a logo for the company and also provides information about what the company does. By adding text to graphic images, your pictures do double duty—providing window-dressing as well as valuable data.

Here we have another photo with text on it. The text is in the process of becoming hotspots that will link to other pages in the site. By drawing the hotspot area tightly around the text, you make it easier for visitors to click the link they need and not accidentally click a nearby link instead.

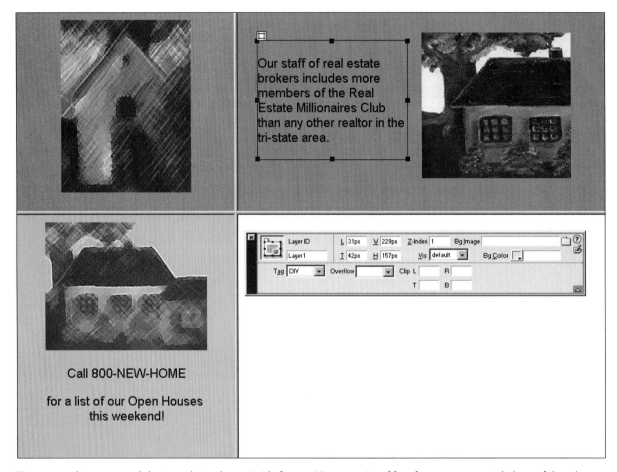

You can combine structural devices, placing layers inside frames. Here, a series of four frames was created; three of them have been filled with colors found in the graphics used. A layer has also been added for paragraph text in the top-right frame so that the desired alignment with the accompanying image can be achieved. The text in the lower-left frame is typed directly into the frame, because it only needs to be centered under the picture.

The Healthy Aging® Campaign

...is supported by public-minded corporations, grants from non-profit corporations, and private contributions.

HEALTHY AGING RESOURCES:
Educational Materials

| Home | Campaign Profile | Directory | Related Sites | Aging Events Calendar | Resources to Order | Order Blank |

The Healthy Aging® educational materials all share one common theme:
It is never too late to improve the physical, mental, social, and financial quality of life.

ORDER

BOOK: Healthy Aging®...Inspirational Letters from Americans

Today's views on aging are told by Americans from across the nation. Adults, ages 50-plus, share their secrets for Healthy Aging®. Candid, original, inspirational -- a must-read for every gerontologist, doctor, or anyone who needs a bit of inspiration as they head toward older ages. It's a great gift or fundraiser for your organization. Quantity discounts are available.

268 pages, hardcover book.
Winner of the Family Channel Seal of Quality
Personal introductions by Jane Brody, Dr. Robert Butler, Dr. James Birren, and Art Linkletter......................$24.95

VIDEO: Healthy Aging®...Redefining America

On-camera host and nationally-acclaimed folk singer Tom Chapin guides the viewer through upbeat, inspirational profiles of middle-aged Americans who are finding ways to deal with what lies ahead.

Meet experts, authors, and educators in this hour-long entertaining and informative video.

This page provides a good example of the use of tables to lay out an entire page. The page consists of two main tables with a nested table inside one of them. The tables contain graphics and text, paired neatly so it's clear which text pertains to which image. There is also a border on the table, which helps provide visual structure for visitors who are shopping at this informative site (**www.healthyaging.net**).

Healthy Aging® Discussion Guide

This educational kit is designed to complement our video, *Our Nation's Health...Healthy Aging®*. The kit contains:

- a 54-page 3-ring binder, providing excellent tools for educating the public about the positive issues of aging
- a written summary of the video
- suggestions for using the video in part of whole
- discussion ideas
- guest speaker suggestions

The kit also includes concrete tips and techniques for healthy aging, including diet tips, suggestions for starting a regular exercise program, and ideas for planning for one's financial future. You also get a copy of the Healthy Aging® brochure.

This kit has been praised by educators and health and aging organizations as an ideal tool to be used in group programs and seminars.

Complete kit: $49.95

Return to Resources

The home page of this site includes thumbnail images that, when clicked, take the visitor to a page like this one. Here users find a larger image and a complete description of the image. Rather than packing one page with too much text, you can create links to additional information and enhanced images. Don't forget the link back to the previous page!

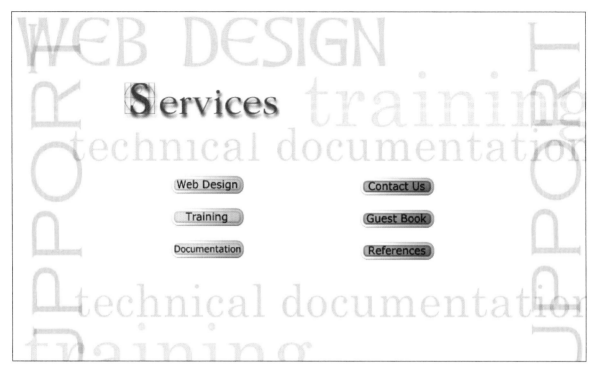

This site uses a background with strategic "holes" (spaces between the background image's graphical text). Layers are nestled in the spaces. Flash buttons were used in two separate layers. Under the layers are text links for visitors who might be using older browsers.

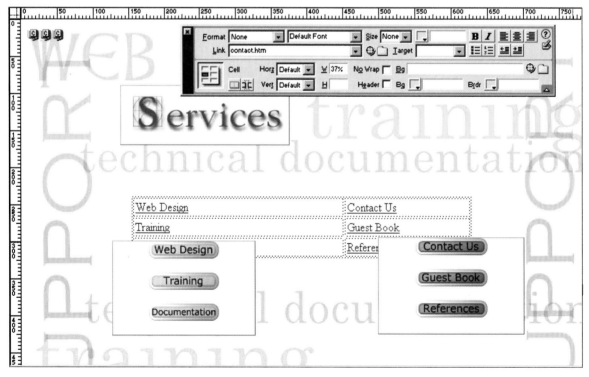

The obscuring layers (which were given a white background fill) have been moved aside to reveal the table cells containing text links. If a visitor can't see the layers, the text links allow them to navigate the site.

Chapter 10

Creating Forms

You want your Web site's visitors to sign your guest book, subscribe to your newsletter, or download a file, and you want a simple, clear, and visually pleasing way for them to comply with your wishes. This chapter will show you how to build forms that are easy to understand and that meet your exacting design standards. You'll also find out what happens after visitors click that Submit button.

Understanding Forms

Your Web pages communicate with your site visitors, giving them information, sharing ideas and opinions, expressing feelings and points of view. The conversation is pretty one-sided, however, with the visitors interacting with content you chose to put on the page. Without forms, visitors' reaction to your content—their interest in the information you're sharing, their desire to buy what you're selling, their willingness to subscribe to a newsletter or join a mailing list—would be a complete mystery to you.

Of course, if your page has a counter on it, you can tell how many times your site is visited—but who visited you, and what drew them there? What did they think of their experience? Were they compelled to read the article or click the link? You can run software on your Web server to keep track of who visited your site and what visitors clicked on, but you cannot electronically watch their mouse and extract their email address to track their feelings, personal information, and intentions to revisit or partake of other products, information, or services you offer.

How do you find out all these things? By providing forms on your site that ask for the information you seek—hopefully, in a compelling way. Do you want to know what visitors thought of your site? Ask them in a form. Do you wish visitors had willingly given you their email addresses, so you can put them on your newsletter mailing list? Provide a form for them to fill out. People resent hearing from sites to which they never knowingly provided information, and you don't want to stoop to that level of subterfuge, when people will generally tell you what you want to know. All you have to do is ask. The key to a successful response is how you ask—how you word the questions, and how you design the form. A well-designed form, such as the one in Figure 10.1, can gently pry virtually any data out of any visitor.

Obviously, the most common use for forms on the Web is in the process of buying and selling. To work, e-commerce requires forms—without forms, people would have to call or send a fax to place an order, and a person would have to manually process the sale. Forms let people choose which product they want, how many they want to buy, which credit card they want to use, and where they want the purchase shipped. On the other side of that process, the form allows Web sites to gather the information and pass it along to one computer to process credit card information; to another computer to generate a pick ticket or other order-processing document, which will make someone pull the item(s) out of inventory for shipment; and, perhaps, to yet another computer to store the customer's information for remarketing purposes. Figure 10.2 shows a form that's really two forms, with each form ultimately sending data to a different database.

To help us serve you better...

Please take just a few minutes to share some information with us.
All information will be kept in total confidence, and will only be used for your benefit.
Thank you!

First Name [   ]   Last Name [   ]   Middle Initial [   ]

How did you hear about us? [from a friend ▼]

Which of our services interests you most?

☐ Instant Real Estate Evaluations   ☐ Dream Home Locator
☐ Find-a-Loan   ☐ Apartment Spotter
☐ Related Services Links   ☐ Live Realtors On-Call

Do you own your own home? ○ Yes ○ No

If Yes, do you plan to sell in the next 6 months? ○ Yes ○ No

What is the current value of your home? [$150,000 - $250,000 ▼]

What is your current annual household income? [$50,000 - $100,000 ▼]

May we send you our list of recommended realtors in your area? ● Yes ○ No
Enter your zip code: [   ]

[Submit] [Reset]

Figure 10.1

People will tell you things through a form that they'd never tell you face to face.

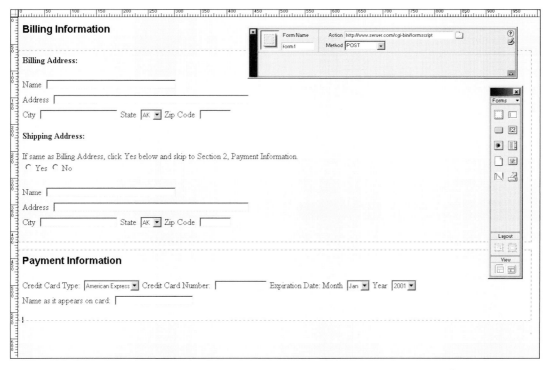

Figure 10.2

E-commerce and the forms that make it possible enable anyone, anywhere in the world, to sell his or her own widgets.

How Forms Work

Forms let people enter data into a database—the people are your site's visitors, and the database is a table of some sort that resides on another computer. The data that the site visitor enters is processed by a script—normally a CGI (Common Gateway Interface) script—and is sent, via your Web server, to the database on another computer. As the HTML code you see in Figure 10.3 shows, when you add a form to a Web page, Dreamweaver creates the tags and attributes necessary for the data that's entered to be routed to the appropriate computer later, via the appropriate CGI script.

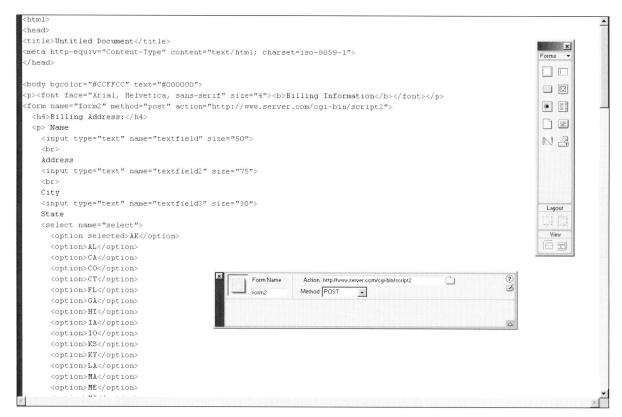

Figure 10.3

The form, with a name you supply, is set to post data to another computer, which you identify through the Action attribute.

The CGI script that handles your form is generally written in Perl, C++, Java, VBScript, or JavaScript. The script, created in any of these programming languages, contains code that looks at each of the pieces of data your user submitted, and then associates that data with a particular field (for example, "Subscribe=Yes" to indicate that the user wants to subscribe to the newsletter). The script then sends that data on to the computer that the Action attribute (in the form tag within the HTML code that makes your page) has identified.

If you plan to have forms on your own Web site, make sure your Web host supports CGI scripts. Although you can create a form and set it up to work on your page without this capability, the data won't go anywhere, which can be a problem if the person entering the data expects something to happen as a result of his or her efforts—e.g., that a newsletter will arrive by email the next week.

When to Use Forms

Forms can be used anywhere, at any time, on any Web page. The word *form* can conjure up images of a long and complex sheet from the IRS, and that can be—to put it mildly—a little disconcerting. In reality, however, a form can be as small and simple as a question such as "Did you enjoy your visit to this site?" and a pair of Yes and No radio buttons, as you see in Figure 10.4, by which visitors can give you their thumbs-up or thumbs-down response.

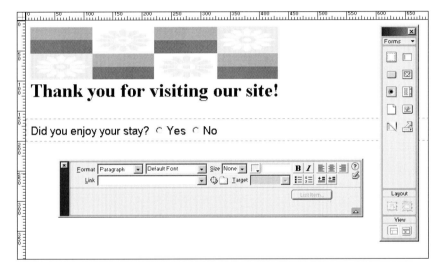

Figure 10.4

A form needn't consist of a list of probing queries—a simple Yes or No response might be all you need.

Forms can also be long and complex if you're looking for a lot of complex information. If you want people to tell you all about their house or car so you can sell it for them or find them a new one, the form that you'll need will probably contain several fields, and several types of fields, as well. The key to a successful long and/or complex form is to make sure the form itself has no role in the complexity. If you clearly word and structure the form, only the nature of the information you seek will give the user pause.

Working with Form Fields

Form fields provide a way for users to respond to your questions or requests for information. Each type of field has a different set of options that you can set—to control the appearance of the field, what kind of data the field will accept, how much data the user can enter into the field, and any default values that the field will contain. For menus and lists, you can also dictate the list of options that the field offers to the user.

Of course, you can insert a form and never put any fields in it, but the form won't do anything but take up space on your page. Until it has fields in it—one or more places for someone to enter data—a form isn't functional. As Figure 10.5 shows, six common field types exist, plus two types of buttons—one for clearing a form and one for submitting the data entered—in addition to checkboxes and radio buttons.

When you're choosing the fields to use in your form, think about how someone would answer the questions you're asking. On the one hand, if you're asking a question that the user could answer in several ways, a radio button (for yes/no responses) obviously isn't appropriate. If you want the answer in the user's words, you don't want the person to choose answers from a list. On the other hand, if you want to control the user's response, providing a simple yes/no way to respond or a restricted list of responses is a great way to keep the data on track.

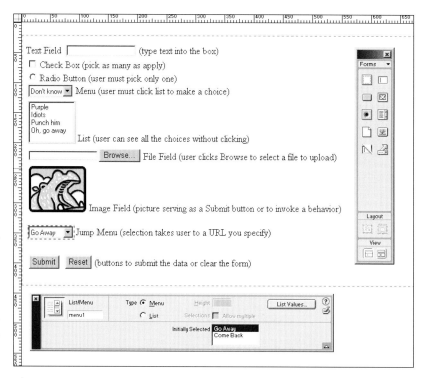

Figure 10.5
Fields accept yes/no (on/off) responses, selections from a list, or strings of text.

Inserting a Form

Inserting a form is rather simple—perhaps deceptively so—considering all that a form does. A form elicits information from people who can be anywhere in the world, and it conveys that data to a specific computer, on which the data is stored and can be used for processing purchases, tracking a site's marketing efforts, developing sales opportunities, or doing a demographic analysis (on which you will base changes to the site).

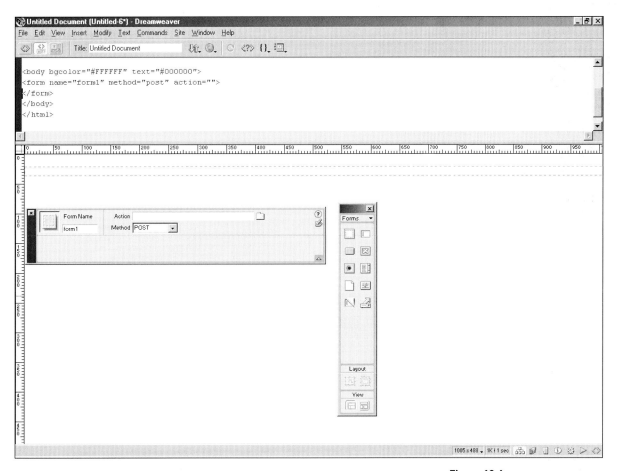

Figure 10.6
A form doesn't do anything until you add fields to it.

A form consists of two parts—the form and the form's fields. The form is simply a container—a box (with a dashed, non-printing border, as Figure 10.6 shows)—that stores the fields. The fields make the form work, but you can't place the fields out loose on the page, because the *form* creation generates the HTML code necessary to funnel the entered data into a database.

The first step in creating a form is to display the appropriate tools. You can convert the Objects panel to a Forms panel, as shown in Figure 10.7. Just click the Common button at the top of the panel, and choose Forms from the resulting menu.

After you display the tools you'll need, click the Insert Form button on the Objects panel. With no fanfare or further effort required from you, a box appears on the page, wherever your cursor was at the time you clicked the button. You can click inside the box, or click its border; clicking the border displays form-related tools on the Properties Inspector, as shown in Figure 10.8.

Setting Up the Form

After you've inserted the form on your page, you'll want to establish a Form Name for the form, a Method for the form to process data, and an Action for the

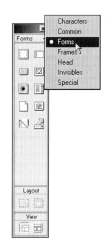

Figure 10.7
All the tools you need to add a form, and a wide variety of field types, is at your disposal on the Forms panel.

Figure 10.8

Click the form border to access the three most important form options on the Properties Inspector.

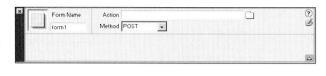

Figure 10.8

Click the form border to access the three most important form options on the Properties Inspector.

Figure 10.9

Give your form a name, choose how it will work, and identify where the data should go.

Either a Borrower or a Lender Be

While you're out there surfing the Web, if you see a form you like, view the HTML code that's behind it by choosing View|Source or View|Page Source (depending on your browser). Within the resulting window, observe the form and field tags—each field will have an input tag, followed by attributes for that particular field, such as names, values, and option tags. You can learn a lot about how forms work by reviewing the underlying HTML code, and you also can borrow the code to use in creating your own form. To borrow the code, highlight it with your mouse, copy it to the Clipboard (Edit|Copy), and then go to your Dreamweaver document and paste (Edit|Paste) the code into your page code, as you view it through Code view or Design and Code views. Be sure to copy the entire form, from the starting <**form**> tag through to the closing </**form**> tag.

form. The Action is simply the path to the CGI script that will handle the data and send it on to the computer that will store the data entered through the form. As Figure 10.9 shows, setting up your form doesn't require much work, but these three basic pieces of information are key to the form's successful use.

Naming a Form

Why is naming your form so important? Because the scripting language that processes the form data will need to refer to the form by name. For this reason, you will want to let the people creating the script know what name you've selected, or ask them what the form name is if they've already set up their end of things.

Form names should be short and relevant, and you shouldn't use spaces. If you need the illusion of a space, use an underscore. Typing in all lowercase letters is also a good idea, because the scripting language will most probably be case-sensitive.

Choosing a Method

A form's method is either **POST** or **GET**, and if you're not the script programmer, you'll want to check with the person who is responsible for the script, to find out which method you should choose. **POST** method means that the data entered into the form will be sent in a message to the server that contains the CGI script. The **GET** method means that the data will be appended to the URL named in the Action field.

If you need to get started on your form design and don't know whether the form will be of the **GET** or **POST** variety, you can always change this setting later. The choice you make won't have any impact on the form's functioning until the form is online and in use by site visitors.

Entering the Action

As I've mentioned, the Action is the URL for the Web server (which contains the CGI script that will process and send the form data on to the database where the user-entered data will be stored and analyzed). As Figure 10.10 shows,

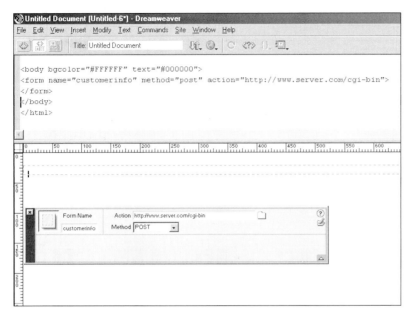

the Action looks like a Web address you'd type into the Link box if you were creating a hyperlink out of text or a graphic.

Again, the Action URL is something someone will have to tell you if you aren't responsible for the database back-end of the Web site. As with the Method, you can hold off entering an Action until you know the exact URL, and you don't need to enter that until you're ready to post to the Web the page that contains the form.

Structuring a Form with Tables

A table is one of the best ways to build a form and set up your fields. Just as tables give your page structure, by enabling you to position text and graphics in either a uniform or free-form grid, a table gives you that same capability when you're positioning fields and their accompanying text. Figure 10.11 shows a form that contains a table filled with fields and instructional text.

You can use either the Standard or Layout view (and each view's associated tools) to build the form table, and you can format the table just as you would any other table—the fact that it's inside a form has no bearing on your ability to resize cells, columns, and rows; to apply color and borders; or to align cell content. When you're using a table to structure your form, think of the fields as graphic elements—pictures you're arranging along with text—and you're using the table cells to control the pictures' placement.

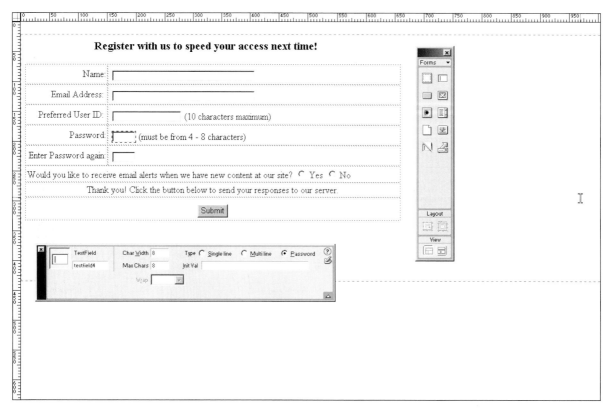

Figure 10.11

Map out the form in your head or on paper, and then create that structure with a table within the form.

Inserting Form Fields

Once you have your table set up within the form (or as soon as you've inserted a form, if you're not using a table), you can begin inserting fields. Assuming you have the Forms panel displayed, you can use the panel's buttons to insert the various types of fields in your form. If you'd prefer, you can use the Insert menu, and the Form Objects command and submenu, as shown in Figure 10.12.

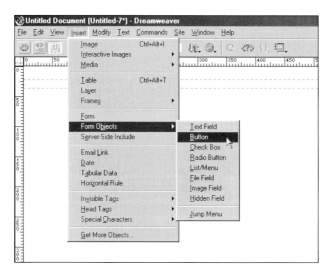

Figure 10.12

Select your fields from a panel or from the Insert|Form Objects submenu.

When you're inserting fields, the position of your cursor will determine where the fields appear. Click to position your cursor in a particular table cell, or in a specific location within the form, before you choose the field type you want to insert. Once you've inserted the field, you can select it by clicking on it (a dashed border will appear around the field), or move it by dragging it. Figure 10.13 shows a field selected and in the process of being dragged to a new location within the form.

Register with us to speed your access next time!

Name:

Email Address:

Preferred User ID: (10 characters maximum)

Password: (must be from 4 - 8 characters) Enter Password again:

Would you like to receive email alerts when we have new content at our site? ○ Yes ○ No

Thank you! Click the button below to send your responses to our server.

Submit

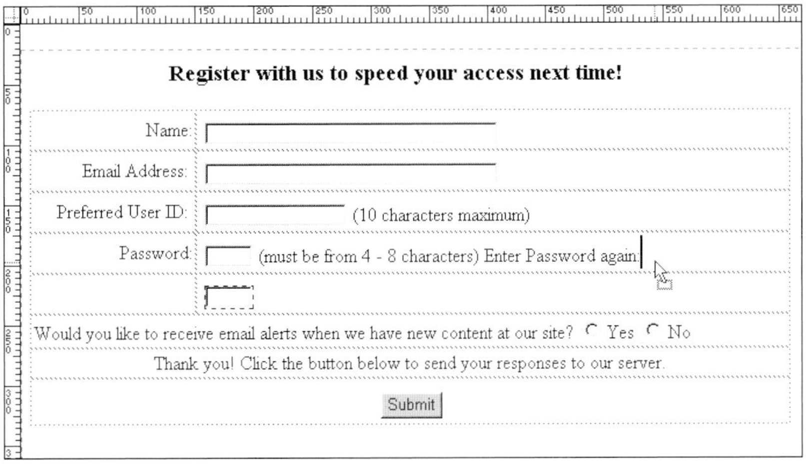

Figure 10.13

Click and drag to rearrange your form fields.

Of course, each field will probably require text to accompany it. How else will the user know what you want to know? Keep your text accompaniments simple and clear, just as you would on a form you design on paper. If you want users to enter their names in two pieces (First Name, and then Last Name in a separate field), type the words "First Name" next to the first field, followed by the words "Last Name" and then the second field. In this example (see Figure 10.14), the placement of the text and associated fields prevents people typing their full name into the First Name field, leaving Last Name blank by mistake.

Figure 10.14

For names, addresses, and credit card numbers, make clear which data goes in which field.

First Name   Last Name   Middle Initial

If you have any instructions for a particular field, be sure to place them close to the field so the user knows to which field the instructions apply. This is where using tables for form structure comes in handy, because you can put the field name or question in one cell, the field in the next cell, and any instruction in the cell with the field itself, so users have no question about which text goes with which field. Figure 10.15 shows a form with a clean, clear arrangement of field labels/questions, fields, and instructional text.

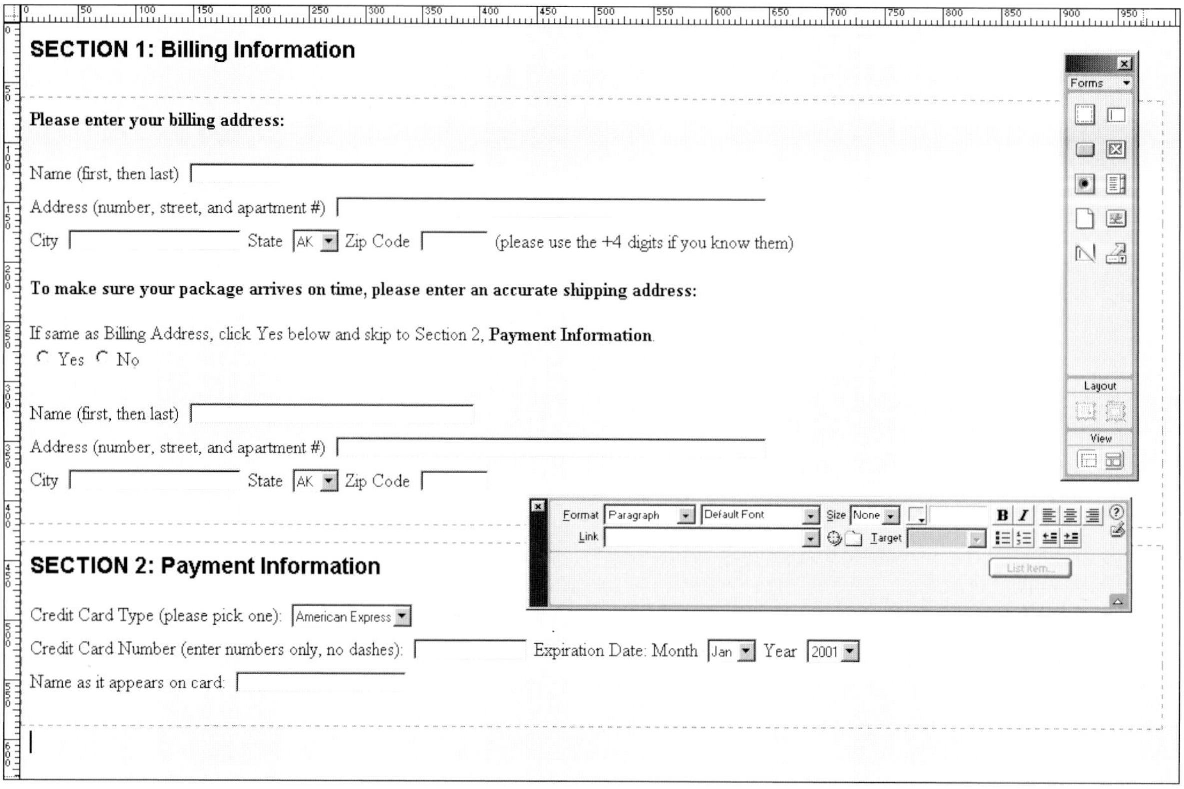

Figure 10.15

Keep things clear, and arrange your text and fields so that users can easily navigate and understand the form.

Although the process of inserting fields is the same for each type of field, what you can do with each field type does vary—and, in some cases, the fields won't work until and unless you address the field's options via the Properties Inspector. For each type of field, the Properties Inspector displays a different set of options, which you activate by clicking on an inserted field within your form.

Text Fields

When you want users to type their own words in response to a question, use a text field. You can use text fields for visitors to enter something short, such as an email address, name, or credit card number, or to type a long string, such as a product review or a comment. Many Web sites will use a large text field to elicit visitor responses or opinions, rather than having the visitor send an email. Why? Because the designer can set up the text field to restrict the length of the response. If you're a senator, for example, and you want to hear the voice of your constituency, you might not want respondents' opinions to appear in the form of an epic—restricting them to a certain number of characters will force them to be concise.

The text field options (as Figure 10.16 shows) include the Type of text field (Single line, Multi line, or Password); an Init Val (initial value), which is content you insert that will appear in the field by default; and options for restricting

Figure 10.16

Set the size of your text field, and establish controls for the amount of data the user can enter.

the size of the field and how much data it will accept (Char Width and Max Chars). You should also give your field a name, so that the CGI script can refer to the field by name, and to make finding the field within your HTML code easier, should you have to do any editing in Code view.

If you choose to make your field a multiple-line text field, the Wrap option will become available, and you can then choose from four options:

- *Off or Default*—prevents the text from wrapping. This option inhibits long responses, but it makes it harder for users to review their entries.

- *Virtual*—wraps the text within the size of the text field, but the wrap information won't be sent with the data in the form of line breaks. The data will be received as a continuous string.

- *Physical*—also wraps the text within the text field, but where the text breaks to wrap onto the next line, a line break will be added to the data.

Radio Buttons and Checkboxes

We all have experience with radio buttons and checkboxes, having used them for years in software dialog boxes. Choosing to turn options on or off to select how to perform a task—the way we communicate with our computers—is very much like the way a site visitor communicates with you through a form. Radio buttons and checkboxes are simple fields that require little or no instruction for the user, which makes them appealing choices when you're building a form. These features do have limitations, however, if only because the user can pick only one (using radio buttons), or pick only from items in a list or array of choices (using checkboxes). When you use these fields in your form, you leave no room for the user's own words.

As soon as you insert a radio button or checkbox, the Properties Inspector changes to display options relevant to the field type you've chosen. As Figures 10.17 and 10.18 show, little difference exists between the Properties Inspector for a radio button and the Properties Inspector for a checkbox.

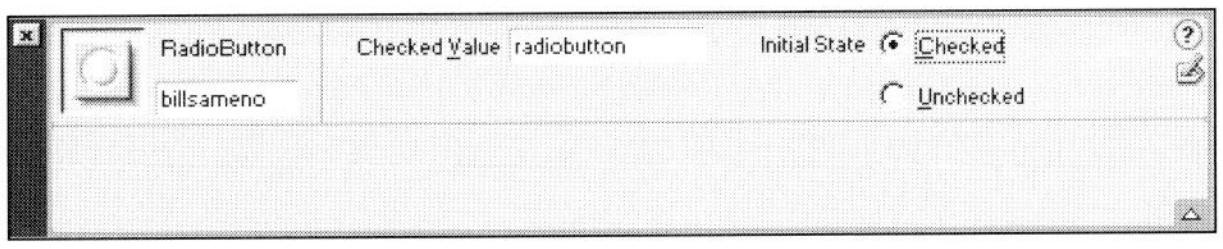

> **Ssssh—It's a Password**
>
> If you choose the Password option for the text-field type, the user's entry will appear as asterisks, which provide security by preventing someone else from observing the user's password as he or she types it.

Figure 10.17

Choose whether the radio button is selected by default, and give the field a name.

Figure 10.18

Choose whether the checkbox will be checked on or off by default. Don't forget to name the field, too.

These figures bring up a good question. Should your radio button or checkbox be on or off by default? The answer depends on the question to which the field accepts a response. If you're asking someone a question to which you hope the answer is Yes, having the Yes radio button on is a good idea, because people are more likely to leave it on than to pick No, unless they're definitely feeling negatively about the question. Setting checkboxes on by default risks that people who are lazy about filling in forms will inadvertently send data that you don't want. Imagine a series of checkboxes for which people are to choose the features they liked most about a product. If you have all the checkboxes selected by default, you might end up with false data if users don't go through and deselect boxes to correctly reflect their opinions.

Lists and Menus

Often referred to as *drop-down* lists, these lists and menus offer form users a list of choices—responses from which to choose when they're answering a question or making a selection. Once you've inserted this type of field, building the list that will appear—choosing when the user clicks the drop-down arrow button to display the menu or whether or not the user will see the whole list all at once—is up to you. You'll also be able to establish the rules for making a selection—to let users make multiple selections, or to force them to pick just one item from the list.

To insert a list or menu, click the Insert List/Menu button on the Forms panel, or choose Insert|Form Objects|List/Menu. A small box with a drop-down arrow button appears, and the options offered in the Properties Inspector change, as shown in Figure 10.19.

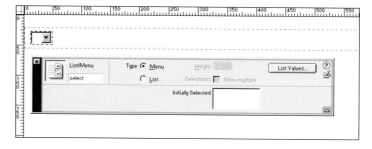

Figure 10.19

You can resize the list or menu box and set up the list of choices it will offer the user.

The big difference between a list and a menu is how the choices appear for the user. If you opt to insert a menu, the user will have to click a drop-down arrow button to see the choices and make a selection. The menu is the best choice when space is limited or if you need to include a long list of choices but don't want to include a list that's an inch or more in length in your form. Figure 10.20 shows a long menu of choices—one that definitely belongs in a menu or a list with a restricted number of choices visible.

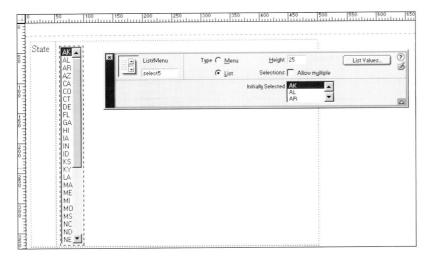

Figure 10.20

Do you have a long list of items for the user to choose from? Save space in the form by placing the items in a menu rather than a list.

A list, however, will display all the choices by default. If the list of choices is long, it will take up significant space on your form. A list is preferable to a menu either when you don't care about the space it takes up, or when you think the user will benefit from seeing all the choices at once without having to click a drop-down menu to see them. Of course, you can also set up short lists of two or three items effectively as a list. As Figure 10.21 shows, if you don't think users will bother to click the menu and you want them to make a choice, show them all their choices in a list—the list requires less effort from users, and their choices are right in front of them as soon as they display the form. Also, if you know what users' most likely choice might be, making that option the default selection might be helpful—if users skip the field, chances are that you're still getting valid data.

Figure 10.21

For short lists, or when users might not bother to make a menu selection, lists are a good alternative.

You'll notice that when you choose List from the Type option, the Height option becomes available. This option lets you restrict the number of items that show in the list. If your list contains 10 choices, but you have room for only 3 of them to show, set the Height to 3. A pair of up and down arrows appears in the field, so the user can scroll up and down in the list of choices. As Figure 10.22 shows, if you set your list Height to 0 (zero), the list will look just like a menu. When you preview the list in a browser (as shown in Figure 10.23), the list (on the left) and the menu (on the right) look the same—a menu has no changeable height setting, and a list with a Height of 0 shows only one choice and must offer a drop-down arrow button so users can see their choices.

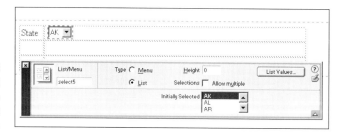

Figure 10.23
Compare a list with a Height of 0 to a menu (for which the height cannot be changed); to the user, these fields look the same.

So why, when we can configure one to look and work just like the other, should we have both lists and menus available as allegedly different field types? Because the List type gives you the capability to set a height to control the number of choices the user sees without interacting with the form, and the Menu type forces the user to interact by clicking the drop-down arrow button.

Jump Menus

Menu fields let users select from a list of responses, normally to complete a query such as "Number of employees at your location" or "Annual household income". A jump menu takes that format a step further and gives the user a list of choices, and each choice results in a jump to a URL (Web address). This added functionality enables you to create forms that link to other Web pages within your site or to someone else's site. You can also make a jump menu wherein each choice leads to another form on another page. This setup lets you make multipage forms in which the subsequent form pages the visitor goes to are of their own choosing. Imagine a form on which you want someone to complete a test and, at the end of the first page, the user can pick whether or not to go on to a history test, a math test, or a science test. This form would let students take tests online—and choose the order in which they take the tests.

To create a jump menu, simply click the Insert Jump Menu button on the Forms panel, or choose Insert|Form Objects|Jump Menu. The resulting field looks just like a regular menu field, but instead of just a new batch of options in the Properties Inspector, the Insert Jump Menu dialog box appears, as you can see in Figure 10.24.

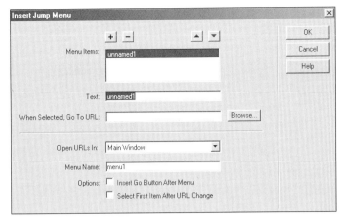

To add menu items to your jump menu, follow these steps within the Insert Jump Menu dialog box:

1. Type the name of your first menu item in the Text box, and click the plus (+) sign at the top of the dialog box. This action adds the menu item to the Menu Items list.

2. Click the Browse button at the end of the When Selected, Go To URL text box. The Select File dialog box opens (looking just like all the other file-selection dialog boxes you've seen in Dreamweaver or any other Windows application), through which you can navigate to a particular HTML file on your local drive or on your company's intranet. Click Select to return to the Insert Jump Menu dialog box. If you know the exact URL of a site on the Web, simply type that address in the box without clicking Browse, as shown in Figure 10.25.

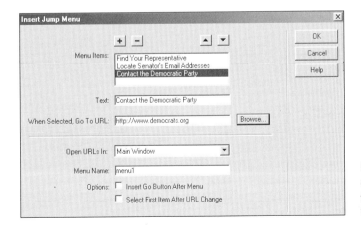

3. If you want a Go button to appear after the menu, click the Insert Go Button After Menu option at the bottom of the dialog box.

To Go or Not to Go

You don't have to include a button after the jump menu—when users make a choice from the menu, releasing their mouse after clicking on one of the menu items automatically will take them to the associated URL. The Go button is a nice touch, but it's not a functional necessity.

4. Repeat Steps 1 and 2 for each item you want on your menu (the Go button, if you applied it, is associated with the entire menu, not with individual items in the menu).

5. When you've built all your menu choices, click OK to create the field and close the dialog box. You'll be returned to your form, with the jump menu you just created in place.

6. Test your jump menu's functionality by pressing F12 to preview your page in the default browser. Make a selection from the menu, and see whether you end up at the site or on the page you wanted.

If you opted for a Go button to accompany your menu, you aren't stuck with the rather simplistic "Go" directive if you don't want it. You can change the text on this button to anything you want, even if you just want to add an exclamation point to create a more convivial "Go!" button instead. To edit the face of the Go button, follow these steps:

Figure 10.26

Look for the input tag with a **<type="button">** attribute, which will be followed by **<value="Go">**, the default button text.

1. With your field selected, click the Code view or Design and Code view button to see the HTML code for your page and for the specific field. Figure 10.26 shows the HTML code for a selected jump menu.

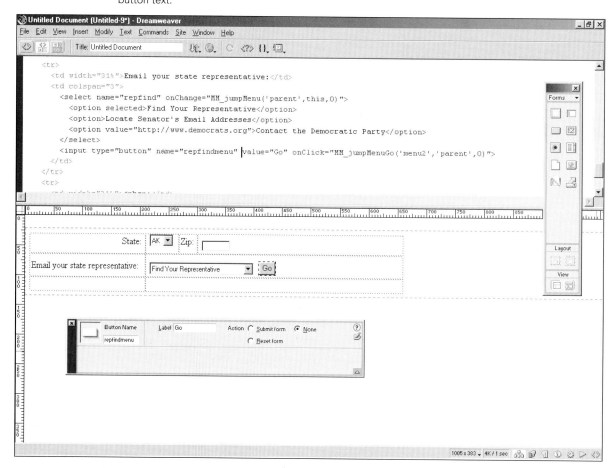

2. Select the button face text (within quotes) and type the replacement text. If you're adding an exclamation point or other characters after the word *Go*, simply click after the *o* and type the added content.

3. The Code view Properties Inspector will appear, prompting you to click the Refresh button to have your changes reflect in Design view, as shown in Figure 10.27. Click Refresh, and return to Design view to see your edited button.

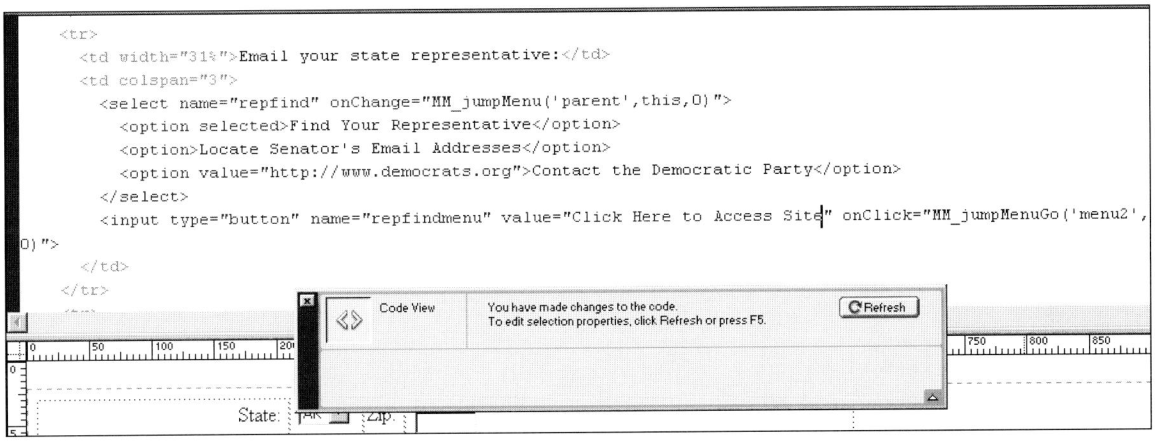

```
<tr>
  <td width="31%">Email your state representative:</td>
  <td colspan="3">
    <select name="repfind" onChange="MM_jumpMenu('parent',this,0)">
      <option selected>Find Your Representative</option>
      <option>Locate Senator's Email Addresses</option>
      <option value="http://www.democrats.org">Contact the Democratic Party</option>
    </select>
    <input type="button" name="repfindmenu" value="Click Here to Access Site" onClick="MM_jumpMenuGo('menu2',
0)">
  </td>
</tr>
```

| | Code View | You have made changes to the code. To edit selection properties, click Refresh or press F5. | ⟳ Refresh |

State:

Figure 10.27
Whenever you edit HTML code in Dreamweaver, you need to refresh Design view to reflect your changes.

If you ever need to edit the URL to which a jump menu item points, select the jump menu field in Design view, and switch to Code view—the associated code will be selected. Look for the **<option value="http://www.domain.com">menu text</option>** code, in which *menu text* is the menu item you want to edit. Figure 10.28 shows this code for an actual form.

```
<tr>
  <td width="31%">Email your state representative:</td>
  <td colspan="3">
    <select name="repfind" onChange="MM_jumpMenu('parent',this,0)">
      <option selected>Find Your Representative</option>
      <option>Locate Senator's Email Addresses</option>
      <option value="http://www.democrats.org">Contact the Democratic Party</option>
```

Figure 10.28
Editing your field's HTML code is easy if you know where to look for the attribute you need to change.

Type a new URL within the quotes, and click the Refresh button in the Properties Inspector. You can then return to Design view and preview your page in a browser to test your change to the menu.

File Fields

Unlike the other fields I've discussed in this chapter, a file field doesn't ask a question or attempt to elicit a response of any kind. Rather, the file field lets the site visitor upload a file to the Web server. You can use this sort of field to let visitors upload documents, graphic images, and even their own HTML files for you (or the server administrator) to post on the Web. A file field, as Figure 10.29 shows, includes a text box for visitors to enter the path and file

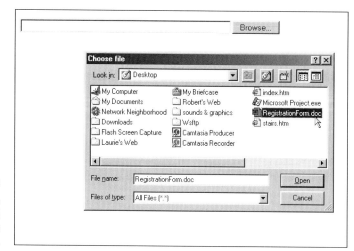

Figure 10.29

If you want a file from site visitors, give them a file field through which to submit the file to you.

HTML-Phobes, Beware

If you exit the Insert Jump Menu dialog box before you've established URLs for each menu item, you'll have to edit the HTML code to associate your menu items with URLs. You'll also have to use the Code view (or Design and Code view) to edit your HTML if you want to change a URL to which a jump menu points. All the other things you can do in the dialog box (add list items, change the order of items) you can also do through the Properties Inspector while the field in question is selected.

name of the file to be uploaded. The field also includes a Browse button that opens a Choose File dialog box, from which the visitor can select the file to be uploaded.

Once you've inserted a file field, you can customize it in terms of its size and how many characters the text box will accept. You can also customize the face of the Browse button—changing it, for example, to read "Click Here to Select a File". Hopefully, you're familiar enough with your anticipated audience to know how much hand-holding your average site visitor will need, and you can design your file-field button (and all your other form text, for that matter) accordingly.

When you insert a file field, the Properties Inspector offers a limited selection of tools, as Figure 10.30 shows—you can change the Char Width (the number of characters it will display) and the Max Chars (the number of characters the field can accept), and you can give the field a name. Naming all your fields is a good idea, if only to help you find them later within your HTML code, should editing the code become necessary.

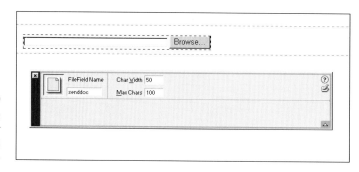

Figure 10.30

A file field should accept a long string of characters, to allow for elaborate paths and long file names.

Submit Buttons

After visitors have filled out all the fields, made their selections, checked the checkboxes, and clicked the radio buttons, everything boils down to the Submit button. Without the Submit button, the data that the visitor has provided will go nowhere—it will just sit on the form. The Submit button sends the data that the visitor entered to the URL listed in the form's Action attribute, where, as I discussed previously, a CGI script is (hopefully) awaiting the data.

When you insert a Submit button, you can choose to leave it as a Submit button (the default) or change it to a Reset (form) button. You can type any text you want to appear on the button face (see the Label field in the Properties Inspector, as shown in Figure 10.31), and you can choose what the button will do—submit the form to the designated URL; reset the form, removing all entries; or do nothing (select None from the Action options).

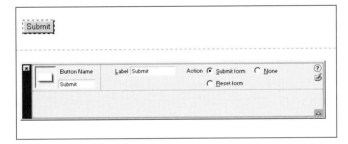

Figure 10.31
Choose what the button will say and what it will do.

A button that does nothing would seem pointless, but such a nonfunctioning button is handy when you're testing a site before you post it to the Web, or while the site's online in a staging area—you aren't ready for the form to do anything, but you want a button in place as you set up your form design. If someone accidentally clicks the button, you don't want an error message to appear, which would happen if a real Submit button were in place. A functioning Reset button can be put in place on a page that's still in the testing/design phase, because for a Reset button to work, no connection to a CGI script is required—it simply clears the form.

Image Fields

Throughout this book, you've read (and you probably already knew) how important color and visual interest are in the design of a Web page. Dreamweaver offers us so many tools to help us make our Web pages compelling and attractive, you'd think the default Submit button would be more visually appealing!

You're not limited, however, to a gray button with Submit or some other black, Arial text on it. You can use a graphic as your Submit button, courtesy of the Image Field. As Figure 10.32 shows, you can use a Submit button you created in Fireworks or some other image-creation/editing software, or you can use a photograph or existing line art (GIF- or JPEG-format, clip-art images).

Jump Menus as Navigation Tools?

Sure. If your site pages are packed with content, and space is at a premium, save the space that a strip of navigation buttons would use, and insert a jump menu instead. Each menu item can take the visitor to a different page in your site. Remember that even though your field is alone, it must be in a form; so insert a form first, then add your lonely jump menu inside the field, with or without a Go button.

Not As Dumb As It Looks

In addition to using a button as a dummy or placeholder during the design phase, you can set a button's Action to None and change the button face to read "Calculate Total", or "Apply Formula", or some other action that will occur when the form data is sent to the CGI script. The function of the button is something you'd have to build into the script yourself or that you'd reflect in the button's face after you spoke with the script programmer. You want to be sure that the button you add to the form works with what's happening once the form data is submitted.

Figure 10.32

Why settle for a boring gray button, when you can have something that matches your color scheme and contributes to your overall design?

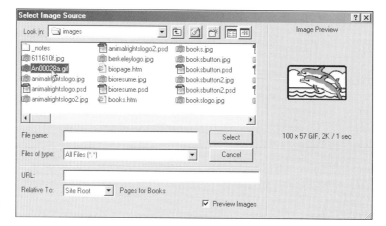

Figure 10.33

Choose the image file you want to use for a button on your form.

To insert an Image Field, click the Image Field button on the Forms panel, or choose Insert|Form Objects|Image Field. A Select Image Source dialog box opens, as Figure 10.33 shows. Navigate to the folder that contains the image you want to use (it must be a GIF or JPEG file, and the same file-size suggestions still apply), double-click the image file name to select the file, and close the dialog box.

Once you've inserted the image on your form, the image appears in the same dashed border you'll see around all other fields. The Properties Inspector changes, too, as Figure 10.34 shows. You can choose another image through the Src box, indicate Alt text that will appear when someone moves the mouse over the field, resize the image with the W and H (width and height) text boxes, Align the image within the form, and give the field a name.

Figure 10.34

Change the field's name to Submit, and your image field is on its way to being a Submit button in disguise.

Oddly, you can't turn an image button into a Reset button, even by tinkering with the HTML code. You can, however, attach other behaviors to an image button, through the Behaviors panel. Simply select the inserted image field, and display the Behaviors panel by choosing Window|Behaviors. In the panel, click the plus sign (+), and a list of the behaviors with which your selected image can be associated is displayed. You can see the list in Figure 10.35.

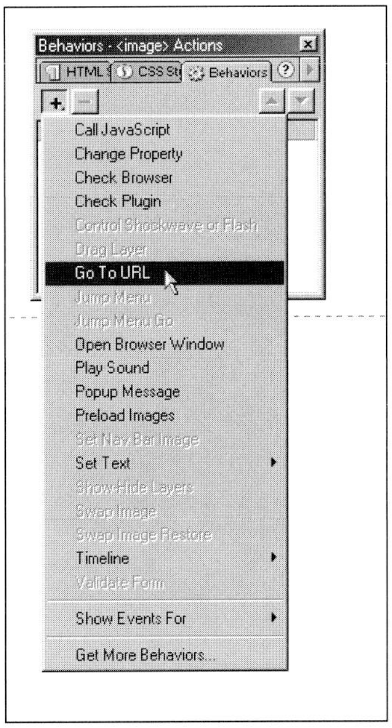

Figure 10.35
Add an image field that takes your users to a different URL when they click the image, or set the image up to play a sound.

Nice Picture, But What Does It Do?

Don't just leave an image field sitting on the page and hope people will stumble onto it and click it. Unless the image has text in it that says "Click me and _____ will happen" (or words to that effect), site visitors might not even realize the image is a button, and they won't click it. If your image is a photo or some other graphic that doesn't offer any instruction from within, add some text above, below, or beside the image that tells people why it's there and what it does. The Alt text (inserted through the Properties Inspector) is also a good tool for telling people what will happen if they click the image, but they'll only see that text if they move their mouse over the image.

Design a Visitor-Feedback Form

In this project, you'll create a form for site visitors to use to rate the site, express interest in more information, and register with the site so they can receive information about site changes and related information via email.

The form will consist of several text fields, list menus, radio buttons, and checkboxes. In addition, you'll turn a graphic into a button for visitors to click to submit the form, and you'll add a jump menu that takes users to another Web site, where they can download a file.

Open a New Document

Create a new blank document using the File|New command.

Insert a Form Title

Create a title for your form:

1. Type "Visitor Feedback" as a heading at the top of the page.

2. Format the title in the Heading 1 style, and center the title.

Insert a Form

Next, insert an empty form on the Web page by doing the following:

1. Display the Objects panel, and switch to the Forms version.

2. With your cursor below the heading, click the Insert Form button on the Forms Object panel.

Insert a Table

To provide structure for your form, insert a table with the following characteristics:

1. Within the form's dashed red border, insert a two-column, five-row table.

2. Set the table width to 100%.

Figure 10.36

Use the table columns and rows to give your form a solid foundation.

3. Center the table, as shown in Figure 10.36.

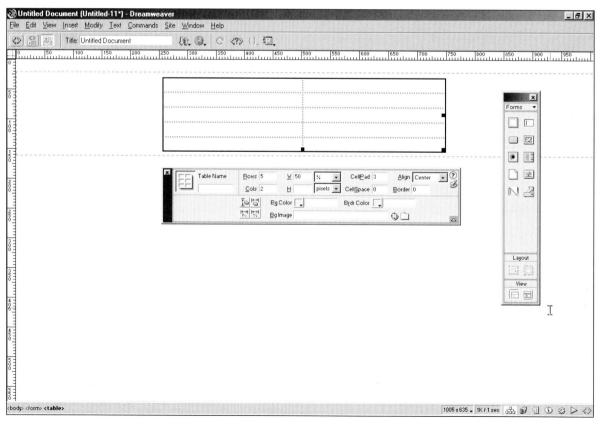

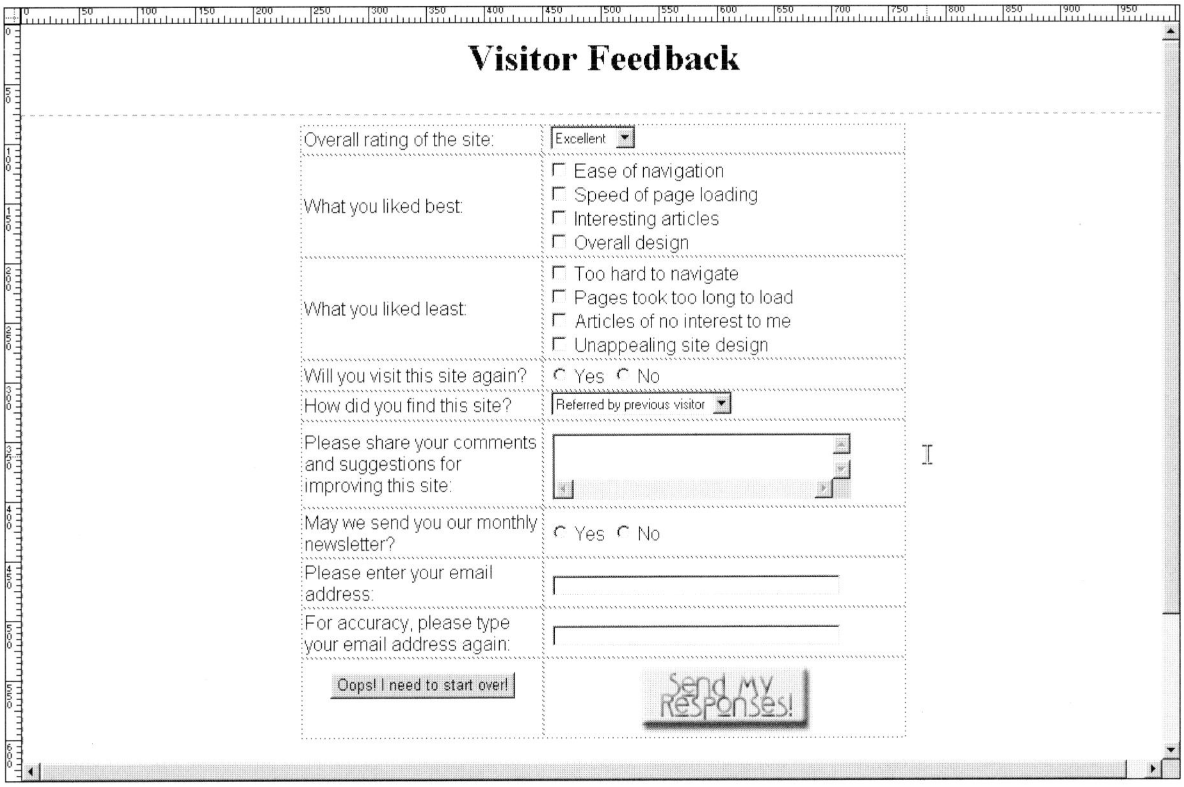

Figure 10.37
This simple form asks a series of questions and makes the method of answering very clear to the user.

Add the Form Fields

Add text and fields to the form as follows:

1. Referring to Figure 10.37, add the following text and fields. The text should be in the first column; the field (and any accompanying text, such as *Yes* or *No*) to which the text refers should be the second column:

   - Overall rating of the site: (Insert a list menu, with ratings of Excellent, Very Good, Good, Fair, and Poor.)

   - What you liked best: (Insert a series of four checkboxes, each accompanied by text: Ease of navigation, Speed of page loading, Interesting articles, Overall design.)

   - What you liked least: (Insert a series of four checkboxes, each accompanied by text: Too hard to navigate, Pages took too long to load, Articles of no interest to me, Unappealing site design.)

   - Will you visit this site again? (Insert two radio buttons, one accompanied by Yes, the other by No.)

   - How did you find this site? (Provide a list menu of choices: Search engine, Clicked a link at another site, Referred by previous visitor, Don't know how I got here.)

- Please share your comments and suggestions for improving this site: (Insert a text box that allows up to 200 characters.)

- May we send you our monthly email newsletter? (Insert two radio buttons, one accompanied by Yes, the other by No.)

- Please enter your email address: (Provide a text box that allows up to 100 characters.)

- For accuracy, please type your email address again: (Repeat the text box from above.)

2. Instead of a Submit button, insert an image field in the form of the graphic called sendresponses.jpg, which you will find on the CD-ROM in the Project 10A folder.

3. Insert a Reset button, and change the face to read "Oops! I need to start over!"

Customize Fields

Make some changes to the fields:

1. The question about the email newsletter should be set to *Yes* by default.

2. The question about revisiting the site should be set to *Yes* by default.

Save the File

Save the Web page, naming it feedbackform.htm.

Preview and Test the Form

While your form won't actually update a database, you can test the form in a browser, working from the local version of the Web page. Press F12 to preview the page in your default browser. Test the form by entering responses to each question and clicking the Send Responses button. Repeat the process, this time clearing your entries with the *Oops!* button.

Moving On

In Chapter 11, you'll learn to speed your design process and maintain consistency between pages in a site by creating and using templates to build your Web pages. You'll also learn to create and stock libraries of page elements, which will make inserting items that appear frequently in your pages and sites faster and easier.

Chapter 11

Working with Dreamweaver Assets

New to Dreamweaver 4 is an Assets panel—a window you can display on the workspace to give you quick access to images, URLs, colors, multimedia objects—anything you want to add to your Web pages. In addition, the Assets panel gives you access to your templates, which you can apply to existing pages or use to start new ones. As you'll discover in this chapter, the Dreamweaver Assets panel might be one of your most convenient and powerful assets as a Web designer.

The Dreamweaver Assets Panel

The Assets panel might run a close second to the Properties Inspector as the most useful on-screen item in the Dreamweaver workspace. The Assets panel offers you the capability to collect elements for individual pages not associated with specific sites. Or, if you're using the Sites capabilities within Dreamweaver, you can use the Assets panel for all the pages in a specified site to help you maintain consistency across any site—where consistency and repetition are called for, you can use the same images, colors, links, and templates.

Displaying the Assets Panel

Despite its usefulness, the Assets panel doesn't display automatically, unless you displayed and left it open the last time you used Dreamweaver. Like all the other panels and palettes, the Assets panel is a floating item: You can move it anywhere on the screen, drag it out of the way while you're not using it, or bring it front and center when you need it. To display the Assets panel, choose Window|Assets, and the panel appears as you see it in Figure 11.1.

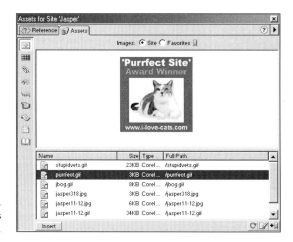

Figure 11.1
The Assets panel has two tabs, nine categories, and thousands of uses.

If you've never seen the Assets panel before (and users of Dreamweaver 3 might have been using Dreamweaver 4 for some time now and never investigated the Assets panel), you'll find that it already has a significant inventory—of images, movies, scripts, URLs, and colors. Go to one of your sites (Sites|Open Site), choose a site from the submenu, and then, for example, click the URL's category button on the left side of the Assets panel. As Figure 11.2 shows, you'll see in the panel all the URLs you used in all the pages associated with your open site.

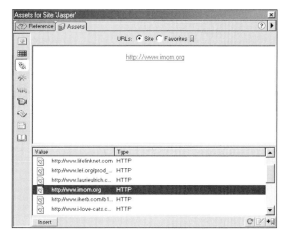

Figure 11.2

Without any effort from you, all the URLs used on any page in the open site appear in the Assets panel.

Viewing the Assets Categories

The nine Assets categories encompass all the different types of elements you'd add to or use within a Web page. To view a category, simply click the button for the category you'd like to explore. The buttons appear vertically on the left side of the Assets panel, as Figure 11.3 shows.

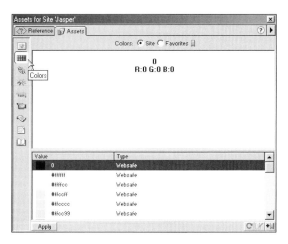

Figure 11.3

Pick a category, any category.

Following are the categories and functions of each button:

- *Images*—Graphics you've used and those you'll add later are all in this category. As I stated earlier, if you've never even displayed your Assets panel, all the images you already put into the pages on a site will be there, ready to insert from within the panel. The images category is also handy for reviewing your images if you forget which ones you've used on all your pages—and you can easily remove items you don't want to keep or risk reusing by mistake.

- *Colors*—A palette of the colors you've used in the creation of a site's pages accumulates in this category. The palette includes colors you've applied to text, links, borders, and backgrounds. If you've used the color-well eyedropper to extract a color from a graphic, that color is in here, too.

- *URLs*—A great way to keep track of the links you've inserted, this category maintains a list of the URLs you've used in your site pages' hyperlinks—including links to scripts, email addresses, pages within your site, and external Web addresses. You can reuse the links from this list, and you can add to the list as you add new links within your pages.

- *Flash Movies*—The SWF (Shockwave Flash) versions of any Flash movies you've added to your site appear here. You can insert these movies from the panel into other pages within your site and if you've saved them with relevant names, you can quickly take an inventory of the movies you have available to use in your pages.

- *Shockwave Movies*—Macromedia Shockwave files are stored in this category. As with any other asset, you can easily insert any Shockwave movie into your pages using the Assets panel just by dragging your mouse (more about this later).

- *MPEG and QuickTime Movies*—If you're using movies in either MPEG or QuickTime format, you'll find them in this category.

- *Scripts*—This category stores independent script files (JavaScript and VBScript), not the scripts that are part of your Dreamweaver files' HTML code. You can, however, add the scripts from this category to your HTML code.

- *Templates*—One of the most labor-saving devices of all time, templates help you build pages quickly and achieve consistency in the pages throughout a site. Any templates you've created while working in the pages for the open site will be stored here.

- *Library*—As if the eight categories above weren't enough, you can create your own libraries to store items you haven't used yet but to which you want quick access for insertion—or to simply keep track of things (images, objects) that you want to be able to use if the need arises.

Viewing and Accumulating Site Assets

To see the assets a particular site has accumulated, simply switch to that site by choosing View|Site|Open Site, and choose the site by name. Display the Assets panel if it isn't already on screen, and view the various categories for the open site. Even the most vanilla Web site will have some accumulated assets—check the Images and Colors categories to see the graphics and colors you've used on the site thus far. Figure 11.4 shows the color palette used on a site. You can see one of the site's pages behind the palette—the colors you see on the page are also in the Assets panel (though they appear in this figure in shades of gray).

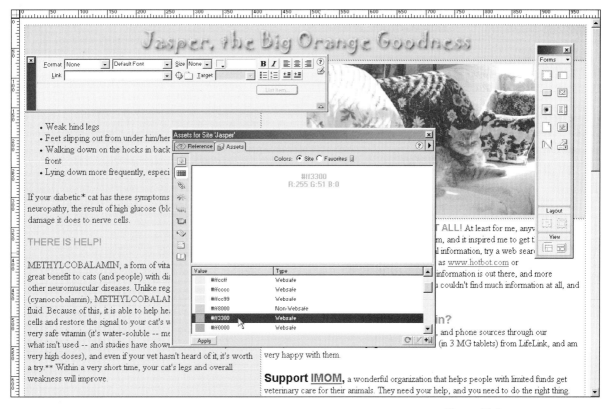

Figure 11.4

Do you want to quickly change a background or text color to another color used on your site? Display the page, and then use the Assets panel to locate the color you used elsewhere.

As you're working on a site—adding pages, editing existing pages—your Assets panel will continue to accumulate items in the appropriate categories. If you don't see something you've recently added to a page reflected in the panel, however, simply click the Refresh button (see Figure 11.5) to update the Assets panel.

Figure 11.5

Make sure your Assets panel is showing the latest and greatest assortment of your site's content.

Working with Favorite Assets

Favorites are those assets that you choose to keep separate from the main group of site assets. You might be keeping these assets separate because you've decided that they represent the best of your assets and, as you go through a redesign, you want to make sure these are the ones you use in the site's pages. Or you might simply want to keep a handful of assets separate from the main group if the main group has become so large that looking through it for often-used items is too time consuming.

Favorites, therefore, are like the Favorites and Bookmarks you accumulate through your Web browser—as with the sites you visit often, these Favorites are images, URLs, colors, movies, and so on that you use often in your pages. Something else that sets your favorite assets apart is the fact that you can add assets to this group without having used the assets in one of your site's pages. When you're in the Favorites view in the Assets panel, you can add colors, URLs, and library items (you can also add library items in Assets view). You can also add templates to the Assets panel (though not to Favorites, as Templates have their own Assets panel category), which makes them as easily accessible as the rest of your Assets. Templates, and their creation and use, are discussed later in this chapter.

Adding Colors to Favorites

Even though the Dreamweaver color-well palette has only 256 colors, it's easy to grab the wrong one. You might inadvertently use a slightly different shade of green or blue in your page and, if you're tired or working in bad lighting, you won't notice. If you're selecting colors from the Assets panel, you don't have to worry that you're picking one that won't "go" with your site colors—by having added the color to the Favorites group, you know it's a color you want to use.

To add a color to your Favorites, follow these steps:

1. Click the Favorites radio button at the top of the Assets panel. This action switches you to Favorites view.

2. Click the Colors category button on the left side of the panel.

3. Click the New Color button. A color palette appears, and your mouse changes to an eyedropper, as Figure 11.6 shows.

4. Select a color from the palette, or click any color on the page—you can click on a color in an image on the page or even on a color from the window's border, such as the title bar or a button on your taskbar. Anything can be a source for colors.

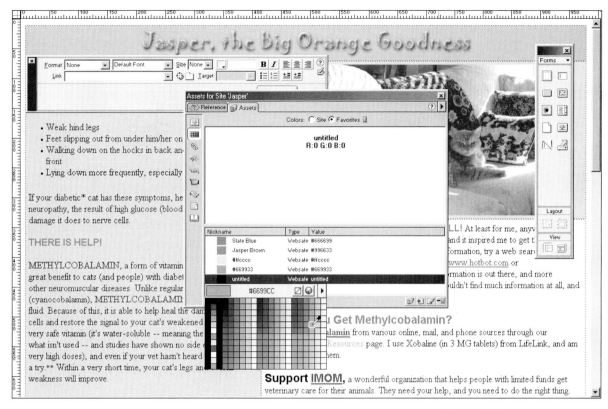

Figure 11.6

Click the New Color button and select a color to add to Favorites.

5. If you'd like to give the color a nickname, right-click the color and its current name in the lower half of the Assets panel, and choose Edit Nickname from the shortcut menu. The color's current name (which is probably its hexadecimal number) becomes highlighted, and a box forms around it (see Figure 11.7).

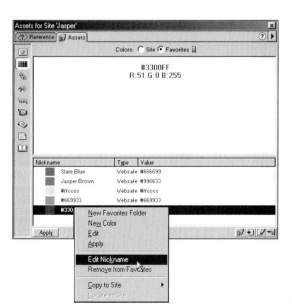

Figure 11.7

Naming colors helps you select them more easily later.

6. Type a new name for your color and press Enter, or click on anything outside of the box around the color's name.

Remember that the colors you add to your Favorites won't appear in the Site Assets until and unless you use them in the site's pages. So until then, to add colors to Favorites or to access colors you've added there, you must enter the Favorites view in the Assets panel.

Adding Favorite URLs

Much like adding a color, adding a URL to your Favorites requires simply that you switch to the Favorites view of the Assets panel and then click the URL category button. Click the New URL button and enter a new URL and any nickname you'd like to give it in the Add URL dialog box (as Figure 11.8 shows). Click OK to confirm the new URL, and close the dialog box.

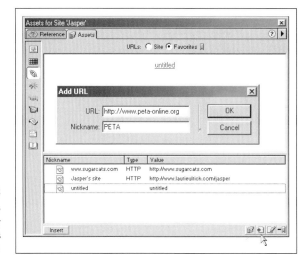

Figure 11.8

Keep track of URLs you intend to use in your site's pages by adding them to your Favorites URL category.

Also like colors, URLs you add to the Favorites won't be available through Site Assets until you use them as a link in one of the site's pages. Until and unless you use them, the URLs you add will remain only in Favorites.

Adding Images and Other Objects to Favorites

The only images, movies, or scripts you can add to your Favorites are those that are already in your Site Assets group. The process of adding these items to Favorites is quite simple:

1. Make sure you're looking at your Site Assets group. If you're not, click the Site radio button at the top of the Assets panel.

2. Click once on the category button for the type of asset you want to add.

3. From the Site Assets group, select the one you want to add to Favorites by clicking once on the asset in the list.

Figure 11.9
The small purple ribbon with a
plus (+) sign means Add
To Favorites.

4. Click the Add To Favorites button at the bottom of the Assets panel (see Figure 11.9), or right-click the button, and choose Add To Favorites from the shortcut menu.

5. A prompt appears, confirming that the selected Asset has been added to your Favorites. Click OK to close the prompt.

Using Your Assets

The assets for your site, as well as those in your Favorites group, are like ingredients in your pantry or on the shelves in your kitchen cabinets. They're nearby, and you can easily pull them down from the shelf for use in any recipe. You've used the assets before (that's how the Site Assets are accumulated), or you've put them up on the shelf, intending to try them for the first time (e.g., in your Favorites group). Using the assets is even easier than using the cooking ingredients you find in your kitchen—with the Site Assets group, you have nothing to unwrap or measure—just drag the assets out of the Assets panel and drop them onto the page where you want to use them.

As Figure 11.10 shows, once your pointer is outside the Assets panel, you can release the mouse to drop the asset wherever you want it to go. A small box follows your cursor until you drop the asset, just as you've seen when you've been dragging images and text around on your page to rearrange them.

When you're using Favorites, you can use the drag-and-drop procedure for images, movies, scripts, and URLs, but not for colors. To use a color from your Favorites, just click the color in the Assets panel after you've clicked the color well for the element—text, a border, a background—sip up the Favorite color with your eyedropper, and it's applied instantly. Figure 11.11 shows a Favorite color being applied to a selected table cell.

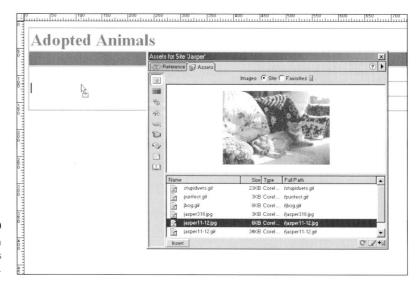

Figure 11.10

Drag and drop your assets from the Site or Favorites categories right onto your page.

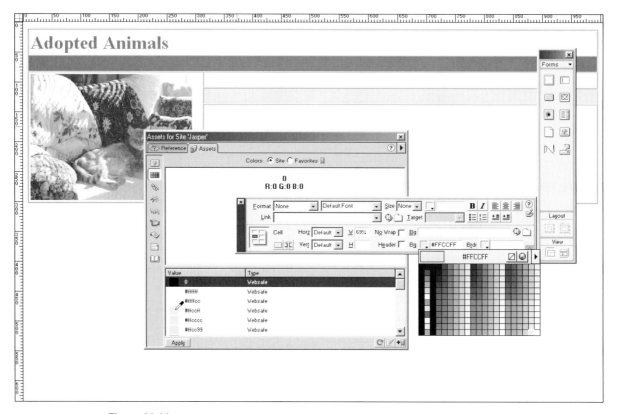

Figure 11.11

You can select any on-screen color while the color well is open—including the colors in your Favorites list.

If dragging and dropping isn't appropriate, you can use the Insert button in the Assets panel. To add an image to your page (or to a table cell, layer, or frame), click once on the asset you want to insert and click the Insert button. If the asset is something that would be applied, rather than inserted, click once on the URL or color, and click the Apply button.

Editing Assets

You can edit your assets in the Images category by double-clicking them. This action will open whatever application Windows associates with the file type—such as Fireworks to edit a GIF or JPEG file. If you double-click a Flash or other movie asset, the application used to create that asset will be opened.

After you make the required edits, save the file and return to Dreamweaver—you'll see your changes reflected in the asset as it appears in the panel, as well as in any places on your pages where you used the image or movie.

What? Windows, Confused?

If Windows doesn't know which application to use to edit your asset, choose Edit|Preferences and select the File Types/Editors category. Choose an application with which to edit the file type in question, and click OK to apply the association. When you double-click the asset from that point on, the selected application will open.

Working with the Library

The last of the Assets panel category buttons is the Library button. This button changes the view of the Assets panel to show only items you've added to a general library (each item is known as a *library item*). The selection of items in the library is entirely up to you, and items can be images, movies, or scripts. They cannot be colors or URLs. You can add items already on your pages to the library, or you can go out and select new items from somewhere on your local drive.

Creating a New Blank Library Item

The lower-right corner of the Assets panel contains four buttons. The button that looks like a small blue piece of paper with a plus (+) sign on it is the New Library Item button. You'll use this button (see Figure 11.12) as you complete these steps to create a blank library item:

1. Make sure nothing is selected on your active Web page. If you're not sure whether anything is selected, click somewhere in an empty area of your page, and wait to see the cursor blink.

2. In the Assets panel, click the Library category button.

3. Click the New Library Item button, as shown in Figure 11.12. The top half of the Library Assets panel changes, directing you to click the Edit button (also in the lower-right corner of the Assets panel). The word Untitled appears in the list of library items, and you can type a name for the library item now—this name will become the file name for the library item later.

From This Point Forward

When you're adding color to text using the Insert button, the color will apply only to any text you type from the current cursor position forward—it won't apply to existing text if you use this method.

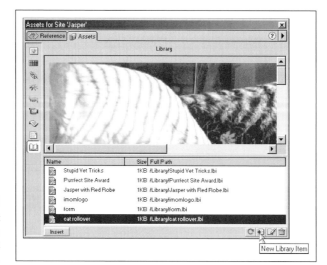

Figure 11.12

When none of your page content is selected, the New Library Item button will create a blank library item.

Figure 11.13

A blank window with a gray background awaits your inserted element, bound for the library.

4. Click the Edit button (the small blue button with the image of a pencil on it). The untitled.lbi (or whatever-you-named-it.lbi) window opens, as Figure 11.13 shows. This is the window in which you'll insert the object you want to add to the library.

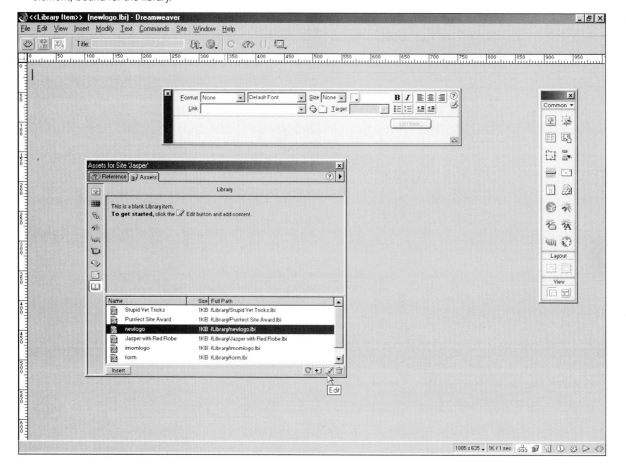

5. Using the Insert menu or the Objects panel, insert an image (including rollover or other interactive images), form (and then form fields, as desired), movie, or other media item.

6. Choose File|Save. If you didn't name the item before you went to the editing window, the Save As dialog box appears, and you must name the library item. If you already named it, no dialog box appears.

7. Close the editing window, and return to your last active Web page. The library item you just created appears in the library.

Adding Page Items to Your Library

If you want to add images, movies, forms, rollovers—any object from your pages—to the library, doing so is simple. Just display the page that currently contains that object, and drag the object into the top half of the Library area of the Assets panel, as Figure 11.14 shows.

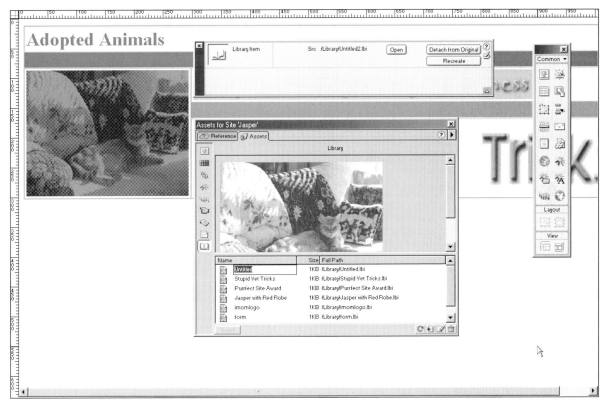

Figure 11.14

Drag and drop any page element into the Assets panel to create a library item.

After you drag the item in, type a new name to replace *Untitled* in the library listing for the item, and press Enter to confirm the new name.

If you prefer, you can instead select the item in the window and click the New Library Item button. The *Untitled* library listing will appear, and you'll see the item in the top half of the Assets panel. Name the new library item, and you're ready to use it anywhere on your site's pages.

Adding Library Content to a Web Page

Library items are easy to add to your Web pages—just select the item you want to insert and click the Insert button at the bottom of the Assets panel. You can also drag the item onto the page. If you're using the Insert button, be sure your cursor is at the spot on the page where you want the library item to be added.

Just as with Assets and Favorites, objects you add to your pages from the Library remain attached to the Assets panel. This attachment is a good thing, generally, because if you edit the item from within the Assets panel, the edited version automatically replaces the original version anywhere within your site's pages. If you want to break that connection, so that you can deal with an instance of a Library-inserted item on its own, select the item and click the Detach From Original button in the Properties Inspector. For more details on this process, see the "Detaching Assets" section earlier in this chapter.

Modifying Library Content

You can edit items in your library just as you would assets in your Site or Favorites groups. Just double-click the item in the Assets panel (either the picture of the item in the top half of the panel, or the listing for the item in the bottom half), and one of two things will happen:

- *If the item is a Dreamweaver item*—such as a form, the Dreamweaver editing window will open, and you can tweak the item as necessary there, and then resave it.

- *If the item was created in another application*—such as Fireworks for a graphic, or Flash for a movie, that application will open, and you can edit and resave the item in the application.

Once you've modified a library item, all instances in which you've used that item in your open site's pages will be updated to reflect the item's edited version—except any instances that you've detached, of course.

Detaching Library Items

If you add an image or other editable item from the Library to your page, that item remains attached to the Library through the Assets panel. This means that you can't edit the item on the page the way you would something you added via the Insert menu and the "normal" means of adding objects to the page. This limitation might seem like a hardship, but consider the benefits—if you want to edit the item, you can edit it through the Assets window (in the case of colors or URLs) or through another application (to adjust size or actions or to edit a script). When the changes are saved, they automatically apply to every instance of the Library item throughout your site. Imagine changing the size of a button you designed in Fireworks. If you added the button to your pages through the Library, editing it once will update all the uses of the button so that it appears in the new size everywhere on your site.

While this attachment to the Library can be a labor-saving feature, it might become problematic for you at some point. Perhaps you really need to change the URL associated with just one instance of a graphic within your site—all the other places the graphic was used should have the original URL associated with them. Or if you want to resize all the instances where an image was used except one, you might want to end the relationship between the Library and that one use of the image in question so that you can resize the image. Another reason you might want to end the connection between the Library and a page element is that the Properties Inspector, which many Dreamweaver users have come to rely on and nearly cherish, is somewhat neutered when a Library-derived element is selected. None of the tools for editing colors, links, alignment, and so on (depending on the type of item selected) are available.

Breaking up the relationship between the item and the Library is called *detaching.* To detach a page element from the Library, click once on the element on a page (in the instance you want to detach), and check the Properties Inspector. As Figure 11.15 shows, the now-bare-bones Properties Inspector offers a Detach From Original button. If you click the button, a prompt appears, reminding you that detaching the image will end your ability to automatically update it when the original image changes. If you really do want to detach the element, click OK.

Figure 11.15
Cut the cord between your image or other Asset-derived element by clicking the Detach From Original button.

Build an Image Library

This project will give you practice creating a library within your Assets panel, naming the library, and filling it with image files. You can then use the image files—which you can easily insert from the Assets panel—in Web pages, which will save users the time it would take them to find and insert images through the Insert menu's commands. All the image files you need to complete this project are on the CD-ROM, in the Project 11A folder.

Collect Image Files for the Library

Rather than start with images that are already on an existing Web page, you'll insert items that you will find on the CD-ROM.

1. Copy the files from Project 11A to a folder on your local drive—this folder will become the source for your new library items.

2. In your Assets panel, with the Library displayed, create a blank library item. Click the Edit button to open the editing window, and go get the images by choosing Insert|Image.

3. For the first library item, choose cat1.jpg, one of the files you copied from the CD into your local folder. Name the library item cat1.lbi.

4. Repeat Steps 1 through 3 for the following images, which you should have copied from the CD-ROM to your local drive:

   - cat2.jpg

   - logo1.jpg

   - brothers.jpg

Insert an Image from the Library

Open a blank, new Web page (or an existing page of your choosing), and insert the brothers.jpg file from the Library into the page. See how easy that was?

Working with Templates

If you've ever used a word processor, you probably know about templates; either you created a template in that application, or you used one that someone else made. Templates in Dreamweaver serve the same purpose as a document, spreadsheet, or presentation template does—to standardize the files you create by providing a "cookie cutter" file on which you can base new files.

Dreamweaver templates are slightly more complex than document or spreadsheet templates, in that you can set up Dreamweaver templates to include sections that are editable and sections that are locked—and, therefore, not editable. When creating templates for yourself or others to use in Dreamweaver, you'll want to think about which sections of the template should be sacrosanct—no one can change anything in them—and which ones can be changed to meet the needs of the new page's designer.

Once created, templates become an asset, and you can apply the templates to existing pages or to new, blank pages. Again, using the drop-and-drag method to say, "Use this here," you can apply templates as easily as you can apply images and library items that are in your Assets panel. In the case of templates, however, the asset is *applied* to the entire page, not simply *added* to a page. Figure 11.16 shows the Assets panel and some items in the Template category.

Creating Templates from Existing Pages

You can save any existing Web page as a template. The process is simple—choose File|Save as Template and, in the resulting Save As Template dialog box (shown in Figure 11.17), enter the template's name and choose a site with which the template should be associated.

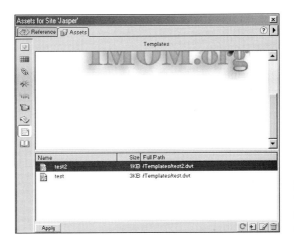

Figure 11.16
Templates are assets that change the layout and content of entire pages.

Figure 11.17
Do you have a page that would be a great start for new pages? Save it as a template.

The Web pages that make the best templates are those that provide a solid foundation for a new page. You probably don't want to turn a page that's jam-packed with content—and very specific links and formatting—into a template, unless you intend to make many pages that are nearly identical to it. Pages that work well as templates have tables or layers in place, which give the page structure; images that should be on every page that you'll make with the template; any text that should be on all pages (such as text links or copyright information across the bottom of a page); and any navigation buttons that you want on every page on which the template is based, as Figure 11.18 shows. If a template has more than that, the person using it will have to remove or change any other content—and, even if that person is you, doing all that will waste time.

Building a New Template

If none of your existing pages fit the bill, you can create a page solely for the purpose of creating a template. You can do this by creating a page as you normally would—choosing File|New, and building the content and structural devices (tables, frames, layers) into the page that should be part of the template. Insert any images where you want them, type any text that all pages using the template should have, and stop there—don't insert anything that's specific to any one page. At this point, you can just save the file by choosing File|Save as Template, and name the file as I described in the previous section.

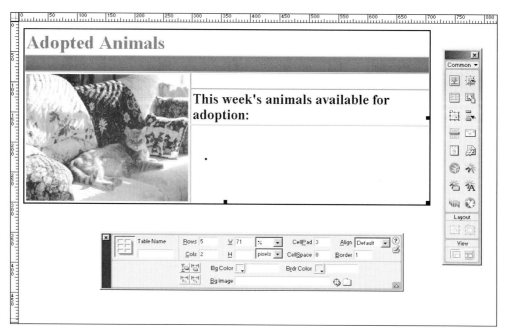

Figure 11.18

The best candidate for a
template is a page that meets
your design requirements for a
site's pages—and that doesn't
have a lot of content you
will have to delete to use the
new pages.

Another way exists, however, to build a template from scratch. This method
involves a Templates panel and some template-specific commands and tools
that help you customize the template from the ground up—rather than
having to do a lot of that customization later, as you'll have to do on any
templates you create from existing pages. To create a blank, new template,
follow these steps:

1. Choose Window|Templates. If it wasn't already on screen, the Assets
   panel will appear, and the Templates category will be selected, as Figure 11.19 shows.

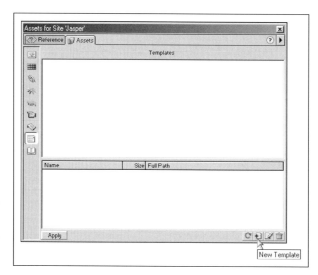

Figure 11.19

If you've never created a
template before, your Templates
list in the Assets panel will be
empty—for now.

2. Click the New Template button at the bottom of the Assets panel. An Untitled template is added to the list of templates, and a box is formed around the word *Untitled.*

3. Type a name for your new template and press Enter. The name is applied, and instructions appear in the top of the Assets panel, suggesting that you click the Edit button to begin building your template (see Figure 11.20).

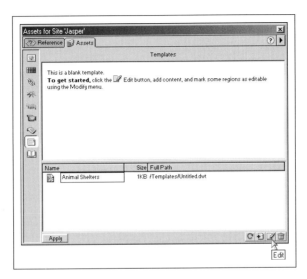

Figure 11.20
Dreamweaver coaches you through the process and suggests you begin editing your new template right away.

4. Click the Edit button (located in the lower-right corner of the Assets panel). The new template opens in its own window. The template has no content or formatting of any kind yet.

5. Build the template page as you desire—insert and format tables, add any images or text you want all pages based on this template to include— and then choose File|Save. Don't exit the document yet, but saving it early is a good idea, so you don't risk losing your work. Figure 11.21 shows a sample template that would provide a simple structure for a new Web page and eliminate much of the groundwork for the designer of that page.

Setting Up Locked and Editable Template Regions

After building the content and structure for your new template, you want to establish which parts of the template the person who creates a new document based on the template can edit. Tables, for example, should be editable, so that they can accommodate page-specific content. Images and text might not

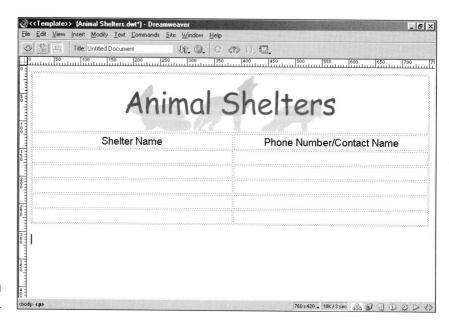

Figure 11.21
A template can consist of a table.

be editable, and you can lock these elements so they can't be edited in any way. To set up which parts of your template can be edited, follow these steps:

1. Select the portion of your template that should be editable—by default, all the parts of a template are locked until you unlock them by designating them editable.

2. Choose Modify|Templates|New Editable Region, or right-click the selected portion of your template, and choose New Editable Region from the shortcut menu. A dialog box opens, as shown in Figure 11.22.

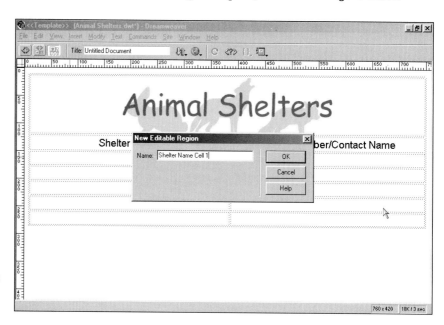

Figure 11.22
Give your editable region a name.

3. Name the editable region, remembering that you must choose unique names for each region you designate as editable. Click OK to close the dialog box.

After you set up which parts of your template can be edited, save the file. The name you gave the file when you chose to create a new template (within the Assets panel) is already assigned, so no dialog box will appear when you save it. You can close the document if you're finished adding content and doing any formatting.

Applying Templates to Pages

You have a few choices for how to apply a template to new or existing pages:

- Drag the template from the Assets panel onto the page. The template will be applied to the page, inserting template content on the page, and placing any existing content (anything you created or inserted before you applied the template) into a single, editable region on the page. The template's editable and locked regions will be in force as they were designated when the template was created, as Figure 11.23 shows.

Figure 11.23

Here's another case for templates that include only the essentials: What happens when you apply a template to a page that already has its own content?

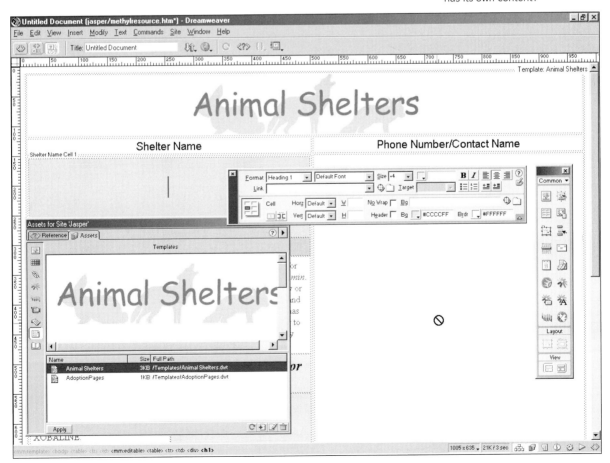

- Click once on the template in the list of templates in the Assets panel, and click the Apply button. Again, the template will be applied to the page, and any existing content will remain as an editable region unto itself.

- Choose File|New From Template to start a new document based on a particular template. The Select Template dialog box will open (see Figure 11.24), from which you can choose the template on which your new document should be based.

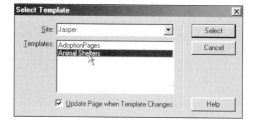

Figure 11.24
Pick a template as the foundation of your new page.

Modifying a Template

As with any asset, all you have to do is double-click a template in the Assets panel, and the template will open in its own window. From this point, you can change the locked or editable status of any region of the page, add or delete content, or change formatting for any of the page elements. After you make your changes, resave and close the file.

If you've applied the modified template to other pages in your site, and you want those pages to reflect the modifications you've made, choose Modify|Templates|Update Pages. If you want to change only a particular page to reflect the template's changes, open that page and, from within it, choose Modify|Templates|Update Current Page. In this latter case, any other pages based on the modified template would remain consistent with the template before you modified it.

Detaching from a Template

Again—another parallel to the rest of your assets—you can separate templates and the pages on which they're based, ending the connection between them. In the case of assets such as images or movies, you perform the separation because you want to edit the inserted asset, with no association to the asset as it's stored in the Assets panel. In the case of template-based documents, the need to detach from the template is normally based on a desire to edit a portion of the page that's locked.

To detach a document from the template on which it was based, choose Modify|Template|Detach From Template. The page is detached, and you can edit any portion of it. What's the potential downside to detaching from a template? If you've edited the template, this particular page can't be automatically updated to reflect the template modifications, even if you execute the Update Pages command. You can, however, reapply the template later—but be aware of the changes doing so might impose as the template content is inserted, and the existing content (even the parts that were originally part of the template) will be set off as a separate editable region. A reapplication of a template rarely works out.

OBJECT Create a Template for Departmental Web Pages

In this project, you'll create a template that each department in a company can use to create its own Web page for the company site. By building the structural elements (a table, in this case) into the template and adding images and text that will be on all departments' pages, the template you create here will help speed the design process for each department—and assure the company of the level of consistency it requires across the pages of its site.

Open a New Document

Open a blank new document by using the File|New command.

Set Up the Page

Now, add the tables.

1. Place a table on the page that's 100 percent the width of the page, five rows tall, and two columns wide. Merge the cells in the top row. The table should have no border, a cell padding value of 3, and no cell spacing.

2. Insert four blank lines by pressing Enter four times.

3. Next, create another table that's 50 percent of the page width, centered. The table should have three columns and two rows. The table should have a border of 0 and cell spacing set to 2. Apply a blue (any shade) background to the whole table, and fill the cells with white—this combination will create the illusion of a 2-pixel, blue border around all the cells.

4. Your finished structure should look like the page shown in Figure 11.25.

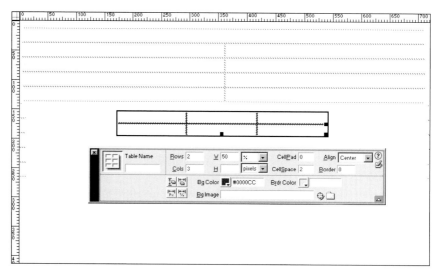

Figure 11.25
Users of this template will thank you for saving them the time of having to create the page structure and the effort of having to make sure the page looks the same as the other departments' pages.

Insert a Company Logo

In the first row of the first table (the one that spans the top of the page), insert the companylogo.jpg image you will find on the CD-ROM in the Project 11B folder. The image should be centered, but it will nearly fill the row from left to right.

Save the Page as a Template

Save the page as a template, adding it to the Assets panel for the page. Call the template deptpages, and make sure that the top row of the first table and the image inside the table are not editable (locked). The rest of the document, including the lines between the tables and the second table, should not be locked, because each department will have different items to add to its page, and the size—and even the number of columns or rows in the table (and blank lines between tables)—might need to change.

Apply the Template to a New Page

Imagine you are the person tasked with designing a page for one of the company's departments. Start a new Web page based on the deptpages template, and save the new page as acctgdept.htm.

Moving On

In Chapter 12, you'll learn to use yet another labor-saving device, Cascading Style Sheets, often referred to by the initials CSS. Much like styles that you apply to text in a word processor, you can use style sheets for Web content to apply universal formatting, so you can maintain consistency throughout related elements in your Web site's pages.

Chapter 12

Creating and Using Style Sheets

Consistency is a cornerstone of good design, whether for printed materials or Web content. Yet the effort and time involved to make sure fonts, colors, headings, backgrounds, borders, and other visual elements are visually related can be daunting to even the most enthusiastic designer. To the rescue? This chapter covers styles and style sheets, which store and give instant access to formatting across a site, making it fast and easy to give your Web designs a consistent look.

Understanding Styles

If you've used any word processor in the last five years, you've used a style. Even if you didn't realize you were using one, you were. If you've used Dreamweaver, even for just five minutes, you've used a style. A style is a group of formats applied to selected content. In both word processors and Dreamweaver, you can pluck any one of a group of styles from the Format drop-down list—Paragraph, Heading 1, Heading 2, and so on, as Figure 12.1 shows. Each style changes the appearance of selected text by applying several formats at once, the same way, every time.

Figure 12.1

Do you need to format a heading? Choose a Heading style from the Properties Inspector Style list.

This process is exactly how style sheets work, but on a smaller level—from the Format drop-down list, you apply formatting to a selection of text in one document, and this action inserts simple formatting attributes and tags into the HTML code that underlies your document.

Styles and Style Sheets Defined

In Web design, styles have even greater power than the styles you've worked with in a word processor, and through the Properties Inspector, you're able to give still greater power to the styles Dreamweaver offers. You can create a style sheet and apply it to all the pages on a site, which results in consistent formatting throughout. You decide which formatting attributes to include in the style, and you can create as many styles as you wish. If you update a style after you have created and applied it, the pages to which you've applied the style will automatically update to reflect those changes. For people responsible for designing and managing large sites, this automatic style update is something they can't really live without. For designers dealing with smaller sites, or separate sections of larger sites (where consistency with the entire site is less of an issue), style sheets are a convenient labor saver, although they're probably not absolutely necessary.

Style sheets have a significant limitation—browsers prior to version 4 (for both Internet Explorer and Netscape) ignore the <**style**> tags that applying a style inserts into your HTML code. This means that some or all of the formatting you've applied through the style(s) can be lost on users of older browsers. Again, for people who must manage many, many pages within a site, this limitation is something they can live with—they'd rather not worry about the ever-decreasing number of people using old browsers than spend several more hours per page applying formats one by one, hoping they don't forget something. If your audience is likely to be using older software, and/or if you have the time to format each page separately, you can work around this limitation by not using style sheets at all.

Creating Styles

Before you actually go through the steps to create a style, you must think about what kind of style you want to create—that is, what you want the style to do, and what scope it will have. Will it apply to a single page? Will it redefine a single HTML tag? Will it redefine two or more tags when they're used together? Will it apply to all the pages in a site? You must have considered all these options because, in the first steps of creating a style, you must make selections—choosing the name, type, and overall impact your style will have.

To begin the style-creation process, you can employ one of several methods:

- Display the CSS (Cascading Style Sheet) Styles panel, and click the New Style button.

- Choose Text|CSS Styles|New Style.

- Right-click your page, and choose CSS Styles|New Style from the shortcut menu.

It's a good idea to have the CSS Styles panel open (see Figure 12.2) on the page, so you have access to your new styles once you've created them; consequently, you might prefer the method that uses the panel's New Style button. To display this panel, choose Window|CSS Styles.

Defining Styles

After you choose to create a new style, the New Style dialog box opens, as you see in Figure 12.3. Your decision-making process begins here, with giving your style a name. The name should serve to remind you what the style does, so don't use generic names such as *style1* or *textstyle*. You're better off with names such as *redheadings* or *majortopics* or *centeredtitles*, which will help you keep several styles separate in your mind.

Figure 12.2

The CSS Styles panel lists your page/site styles and offers tools for creating and editing them.

Figure 12.3

You have three decisions to make when you're building a new style: what you want to call the style, what you want it to do, and when and where it can be used.

And That's What I Want to Call It, Period

You'll notice that the *unnamed1* text in the Name box is preceded by a period (.unnamed1). You should leave the period there when you insert the name. As with most Web-related names, use lowercase letters and avoid spaces (use an underscore, if you must) in your style names.

After you have named your new style, you have to decide what type of style you want to create. You have three choices:

- Make Custom Style (Class)
- Redefine HTML Tag
- Use CSS Selector

The names for these options aren't terribly revealing even after you hear what each of them does—you might wonder who chose the wording for the options. In any case, here goes:

- *Make Custom Style*—As I stated previously, a custom style is similar to a style you'd create and use in a word processor. A custom style is a group of formats with a specific name, which you can apply to text in a document. You can apply a custom style to a single letter, word, paragraph, or group of paragraphs. If you apply the style to a paragraph (a distinct group of characters between existing <**p**> and </**p**> tags in your document—or, to those not familiar with paragraph tags in HTML, a group of characters followed by a hard return), a <**class**> tag, <**p class="stylename"**>, is added to the HTML (see Figure 12.4). If you apply the custom style to text within a paragraph, a <**span**> tag is applied before and after the selected text. You can save custom styles as part of a style sheet (in which case, they are applicable to any page in a site), or as individual styles, applicable to the active page only.

```
<html>
<head>
<title>Untitled Document</title>
<meta http-equiv="Content-Type" content="text/html; charset=iso-8859-1">
<link rel="stylesheet" href="/headingstyles.css" type="text/css">
</head>

<body bgcolor="#FFFFFF" text="#000000">
<p class="boldredheadings">text</p>
</body>
</html>
```

Figure 12.4
If you apply a style to a paragraph, Dreamweaver inserts a <class> tag, along with your style name.

- Redefine HTML Tag—This option means that you want to add to, or entirely change, an HTML tag that currently applies one set of formats. For example, if you want to redefine the <**h2**> (Heading 2) tag so that it not only changes the size of text, but also turns the text blue and centers it, you can choose this option. The result? You'll apply the style through the Format drop-down list, and every time after that, when you choose <**h2**> as the format for selected text, your style will be applied, redefining the tag's original intent.
- *CSS Selector*—Here's where the name of the option doesn't begin to explain what it does. If you choose CSS Selector, you're opting to redefine a group of HTML tags. For example, if you want to redefine the <**h2**> tag,

but only when it's applied in a table cell, you would use the CSS Selector option. If you used this option, and then applied <**h2**> outside of a table, the original <**h2**> formatting would be applied. If you applied <**h2**> within a table cell, the style would kick in.

Did you get all that? Dreamweaver's style sheets feature can be a conceptual roller coaster. First, the idea is simple—a style lets you apply a group of formats all at once, with one command. Great, simple, no problem. Second, the style asks a bunch of questions, and you must have all your intentions for using the style worked out ahead of time—and you get the feeling that if you don't know a lot of HTML, you'll be lost. Then, once you've built a style and applied it (and you'll learn to do that next), you think, "OK, I can handle this. This might even come in handy." At this point, though, you're in the second phase of the style concept, the screaming-down-the-steep-drop portion of the roller coaster. But the concept gets easier if you bear with me.

Creating a Style Class

For those designers with a less-than-extensive knowledge of HTML (who are many in number), using the Custom Style Class is probably the way to go. This way, you can choose from a variety of formats to include in the style, and you will use a simple dialog box to do so. After you choose Make Custom Style (Class) in the New Style dialog box, all that's left is choosing whether you want the style to be available to all pages on your site (choose New Style Sheet from the Define In list), or whether you want the style to be available in the active page only (choose This Document Only).

After you make your choice, click OK. If you choose New Style Sheet, a dialog box appears, asking you to name and save the style sheet (see Figure 12.5). This action might seem redundant with naming the style, but remember—a style *sheet* can contain several styles. So, name the style sheet accordingly— *headingstyles* or *textcolors* are examples of appropriate names that will define the styles you add to the sheets later.

Figure 12.5

Name your style sheet, giving it a name that will express the nature of the styles it will contain.

After you name your sheet, click Save. The Save Style Sheet File As dialog box closes, and the Style Definition dialog box opens, as Figure 12.6 shows. (If you opted to create the style in This Document Only, you'll get the Style Definition dialog box as soon as you click OK in the New Style dialog box.)

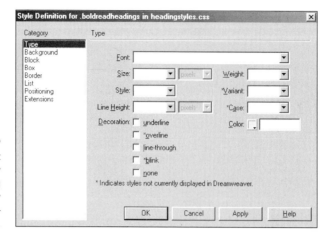

Figure 12.6

Your new style includes eight categories, and each category provides several formatting options. You can completely customize text, tables, pages— any aspect of the design process.

To begin defining your style, choose an item from the Category list. If you're setting up a style that will apply to text, you'll do most of your work in the Type category, although you might also use Block and List. If you're setting up a style that will apply to an entire page or a frame, choose Background, from which you can pick background colors and images. To get acquainted, poke around in the categories, clicking on each one and looking at the options it offers you.

Type Attributes

The Type category, as you see in use in Figure 12.7, shows the basic formatting options for text—font, size, color—most of which are available through the Properties Inspector, so you're used to setting them for selected text. Text attributes that aren't available through the Properties Inspector are marked with an asterisk—evidence that applying them through a style is your only way to do so via Dreamweaver.

Background Attributes

The attributes available through the Background category apply to pages and frames (which are pages unto themselves). You can choose the typical options (attributes you can also set through the Page Properties dialog box), and a few more, which, as you saw in the Type category, are marked with an asterisk (see Figure 12.8). You can set the page background color, background image, and whether (or how/how often) the background image repeats over the surface of the page. You can also choose whether to have a scrollbar on your frame with the Attachment option, and you can choose the Horizontal and Vertical position of the background image. This positioning is especially important

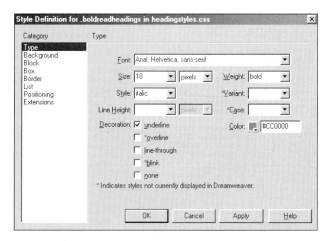

Figure 12.7
Choose how your style will apply to text.

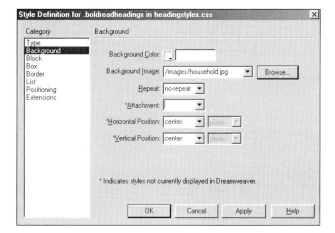

Figure 12.8
Set up the way your style will apply to an entire page or frame.

to set if you've chosen not to have your image repeat, and that it will appear once, perhaps centered, on your page.

Block Attributes

The Block Attributes category applies to text, but specifically to the treatment of text in a block, or paragraph, rather than to single characters or words within a paragraph. You can adjust word spacing (*tracking*, to designers from the print or typesetting world), letter spacing (known as *kerning* in typesetting lingo), and set alignment and indents, as Figure 12.9 shows. The Whitespace option refers to the handling of white space within a block, and how line breaks and wrapping are handled. Internet Explorer will ignore Whitespace settings, but Netscape honors them.

Box Attributes

If your pages will contain layers, you might want to tweak the way the style affects each layer by making adjustments in the Box category. You can adjust the Width and Height settings to apply a size when the style is applied, choose how the layers will float on the page, and how surrounding content will react

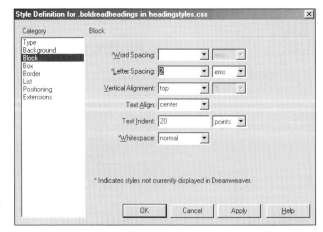

Figure 12.9

Adjust your style's treatment of blocks or paragraphs.

No, It's Not Aunty EMS

The "ems" you see next to the Word Spacing and Letter Spacing options in the Block Attributes category refer to *em-spaces*, or the width of the letter *m*. You may have heard of *em-dashes*—dashes the width of the letter *m*—used (as in this sentence) on either side of a parenthetical statement to separate the statement from the rest of the sentence. In terms of spacing between letters and words, you can choose how many em-spaces you want by entering a number in either or both of these two option boxes.

Figure 12.10

Margin and Padding options let you control the distance between the border (padding), or edges with no border (margin), and the content of layers to which your style is applied.

to the layers in terms of wrapping around them (think of a picture in a magazine—the text wraps around it within an article—here, the layer is analogous to the picture). Figure 12.10 shows the full selection of Box category options.

Border Attributes

As Figure 12.11 shows, only three options are available in the Border category—Width, Color, and Style. Width pertains to the thickness of borders; Color (obviously) pertains to the color of borders (but, remember, only Internet Explorer honors color settings for table borders—both IE and Netscape will honor the settings for frames); and Style lets you choose from dotted, dashed, double, and a variety of other line effects for your borders.

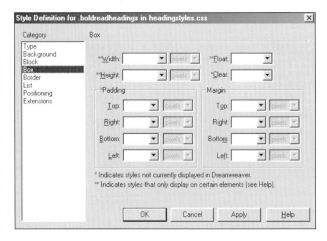

List Attributes

Another text-related category, the List category pertains to unordered lists (bulleted lists) and ordered lists (numbered lists). As Figure 12.12 shows, you can choose the type of list to which your style will apply, choose a Bullet Image, and set the position of the bullet or number by choosing how the list items wrap—*inside* means the text will wrap to the margin, and *outside* means the

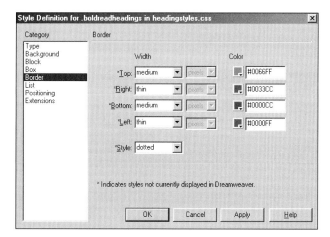

Figure 12.11
Tables, frames, and layers can have visible borders, and the Border category helps you define how your style will format these entities.

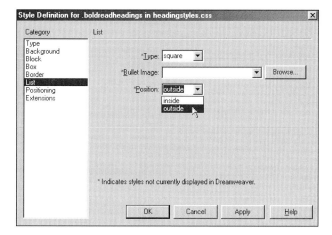

Figure 12.12
Set your style's options for dealing with numbered and bulleted lists.

text in the bulleted or numbered item will indent and wrap under the bullet or number that precedes the text.

Positioning Attributes

Netscape does not support Positioning-category options, and Internet Explorer supports them only if you use a Custom Class style. The options apply only to layers, so you're up against two browser-compatibility issues—only the latest versions of IE and Netscape recognize layers at all and, by using these options in your style, you cut Netscape out entirely. If you decide to dabble in this category, the options (as Figure 12.13 shows) let you adjust layer placement, display, and the stacking order (Z-Index) of overlapping layers. You can also adjust how layers with more content than they're currently sized to display handle the overflow, and the use of timelines to apply special effects, such as a wiping effect that animates the visibility of the text or graphics in a layer.

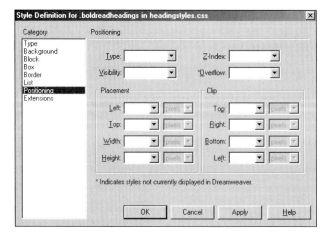

Figure 12.13

Although not well supported by browsers, the Positioning category offers interesting layer controls.

Extension Attributes

Browser support for the options set in the Extension category is spotty, so your use of this category will be rather limited. Theoretically, you can control how page breaks will be inserted when someone prints your page and how the cursor will look. You can also apply special effects such as blurring and color inversion. Cursor control and Filter settings are supported in Internet Explorer 4, but no browser (or any version thereof) supports the Pagebreak option. You can see this category's options in Figure 12.14.

Perhaps the next generations of Internet Explorer and Netscape will honor these formats; but, at this time, using them in your style will only lead to unexpected (and potentially unpleasant) results, especially if you apply them in such a way that your design's effectiveness hinges on their effects. Why would Dreamweaver include features that are either poorly supported or not supported at all? Because potentially, these features are of value to designers, and it's simply a matter of pushing the technology along. If the Web-design software manufacturers don't aim for a higher mark than the current technology supports, the supported technology would progress at a much slower rate, if at all.

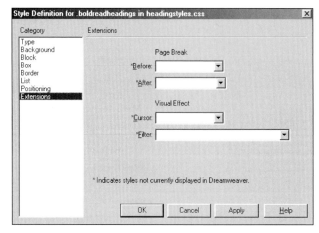

Figure 12.14

You probably won't bother with Extension attributes, because neither Internet Explorer nor Netscape currently recognizes them.

Redefining HTML Tags

If you elect not to create a Custom Style Class, but choose instead to change the way an HTML tag will apply formatting, choose Redefine HTML Tag in the New Style dialog box (refer back to Figure 12.3). As soon as you click the Redefine HTML Tag radio button in the New Style dialog box, the Name box changes to a Tag list, from which you can select the tag you wish to redefine (see Figure 12.15). After you make that selection, you must still choose whether to make this redefinition part of a style that applies only to the open document, or to make it part of a style sheet (in which case, you can apply it to all pages within your site).

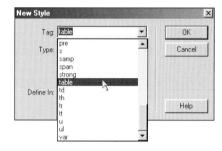

Figure 12.15
Pick a tag to redefine with your new style.

Once you click OK in the New Style dialog box, the Style Definition dialog box appears again, this time listing the tag you chose to redefine in the dialog-box title bar. You can use the categories (as I described previously in this chapter) to determine how the tag you've selected will be applied. For example, if you opt to redefine a **<blockquote>** tag, you can add to what that tag does by default, which is indent blocks of text from both the left and right. You can redefine the tag so that it applies formatting and settings from all eight, style-definition categories.

Of course, making wild redefinitions to tags is not a good idea—if you've already used a tag somewhere else on any page in your site (and you're dealing with a style sheet, which will apply to all pages in your site), you risk making undesirable changes. Imagine changing the **<p>** tag to include an extra indent. Then, all of your pages with any hard returns (places you've pressed Enter while typing text on the page, between graphics, within tables—anywhere at all) will include that extra indent. You could end up with some bizarre-looking text.

Defining Groups of Tags with Selector Styles

The Selector style option within the New Style dialog box lets you redefine tags as they're used in groups (with a group being two or more tags used together). For example, by typing "blockquote td" in the Selector box, as Figure 12.16 shows, you can create a Selector style that applies only to block quotes when they're applied within a table. If you click the drop-down arrow on the Selector

What's in a Name

If you do redefine a tag, choose a name wisely for the style. Give the style a name that explains what the redefinition does, such as *blueheading1italic* for an **<h1>** redefinition that now includes making the text italic and blue. The more revealing the style names are, the less likely you are to apply a style in error.

box, you'll see that Dreamweaver offers only link-related tags, such as **a:hover**, **a:link**, and so on. But you can type any grouping of tags that you want into the Selector box.

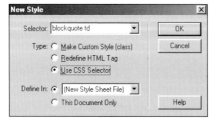

Figure 12.16

Type a pair or group of tags (with each tag separated by a space) in the Selector box, and click OK to access the Style Definition categories and redefine how the tags will work together.

Figure 12.17

Auto Apply is on by default, which means that your style and any changes to it will be applied automatically.

Applying Styles

If you want to use a style you've created, simply select the element to which you want the style to apply, and click the style by name in the CSS Styles panel. If you've redefined a tag, make sure the Auto Apply option is on (see the lower-left corner of the CSS Styles panel shown in Figure 12.17). Then, when you insert that tag (by virtue of a menu selection, Properties Inspector action, or typing), the style you set up for that redefined tag will be applied.

If you make changes to a style after it has been applied, those changes will apply automatically to all the places in your page(s) where you used the style, whether or not Auto Apply is on.

Editing Styles and Style Sheets

To edit a style, simply double-click it by name in the CSS Styles panel. The Style Definition dialog box opens, and you can adjust the settings you put in place within the categories and their options, or add to the effects of the style by using categories you didn't tinker with when you built the style in the first place.

When you're editing style sheets, you can double-click them by name and go right to the Style Definition dialog box. Or you can choose, from within the style sheet, which style you want to edit. To give yourself access to the list of styles included in a style sheet, click once on the style sheet, and click the Edit Style Sheet button in the lower-right corner of the CSS Styles palette (see Figure 12.18). The Edit Style Sheet dialog box opens, displaying the list of styles you can edit.

Figure 12.18

Click the Edit Style Sheet button to open the Edit Style Sheet dialog box.

To select a style to edit, click once on the style, and then click the Edit button. The Style Definition dialog box will open, and you can make changes to the style, as desired. When you're finished making your changes, click OK, and then click Save in the Edit Style Sheet dialog box. Your changes to the style are stored and, if you've applied the style anywhere in your pages, the elements to which you applied it will be updated. Of course this automatic update applies only to style sheets, which apply to all the pages in a site. If your changes are to a style that was active only in a single document, only that document will be updated to reflect your changes.

Handling Style Conflicts

At times, two or more styles might be applied to the same text, which creates the potential for conflict. For example, you might have one style that makes text bold, blue, and centered, and another style that italicizes text and turns it red. If you apply both styles, the color aspect is in conflict. Which style will win? Dreamweaver applies the following criteria to settle such disputes:

If two styles that have a conflicting attribute are applied, the attribute closest to the text within the HTML code wins. For example, say your code appears as follows:

```
<p class="boldbluecenter"><span class="reditalic">
Events and Activities </span></p>
```

The attributes in the style called *reditalic* will win, and the conflicting attributes will override those applied by *blueboldcenter*. The text will still be bold and centered (and also italic), because those attributes weren't in conflict, but it will be red rather than blue.

Copying Style Sheets

Duplicating a style sheet is simple. Right-click the style sheet by name in the CSS Styles panel, and choose Duplicate from the shortcut menu (see Figure 12.19). In the resulting Duplicate dialog box, give the duplicate style a name (the screen suggests merely adding the word *copy* to the existing name, although you can override that name entirely if you wish). You can change the nature of the duplicate by choosing a different Type and making a different selection from the Define In options.

Attaching Style Sheets

If a style sheet exists in one site, and you want to have it available on another site, display the CSS Styles panel on the site in which you want the style sheet, and right-click the *area* of the panel that lists styles and style sheets (don't right-click on any particular style or sheet). Choose Attach Style Sheet from the shortcut menu (see Figure 12.20).

Figure 12.19
Get two styles for the price of one: Take what's great about one style, and add to it by duplicating the style and then making adjustments.

Figure 12.20
You can choose to attach a style sheet using this menu, or by clicking the Attach Style Sheet button in the lower-right corner of the CSS Styles panel.

Figure 12.21
Navigate to and select the CSS file you want to attach.

In the resulting Select Style Sheet File dialog box (see Figure 12.21), double-click the name of that file that you want to attach (or click the file name once, and then click the Select button). The style sheet will now be available on the open site, and you can apply it to that site's pages.

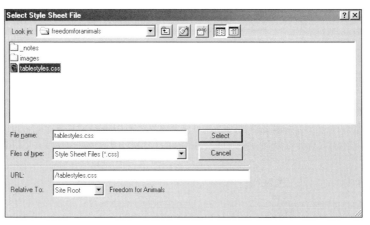

Create a Style Sheet to Format Site Headings

In most cases, heading text should have the same formatting throughout the pages on a site—standardized heading text provides the sort of consistency that makes it easier for people to navigate your site, and the standardization gives your overall design a cohesive look and feel.

Name and Build a Custom Heading Style

Create a style sheet that will apply a heading style to all the pages on your site.

1. Open the New Style dialog box and give the style sheet the following attributes:

    • Name: specialheads

    • Type: Make Custom Style (Class)

    • Define In: New Style Sheet File

2. Save the style sheet file as headingstyles.css.

3. In the Style Definitions dialog box, apply the following formats to the new style:

    • Font: Arial

    • Size: 20 pixels

    • Color: #330099

    • Alignment: Centered

Name and Build a Page Style

Create a new style sheet to format backgrounds and frame borders in all pages on your site.

1. Open the New Style dialog box and give the style sheet the following attributes:

   - Name: specialpages

   - Type: Make Custom Style (Class)

   - Define In: New Style Sheet File

2. Save the style sheet file as pagestyles.css.

3. In the Style Definitions dialog box, choose the Background category and set the Background Color to #FFFFCC.

4. Choose the Border category and apply these settings:

   - Style: Dotted

   - Colors (set all for Top, Bottom, Left, and Right): #66CC99

Apply the Style to Site Pages

To apply the style you've created to your site pages, follow these steps:

1. Open two blank pages within an existing site on your local drive. Type "Our People" at the top of one page and "Products and Services" at the top of the other. Apply the Heading 1 style to each, using the Properties Inspector.

2. Apply the allheadings style sheet to the pages, and observe the changes in the Heading 1 text.

3. Apply the specialpages style to both pages, and observe the changes in background color. Insert a frame, and observe the border style.

Moving On

In Chapter 13, you'll learn to add multimedia objects—sound and movies—to your Web pages. You'll employ skills you've learned throughout this book to create links between page elements and files, and you'll learn how to improve visitors' experiences at your site by involving more of their senses in the process of viewing—and now hearing—what you have to say.

Chapter 13

Using Multimedia Objects

The term "multimedia" refers to a variety of media. As soon as your Web pages include anything other than static text and graphics—such as sound and movies—your pages contain multimedia. This chapter shows you both how to add multimedia objects to your pages, and when and where to use such objects to your advantage.

Multimedia from a Design Point of View

My intent is not to sound like someone's mother ("If all your friends jump off a cliff, does that mean you have to do it, too?"), but I'm a firm believer in the idea that, just because something's possible, or other people are doing it, doesn't mean I should automatically do it, too. Although I'm not comparing the use of multimedia to jumping off a cliff, I am saying that not all Web sites require multimedia, and many site visitors won't be able to appreciate it, so you should carefully consider its use.

From a design perspective, saying that what looks good *is* good for a design is easy, but not always true. It's certainly true for printed materials, where how the information looks on paper is really all that matters (other than the expense of getting it there). For the Web, however, design involves not just how something looks, but also how it works. With the wide variety of Web users and computers out there visiting our sites, whether something works at all is just as important. The fact that a movie you add to your Web page might take a long time to load—or might require visitors to download a program or an update of a program they already have—just to see your movie, is a significant factor in your decision to use or not use a movie in your site's pages.

If I sound as though I'm warning you against using multimedia, I'm not. If your site pertains to a cutting-edge topic—something high-tech, or entertainment-oriented, or pertaining to multimedia—use movies and sound to your heart's content. Why? Because people who visit cutting-edge sites tend to have more cutting-edge computers than other people. And, even if they don't, they don't blame your site for taking so long to load. Because these visitors are more technologically savvy, they know their modem or Internet connection method is to blame.

On the other hand, if your site pertains to a nontechnical topic and/or has an intended audience likely to be using dial-up connections to the Internet on older computers, don't make your page design dependent on something many of those people won't be able to see or hear (at least not without a tedious download time). Just as making color, font, and image choices to match the tone, intent, and audience you anticipate for your site requires judgment, the decision to use multimedia objects is a judgment call—and, often, quite a subjective one.

Multimedia Defined

Of course, *multimedia* means a variety of media, but that's not where the definition ends. As Web designers, you need to know what kinds of multimedia are at your disposal, and begin to think about appropriate places and

---

The Times, They Are A-Changin'

As I warn you about catering to the needs of people with older, slower computers and Internet connections, I must also say that, every day, one fewer person is using a slow computer with no capability to view Flash movies or play sound. Every time someone buys a new computer for his business or his family, the technical capabilities (if not the technical knowledge) of your audience are raised another notch. In a few short years, we might be able to remove from our design checklist "Works for browsers prior to version 4?" and questions about users' ability to download and play movies via Web sites.

situations in which to use multimedia. The major multimedia objects that should fall under your consideration as a designer are the following:

- Flash and Shockwave movies

- Flash buttons

- Flash text

- Sound

Adding Motion with Movies

Flash movies are meant for the Web—their sole purpose in life is to add motion to Web pages, and their file-format design creates the smallest possible file, which increases the viability of Flash movies for general Web consumption. Shockwave movies are created in Macromedia Director, which is not an application solely for developing content bound for the Web. You can insert both Flash and Shockwave movies into your Web pages, however, and most popular browsers will deal with both kinds of objects. Your only limitations with these objects are the audience and their individual connections to the Internet—dial-up connections tend to be slow and, if the movie file is large, the download time might be prohibitive.

What's good about movies on your Web site? You can say so much more with a movie than you can with static images. Do you want to show how your company's products move from customer purchase to delivery? Sure, you can use an image of a production flowchart, or even a series of graphics showing each stage of the process. But wouldn't you (and your site visitors) rather watch a movie that shows the process, including scenes of someone placing an order and processing it, pulling the inventory, and loading the package on a truck and delivering it to a happy customer? If you want to tell a compelling story, nothing beats movies. Of course, anyone who's seen a movie made from a book will generally disagree with that, but not until books are as easy to read online as they are in print will that be a valid argument against movies on the Web.

If you're in doubt about the two sides (pro and con) of movie use on Web pages, go to a news site, such as **www.cnn.com** or **www.abcnews.com**. Try accessing the site with a dial-up connection, and click one of the links that shows the video of a news conference or speech, or of news footage from somewhere in the world. The movie will take quite a while to load. Once it runs, it will be choppy, and any sound might be out of synch with the action on screen. Even choppy movement, however, can be more compelling than a static image from the same news story.

Creating Interactivity with Buttons and Text

Flash buttons are predesigned rollover buttons that you can add to your pages. What's the benefit of using Flash buttons? They're snazzy looking, and even a

But What About . . .

Issues arise around server support of various multimedia objects, such as Microsoft's ActiveX controls and Macromedia's Generator tools. These topics might come up for the server administrator of a site or Web host, but they are, at best, on the periphery of what you as a designer should be concerned about.

seasoned Photoshop or Fireworks user would be challenged to create them anywhere close to as quickly as you can insert them using the Flash Button choice on the Common Objects panel. Flash text is rollover text—you pick the font, the color, and the color the font changes to when it rolls over, and you're set to go. Saving the text in two colors, and then setting up both files to be the original and rollover versions of a graphic, is much faster than creating graphic text in a program such as Photoshop. You can insert both Flash buttons and text in less time than it took you to read this paragraph, and that's what makes the buttons useful.

Giving Pages a Voice with Sound

Sound is something you don't run into much online, other than at sites through which you can download MP3 files, or where people go to purchase audio CDs and movies on tape or DVD. At sites such as these, sounds are playable on demand as product demos. But that's not a design feature—that's a sales tool.

When you're designing with sound, be careful. Most sites that use sound are homemade sites, and either visitors will turn off their speakers as soon as they hear the song start, or they'll click Back to return to the previous page, where blissful silence reigned. The only sound that's generally acceptable on Web pages is sound that plays with a Flash or Shockwave movie, and then only when the sound is integral to the experience of the movie.

One exception to the above rule-like statement is narration. If your page would benefit from someone standing next to the visitor, pointing out cool things to click, or giving some sort of narrated tour, then by all means, record a narration, and set it to play when someone clicks a button (so that listening to the sound is optional). Or, if the narration is short and pleasing to the ear, set it to play automatically upon page load.

You can insert sounds on a page, link them to objects on a page, or embed them into a page, which results in a sound-playing application starting when someone clicks a button or link (as Figure 13.1 shows). Depending on how willing your site's visitors are to wait for an application to start and the sound file to buffer, and then to listen to what might be a halting, choppy sound experience, you can choose how and when your sound will play.

Inserting Multimedia Objects

Dreamweaver doesn't use the word *multimedia*. Rather, it refers to sound and movie objects as simply being in the *media* category. Therefore, you've seen the word *multimedia* for the last time in this chapter. Adding media objects to a Web page in Dreamweaver is a similarly pared-down process, and the method you choose will likely follow one of these paths:

Figure 13.1

When visitors are serious about hearing your sound, they'll be willing to wait for an application to load and for the sound to finally play.

- Using the Objects panel (with its Common face forward), drag the button that represents the type of object you want to insert onto your page to the specific location where you want the object to appear or begin playing when the page is viewed in a browser.

- Click to position your cursor on the page where the object should go, and then click the corresponding button on the Common Objects panel.

- Use the Insert menu for a more methodical approach. Position your cursor on the page at the point where the object should go, and then choose Media or Interactive Images from the Insert submenu.

Whichever method you use, you'll insert an object with distinct properties, which you can easily adjust through the Properties Inspector. You can then preview your page to see or hear the media object as it will look or sound on the Web, and you can return to Dreamweaver to make any desired changes to the object's settings.

Working with Flash and Shockwave Objects

You can insert Flash and Shockwave movies from the Insert menu or the Common Objects panel (see Figure 13.2). When you issue the command (either way) to insert the object, a dialog box opens, and you must select the Flash movie file (in SWF format) or Shockwave movie file (in SWF format) to insert, as you see in Figure 13.3.

When you insert a Flash or Shockwave movie object, the object doesn't simply appear on the page as a graphic would. Rather, you see a placeholder with either a Flash or Shockwave object symbol in the middle of it, as Figure 13.4 shows. You can't see the movie without playing it from the Properties Inspector or previewing the Web page in a browser.

Figure 13.2

Click the Insert Flash or Insert Shockwave button.

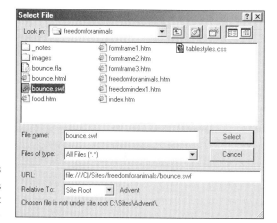

Figure 13.3
The Select File dialog box helps
you choose the movie object that
will run on your Web page.

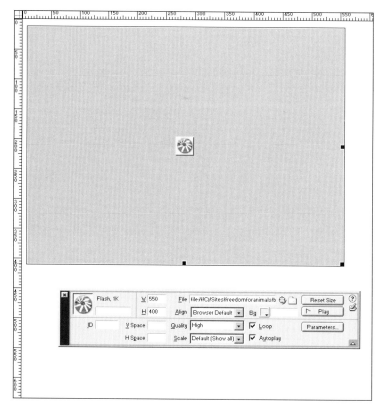

Figure 13.4
A placeholder appears in the
Dreamweaver workspace to
indicate where a movie object
has been inserted.

Understanding Flash Object Controls

The Properties Inspector offers several controls for Flash movie objects. As Figure 13.5 shows, some of the controls are familiar (Name, W and H, Align, Bg, V Space, H Space). Some new options let you play (and stop) the movie, associate the file with an ActiveX control, set the quality of the movie's appearance, and scale the movie object to control possible distortion created by changes in the size of the page-display window.

Figure 13.5

You can control where the movie plays on the page and how good it looks while it's playing.

The two controls you'll probably be most tempted to use are Play (to see the movie happen on the page without previewing it in a browser), and Quality. When you're adjusting the Quality option (see Figure 13.6), resist the temptation to choose a high setting, because doing so will mean that only visitors with fast processors will be able to view the movie properly—you're essentially setting the bar for who (or, rather, which computers) can watch the movie. The best choice is Auto Low, which starts the movie out at a low-quality setting, but will take advantage of a better processor as the movie begins and progresses. The bottom line is that if your visitors are running low-end computers, they will be able to see the movie in the best quality their computers are capable of. And visitors with newer, more powerful computers will see the movie at the best their computers are capable of.

Figure 13.6

Set the Quality option to Auto Low so that all visitors get the best view of the movie their computers can provide.

As Figure 13.7 shows, the Scale option lets you control how the movie will display within the set W (width) and H (height) values. If the movie's screen is wider than it is tall, and you accidentally make your width lower than your height, a Quality setting of Show All will make sure the entire movie shows in the appropriate width/height proportions to prevent distorting the movie's image. The No Borders option can have the same effect as Show All, but you might notice the edges of the movie screen are cut off, which makes this option risky. The only reason to choose No Borders is if all the borders that might appear on the sides of a movie set to Show All are unacceptable within your design.

Figure 13.7

Your Scale setting is best set to Show All, so any changes to the screen area don't end up distorting movie content.

Working with Flash Buttons and Text

Of course, the Flash movies you insert and run on your Web pages are created externally to Dreamweaver—you or someone else creates the movies in Flash and saves them, and then you insert them into your Web page. As is the case for all graphical content for your page, you should copy the file to your site folder, so you can easily upload the page and the media content, and maintain the same file locations on the server that you've created locally.

Flash buttons and text, however, are made from within Dreamweaver, which creates a file that's automatically saved to the active site folder. This means that when you're working on your page and realize you need a special effect, you don't need to fire up another application to create the effect, or call a Flash expert in to create a special effect for you.

Flash buttons, as I stated earlier, are rollover buttons. Dreamweaver comes with a large selection of predesigned buttons—some with text, some without, some that look like controls on a VCR. The buttons come in a variety of colors and styles, and you can tweak how they look and work when you insert them into your page. Figure 13.8 shows the dialog box that results when you click Insert Flash Button on the Objects panel.

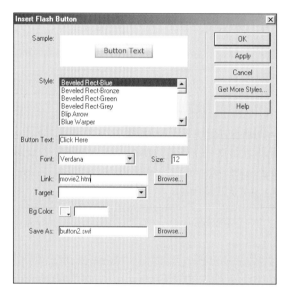

Figure 13.8

Scroll through the available buttons, and customize them as necessary.

If the button you choose has text on it, you can insert your own replacement text, and you can turn any button into a link. For example, you can link a button that looks like a play button on a VCR to a movie or sound file, so that the button appears to run the sound or movie (when, in fact, it's just opening a page that contains that object).

Flash text also has a rollover effect. Rather than going out to Fireworks or Photoshop to create a graphic text image, you can create one through the dialog box that appears when you click the Insert Flash Text button on the Objects panel (see Figure 13.9). Because you're creating an object, not typing page text, all the fonts on your computer are available (rather than the small group of Web-safe fonts to which you're normally restricted for page text). You can choose the size of the text, the color in which it will appear when it's not active, and the color to which the text will change when someone moves his mouse over it.

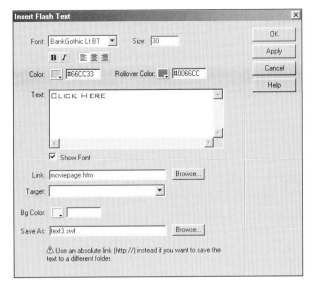

Figure 13.9

Create a snazzy, graphic text object, and turn it into a link, all from within the Insert Flash Text dialog box.

As you insert Flash text and Flash buttons, files are being created, although you're never asked to name a file or choose where to store it. If you click on an existing button or text, you'll see the automatically assigned name (as Figure 13.10 shows), with an .swf extension—just like a Flash movie has. The files are saved to the site folder, no questions asked. But you can change the location of the file as well as its name. Just enter your desired information in the Save As box in the Insert Flash Text (or Button) dialog box.

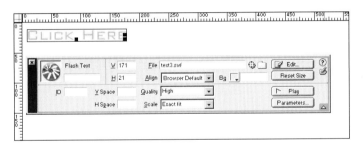

Figure 13.10

You don't need to name and navigate to an images folder to save your Flash buttons and text—Dreamweaver sees to all that for you.

Controlling Shockwave Movies

Just as the processes for inserting Flash and Shockwave movies are similar to each other, so are the controls available to you once the objects are inserted. As Figure 13.11 shows, the Properties Inspector offers options for controlling the size of the movie screen area, the alignment, the background color, and the white space around the image (through V Space and H Space); and for appointing a specific ActiveX control (through the ID option).

Figure 13.11

You can't control Shockwave movie quality, so your visitors are on their own in terms of how well their particular processors can deal with your movie file.

The Parameters button opens a Parameters dialog box, through which you can adjust the HTML <**param**> tag, which, essentially, lists the settings you've established for the quality of the movie's display.

Previewing Your Flash and Shockwave Content

You can watch your movie from within the Dreamweaver window by clicking the Play button on the Properties Inspector. Of course, this button is available only when the object is selected and the Properties Inspector is displayed.

If you prefer to see your page and the movie within the context of a Web browser, preview your page by choosing File|Preview In Browser. You can also press F12 to see the page previewed in the browser that is established as the default. Figure 13.12 shows the movie bounce.swf playing in a browser window.

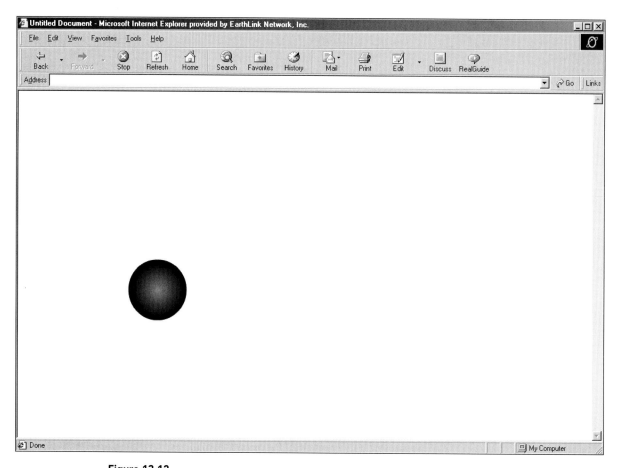

Figure 13.12
Your movie plays in the space allocated by the current W (width) and H (height) settings for the object.

Adding User Controls for Playing Movies

You can use the Behaviors panel to create user controls—to let users stop, play, rewind, or move to a specific frame within your Flash or Shockwave movie. You can choose how these controls are invoked, and you can even select from a list of controls based on the version of the browser you feel most of your site visitors will have. Obviously, the list of controls available for version 5 and later of Internet Explorer and Netscape is much more extensive than the list for versions 4 and earlier. In fact, only the onLoad control (which means that the movie can be played, stopped, rewound, or moved to a particular frame as soon as it's loaded) is worthwhile from within the version-4-and-earlier list.

To apply Behaviors to your movie and give users (or at least their browsers) some control over the action of the movie, follow these steps:

1. Choose Window|Behaviors to display the Behaviors panel.

2. Be sure the movie object you're about to work with has been named through the Properties Inspector. If it hasn't, give it a name now, as Figure 13.13 demonstrates.

Figure 13.13

Name your movie so that your page code has a way to refer to it when it applies the behaviors you're about to associate with the object.

3. Click once on the movie object to select it.

4. Click the plus sign (+) in the Behaviors panel, and choose Control Shockwave Or Flash from the resulting list, as Figure 13.14 shows.

5. In the dialog box that appears, choose the movie by name from the Movie list (see Figure 13.15).

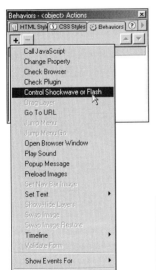

Figure 13.14

(Left) Choose which behavior you'll add to your selected object.

Figure 13.15

(Right) Choose the movie by name from the Movie list.

6. Choose the action that will occur when the control is applied. You can choose Play, Stop, Rewind, or Go To Frame (and enter a frame number).

7. Click OK to close the dialog box.

8. In the Behaviors panel, click the listed event (it defaults to onLoad) in the Events list. A long list of events, such as onClick or onMouseOver, appears, as shown in Figure 13.16.

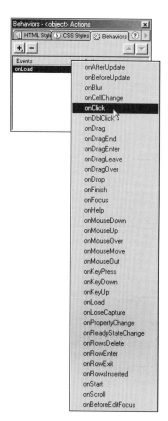

Figure 13.16

Choose what the visitor must do for the selected control to occur.

9. Choose an event from the list. This event is what must occur for the selected action—Play, Stop, Rewind, and so on—to happen.

Using Sound on a Web Page

You can use sound on any Web page—to provide atmosphere, or to showcase a musician or performer to which the page pertains. As I said earlier in the chapter, you rarely find sound used indiscriminately on professionally designed or professional-looking Web sites. A sound playing just for the heck of it on a Web page is usually the sign of an amateur designer, or of a designer who was designing a page for a group of friends who knew what they'd like and who had no interest in the outside world's impressions of the site.

My comments are not intended to sound condescending or to inhibit anyone's design impulses—if you want to create a personal or family Web site that plays the music you love when the page loads or when someone moves a mouse over a picture, more power to you. Not every Web site needs to be professionally designed or used for a commercial purpose. Fun Web sites that provide a place in cyberspace for friends and family to share information have a legitimate place, too.

However, if you've been hired to design a site for a business or organization, you probably don't want to insert sound objects unless you're asked to. Even if a site seems to cry out for a "theme song," be careful about using sound unless you know that the site owner and visitors will appreciate it. I've seen many people turn their speaker volume down or off as soon as a page with sound is loaded. (A possible exception is the **www.hamsterdance.com** site, which people used to open and leave running at their desks to annoy co-workers. The music, supposedly the song of dancing hamsters, could drive anyone mad in short order.)

If, however, sound is the right thing for your site, go for it. Sound doesn't have to be in the form of music—it can take the form of a narration, such as, "Welcome to the ABC Company Site. Click the About Us link to find out more about our organization, our goals, and our accomplishments." If you want to use music, use something universally appealing, preferably instrumental, which matches the tone of your site. A jazzy, upbeat tune probably isn't great for a funeral home's site, while a somber, cello solo might be too serious for the site that tells you all about a chain of party-supply stores.

Sounds can play as soon as the page containing them loads, or when someone moves a mouse over a graphic or clicks a link. The timing of the sound is up to you, as is the number of times the sound plays.

Sound File Formats

You can add sound files in any of the following formats to your Web page:

- *WAV files*—These files have good sound quality, and they require no special plug-ins. Most (perhaps all) browsers support WAV files, and they're easy to create—a plus if the sound is one you have to record yourself. You can create a WAV file with the Sound Recorder program that comes with Windows Accessories, and the only equipment you need is a microphone. The downside to these sound files is their large file sizes. Any sound that plays longer than 30 seconds will take forever to load on a dial-up connection.

- *MIDI*—These files are like WAV files in that browsers nearly universally support them, and they don't require a plug-in. Another plus with MIDI files is that the file sizes are small, and the sound quality is very good.

Are the Mouse Actions Missing?

If a smaller list of events appears and doesn't include useful choices such as onClick or onMouseOver, click the Show Events For command at the foot of the list and choose a later-version browser. Of course, you don't want to do this if you know a number of your visitors will have older browsers. If you do pick events that older browsers don't support, those visitors won't be able to take advantage of the behaviors you've set up. A good idea, therefore, is to leave onLoad as one of the events for the selected movie, so that the movie plays when the page loads, regardless of the visitor's browser version. Even very old browsers honor onLoad.

You knew there had to be a catch, though, right? You can create MIDI files only with a computer using special hardware and software. You can't just belt out a tune or read a script and save the recording, as you can in the case of a WAV file.

- *MP3*—These files are small, and the sound quality is good. To create MP3 files, you need special software. And to play them, you also need special software and a plug-in, such as RealPlayer or the Windows Media Player.

- *AIF*—These files are like WAV files in every respect—they have good sound, are easily created, and don't require special software or plug-ins. AIF files are also large files, so for Web use, they're not a great choice.

- *RAM, RPM (RealAudio)*—These files create small files—even smaller than MP3 files. You can stream RealAudio files so that the music starts before all the page images are finished loading, which is a nice thing. MP3 files have better sound quality than these files, but that's an issue only if you think people are going to want to download the sound for their own en-joyment—if the sound is just background noise at your site, the quality is fine. To record and play RealAudio files, you need to download and in-stall RealPlayer.

You can insert any of these sound files into a page by embedding the player software that is required for the sound format, or by inserting a link that will play the sound file itself. Of course, the latter option requires that you use a sound format that doesn't need a plug-in, or that you're fairly certain your visi-tors will have the capability to download, and not mind downloading, the files.

Inserting a Sound

To set up a sound to play when your page loads, follow these steps:

1. In the page that should include the sound that plays as the page loads, display the Behaviors panel by choosing Windows|Behaviors.

2. Click the plus (+) sign in the Behaviors panel and choose Play Sound. The Play Sound dialog box opens, as Figure 13.17 shows.

Figure 13.17
Pick a sound to play as your page loads.

3. Type the path to and file name of the sound file you want to play, or click the Browse button to find and select the file.

4. Click OK in the Play Sound dialog box.

5. To make sure the behavior associated with the sound is set to onLoad, click the drop-down arrow on the Events button in the Behaviors panel, and choose onLoad from the list, as Figure 13.18 shows.

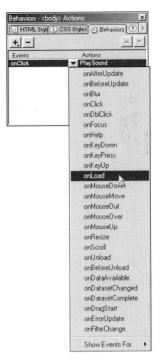

Figure 13.18

Most browsers, even the old versions, will handle the onLoad behavior.

6. Save and preview your page—the sound will play as soon as the sound file has a chance to load.

Obviously, such a technique requires using a sound-file format that doesn't need a plug-in. With this approach, you must use the WAV, MIDI, or AIF file format, and these formats produce large files. That's the tradeoff—if you don't want the visitor potentially forced to download a plug-in or some special software to play the sound (which would kill the spontaneous effect of a sound that plays automatically when a page loads), you must use a file format that takes a long time to load anyway. (Of course, if the page contains a lot of graphics, by the time they've loaded, the sound file might be ready to play.)

Linking to Sound Files

One way to add sound to a Web page is to link the page to a sound file. To do this, simply select the image or text that will serve as the link, and enter the Link information—the path to and file name of the sound file (see Figure 13.19). Of course, like all other Web page content, you need the sound file to be in the site folder to facilitate uploading to the Web server. So, either copy the file there before you set up the link, or accept Dreamweaver's offer to copy it there for you.

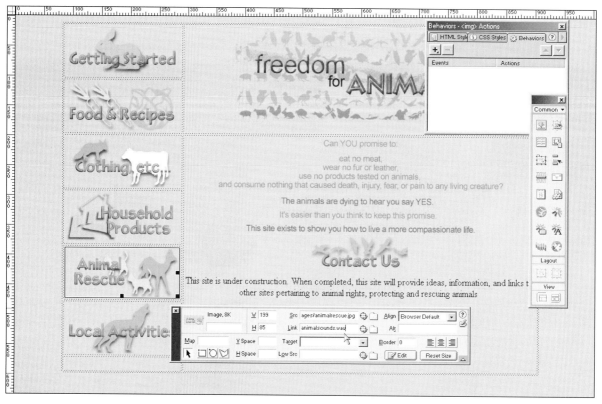

Figure 13.19

Unlike what you can do with a movie, which must be on a page, you can link directly to a sound file.

When visitors click the link, they will see a prompt appear on their screen, which asks whether they want to open the file or save it to their disk (see Figure 13.20). This option is obviously a good choice only if you think visitors want to go to that much trouble to hear the sound, or if they want to keep a copy of the sound file itself. Otherwise, linking a sound file to your page isn't your best choice for providing ambient music on a Web page.

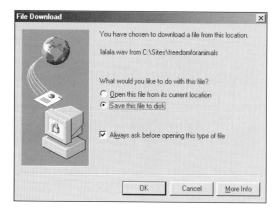

Figure 13.20

Is your sound one that visitors want to download for their own use? Unless it is, you don't want to link the sound to your page.

Embedding Sound Objects

An embedded sound file brings a lot of baggage with it in terms of the software required to play the sound. You need to embed files only if the file type you're using requires special software. If your visitor doesn't have that software, the page provides it, by virtue of the embedding. If the visitor doesn't have a plug-in to make his browser talk to that software, however, he'll need to download the plug-in.

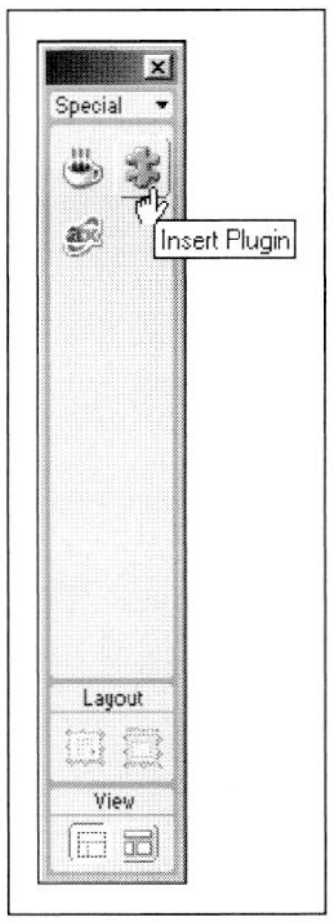

To embed a sound object, follow these steps:

1. Click to place your cursor on the spot where you want the embedded file to appear.

2. Click the Insert Plugin button on the Objects panel (see Figure 13.21). You can also choose Insert|Media|Plugin.

3. The Properties Inspector will change to offer you tools that pertain to the selected plug-in, as Figure 13.22 shows. Click the folder icon next to the Src box to browse for the audio file—or, if you know it, type the path to and file name of the audio file.

Figure 13.21

The Insert Plugin button will let you insert any object that requires a plug-in to play.

Figure 13.22

Set up the plug-in options through the Properties Inspector.

4. Adjust the W (width) and H (height) settings to create the space in which the embedded audio software will appear on the page. You can also resize the object placeholder by dragging its handles with your mouse.

Once you've inserted the plug-in, a placeholder for the plug-in controls will appear on screen, as shown in Figure 13.23. If you know the approximate size of the eventual plug-in object, resize the placeholder accordingly. You won't see the actual controls until you preview the page.

Figure 13.23

A plug-in placeholder tells you where your plug-in will appear when the page is viewed online or previewed locally.

When you preview or visitors see your page online, the plug-in controls replace the placeholder, and visitors can stop, rewind, play, and fast-forward the sound (see Figure 13.24). The controls that appear depend on the file type you choose. For a basic WAV or MIDI file, a simple set of controls will appear, with no logo or indication of the software behind the controls. If you choose a format that requires special software, the plug-in controls will reflect that. When you're designing your page, be prepared to accommodate larger control objects or have the colors within the control object clash with your site colors. This reality can affect your choice of file formats, or you can adjust some of your surrounding colors (if that's possible) so the plug-in doesn't stand out like a sore thumb.

Figure 13.24

Some plug-in objects are simple and don't present a design dilemma; others are more complex and can create design challenges.

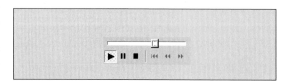

PROJECT Insert and Run a Flash Movie

In this project, you'll insert a Flash movie on a page, and then on another page, you'll insert a Flash button that links to the page that contains the movie. Using a Behavior option, you'll set the movie to run as soon as the page containing it is loaded.

Create the Movie Page

Follow these steps to create the Flash movie page.

1. Open a blank new page, and insert the Flash movie bounce.swf, which you'll find in the Project 13A folder on the CD-ROM. This is a simple Flash movie of a ball bouncing within a square space.

2. Display the Behaviors panel, and associate the Play control with the movie, set to occur onLoad.

3. Set up a sound to play when the page loads. To accomplish this, copy the sound file boing.wav from the CD-ROM to your site folder, and then select that sound from the Play Sound dialog box that appears when you choose the Play Sound list of behaviors—click the plus sign (+) to see the list. Using the Behaviors panel, select onLoad as the event associated with the sound.

4. Save the page as bounce.htm.

Create a Flash Button

Create and insert the Flash button that will open the movie page.

1. Open a blank new page.

2. Type "Try Before You Buy" as the heading.

3. On a line below the heading, insert a centered Flash button. Choose one of the buttons that has text on it, and change that text to "Play Movie".

4. Link the button to bounce.htm.

5. Save the page as trymovie.htm.

Preview and Test

Preview the page in a browser, and test the link to the movie page.

1. Press F12 while you're in trymovie.htm. The page will open in your default browser.

2. Click on the Play Movie button. The page bounce.htm should load. After bounce.htm loads, the sound boing.wav should play, and the movie (bounce.swf) should start.

Appendix A

What's New in Dreamweaver 4?

This Appendix lays out Dreamweaver 4's improvements: new tools and windows, simplified features, improved access to underlying HTML, and new features for better site management.

The New Dreamweaver

Dreamweaver 4 was nicknamed "Notorious" throughout its beta program. While the word *notorious* generally has negative connotations—we think of notorious things and people as being involved with scandal and gossip—the term's a good one for the new Dreamweaver. Why? Because Version 4 solidifies Dreamweaver's reputation as a great design application for the Web. This version gives Web designers an environment and set of tools that will enable them to create scandalously great Web sites, which will generate a lot of gossip about how wonderful the designers are.

General Improvements

The new features in Dreamweaver 4 include changes and improvements in the following areas:

- More streamlined interface, offering a new toolbar, new windows, and a more cohesive look.

- Improved site-management tools.

- Enhanced ability to add multimedia elements, such as Flash objects.

- Better tools for simplifying workflow and collaboration.

- Simplified methods for viewing and editing HTML code.

Throughout this Appendix, you'll find out more about these improved aspects of the Dreamweaver application.

New Tools and Windows

Something as simple as a toolbar button for previewing your page in a browser might not seem like much, but it's a tremendous addition to Dreamweaver 4. The new Dreamweaver toolbar puts tools such as this within easy reach, eliminating much of the need for opening menus. Figure A.1 shows the new toolbar.

Another improvement is the addition of a keyboard-shortcut interface. What's great about this improvement is that it's supported across the entire Macromedia Web-publishing product line—take the time to learn the shortcuts in Dreamweaver; apply many of them in Flash and Fireworks. The shortcuts are customizable: choose Edit|Keyboard Shortcuts to open this dialog box (see Figure A.2). You can create your own shortcuts, change the existing shortcuts, and create entire sets of shortcuts—and choose which set to use under a given set of circumstances. The need for speed in Web design has never been better understood or supported.

Dreamweaver's windows and panels now coexist more effectively, too. When you open a window—a new document, for example—the window won't obscure your panels and palettes. This improved arrangement makes it easy to

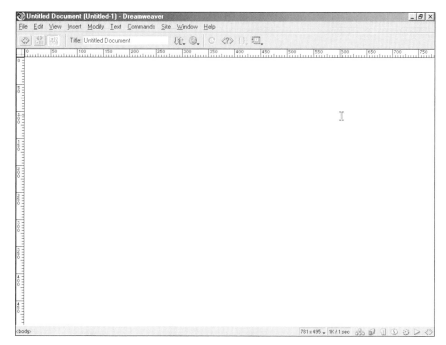

Figure A.1

From left to right, enjoy the use of Code view, Design and Code views, Design view, a Title text box, File Status, Preview In Browser, Refresh Design view, Reference, Code Navigation, and access to a list of Options.

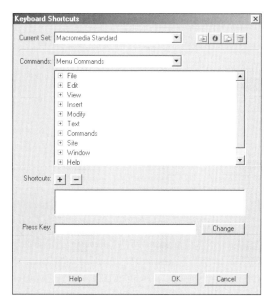

Figure A.2

Even if you use only the new set of Macromedia Standard shortcuts, you'll be saving time and effort as you work in both Design and Code views to create and edit page content and appearance.

format content and set up links (using the Properties Inspector) on two or more Web pages. You won't have to drag palettes and panels around, and rearrange the stacking order of your windows and on-screen tools, every time you want to work with a different page or page element.

Simplified Design Features and Tools

The key to any good software package is ease of use. Dreamweaver has always been a powerful product, and its power is increased with the release of Dreamweaver 4. All that power, however, would be lost on many users if access to and use of the powerful features weren't easy enough to learn, master, and put to everyday use. Consider the following key areas where Dreamweaver has improved existing features and added access to new tools.

Table Layout

Dreamweaver 4 provides new and better tools for page design and layout. Through the use of Layout view, you can set up tables quickly and easily, drawing table cells, nesting tables, or moving and resizing the tables and their content as you go. You can access Layout view and the related Layout tools near the bottom of the Objects panel, as shown in Figure A.3.

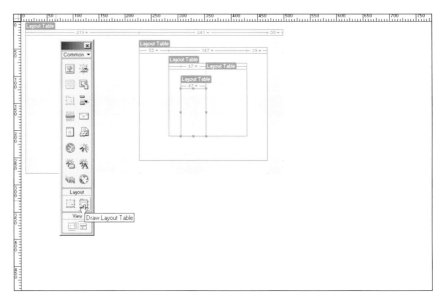

Figure A.3

When Dreamweaver is in Layout view, use the Table Layout tools to draw tables, nested tables, and free-roaming table cells.

Figure A.4

The Objects panel offers a variety of Flash buttons and related tools.

Flash Buttons

To support the growing number of designers who want to use Flash in their pages (and the growing number of site visitors who already have the Flash plug-ins and can therefore view Flash content without stopping to download a file), Dreamweaver 4 has added Flash buttons. You can use Flash buttons to create Flash movies right within Dreamweaver, choosing from a comprehensive set of Flash styles or using Flash styles you've created externally in Flash. You'll find the Flash buttons in the Objects panel, in the Common group, as Figure A.4 shows.

Better Template Tools

When you use a template in Dreamweaver 4, you can now easily see which portions of that template are editable. An outlining rectangle and tab that contain the name of the editable region let you visually identify the parts of the template you can edit, as Figure A.5 shows.

Figure A.5
Find out which regions of your template you can edit by observing new on-screen cues.

Make That ECSS, As in Easy Cascading Style Sheets

While many designers are not fans of the whole Cascading Style Sheet (CSS) concept, Dreamweaver 4 has made significant strides in simplifying the process to create and apply cascading style sheets.

You can now set up an external style sheet whenever you make a new style. With the press of a button, you can also attach a CSS style sheet to the CSS Styles panel. When you want to apply that CSS, just click that button. What could be simpler?

To Fireworks and Back Again

If you're a Fireworks user (and if you're not, you can get a leg up on the learning curve in Appendix C), you'll like the fact that you can launch Fireworks from within Dreamweaver simply by double-clicking a PNG image on your Web page (in Design view, as shown in Figure A.6). Once you're finished editing the selected image in Fireworks, you can get back to Dreamweaver easily, where changes to the graphic are immediately reflected in both the Design and Code views.

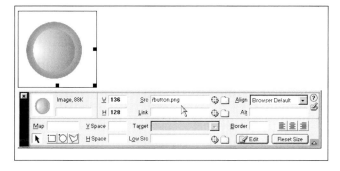

Figure A.6
View the format of your selected PNG graphic, then double-click the graphic to either open or return to Fireworks to edit the image.

Improved Site, Collaboration, Library, and Reference Tools

Dreamweaver 4 offers new and improved features for creating and managing a site, accessing reference materials, accumulating and controlling page assets (graphics, objects), and communicating with others during the design process.

Site Management Reality

Create a site, set up folders, create and name pages, establish links, and develop a site map—all in one handy and powerful Site window, as you can see in Figure A.7. I discuss the use and function of this window in detail in Chapter 2.

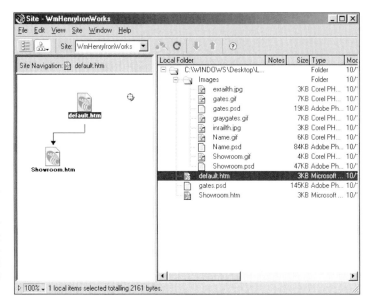

Figure A.7

Keep each of your sites separate, and create a simple folder hierarchy that you can repeat on your Web server, to make uploading sites, pages, and images much easier—and have everything work online.

Manage Your Assets

The standards for good Web design have been raised in the past few years, and most Web pages are busy places—filled with text, graphics, movies, sounds, templates, animations, and a variety of other objects. To keep track of this cornucopia of *assets*, Dreamweaver 4 gives you the Assets panel, as Figure A.8 shows.

The Assets panel lets you view and manage all the graphics; JavaScript; colors; Flash, Shockwave, and QuickTime objects; URLs; Templates; and Library items in one floating window. You can preview your assets and then drag them onto your Web page. You can also set up Favorites for items you plan to use often throughout a site or across sites.

Figure A.8

Anything you'd want to add to your page is just a click and drag away in the Assets panel.

Look It Up

Want to know what a **
** tag does? Curious about how tag attributes should be expressed? Don't know what I'm talking about? Try the Reference panel. Just a tab away from the Assets panel, the Reference panel provides information on CSS, HTML, and JavaScript, and lets you look up specific topics by category and read the related text. Figure A.9 shows the Reference panel and the material related to an HTML tag displayed.

Figure A.9

Learn what the code does and how to use it through the Reference panel.

Write to Me

Dreamweaver 4 provides collaborative tools to help you stay in touch and compare notes with one or more coworkers on any design project. If you're working with others on a Web page or site, you can click on the collaborator's name to send him or her an email. You can set up the email through the Workflow tab in the Site Definition dialog box.

More and Better Access to Underlying HTML Code

Whether you already know HTML or are hoping to learn a little about it, Dreamweaver 4 makes it much easier to get at and edit your HTML code. Some new features help to make this possible.

New Code Views

Choose from two views that show you the code you've created while working in the WYSIWYG Dreamweaver environment: Code view (see nothing but your code, as shown in Figure A.10) and Design and Code views (see a split screen that shows both your page in the Dreamweaver Design view and the corresponding HTML code, as shown in Figure A.11). You can scroll each screen independently, but you can select content in either screen and see the corresponding content. For example, if you select something—a graphic, some text—in the Design view screen, the Code view screen immediately displays the code associated with that element of the page.

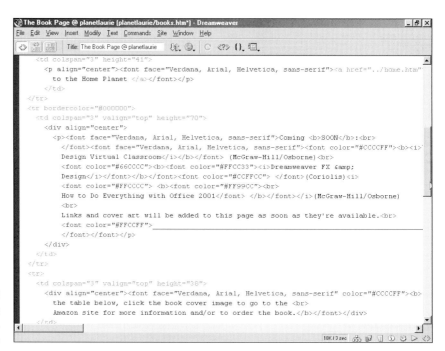

Figure A.10

Roll up your sleeves and work with nothing but your HTML code in Code view.

Full-Fledged Text Editing

The Code view window reveals real text-editing software, complete with tools for quickly locating tags (see Figure A.12), correcting mismatched tags and punctuation, and editing the colors of different code elements (use the Code Colors tab in the Edit|Preferences dialog box). You can also use the text editor to edit JavasScript and XML code.

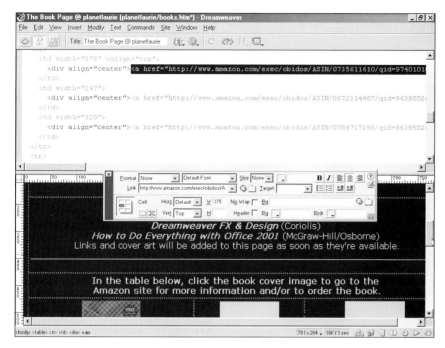

Figure A.11

Straddle the environment-preference fence by working in and viewing Design and Code views at the same time.

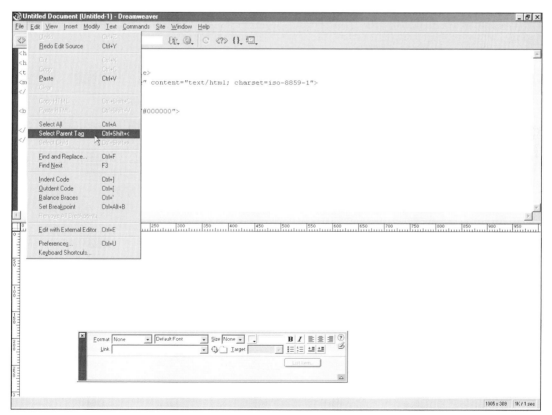

Figure A.12

Choose Edit|Select Parent Tag to find the beginning of the tags that pertain to a selected page element or text within Code view.

Appendix B

Do I Have to Know HTML to Use Dreamweaver?

In this Appendix, you'll discover the basic concepts behind the HTML language that makes your Web designs possible. Even if you decide that learning HTML isn't for you, it's a good idea to at least understand enough of the language to get along in a pinch—sort of like being able to ask directions to your hotel in a foreign country.

How Important Is HTML?

Many users ask if they must have HTML knowledge to use Dreamweaver, and the answer is "No, but . . ." Plenty of people who don't know much about HTML (the Hypertext Markup Language that is the backbone of Web content) use Dreamweaver to create Web pages. However, if simple curiosity doesn't lure you in to check out Code view and see the HTML code that's being created while you build your Web page in Dreamweaver, the need for you to understand HTML will surface at some point. So you might as well be prepared.

What happens if you design a Web site for someone and you're called upon to edit the site on a computer with no Dreamweaver? What if a Web page you're designing contains something funky—a graphic that won't move, a table cell that won't resize—and you can't seem to get Dreamweaver to respond to your attempts to solve the problem? HTML might end up being the only weapon you have. As with any weapon, understanding how HTML works is a good idea before you have to use it.

HTML Basics

HTML is a language that consists of *tags*, *attributes*, and *values*. You type the tags, attributes, and values as simple text, and save the file with an .htm or .html extension. To edit HTML, you can use NotePad, which comes with Windows and is accessible via the Accessories submenu. You can also use programs such as TextPad (from Helios Software Solutions), or you can use Dreamweaver's Code view window. Although NotePad seems to allow only a text (TXT) format in which to save your file, you can save it with an .htm extension by typing the file name followed by .htm.

An HTML tag is a statement that says either "This is here," or "Do this." For example, a Web page starts with a tag that tells the Web browser that will display the page, "This is in HTML." The tag is <**html**>, and it's the first line of any Web-page code. A closing tag, <**/html**>, which basically says "The HTML ends here," is placed at the very end of the page. The closing tag is the same as the opening tag, except that a slash precedes the **html** in the closing tag.

Most tags require both an opening tag and a closing tag, but some do not. Many tags are accompanied by attributes and values, settings that dictate how a tag's purpose will be fulfilled. For example, if you use a tag to say "Here is a table," that tag may include information about that table—its size, how thick its cell borders will be, and how the table is aligned on the page. Figure B.1 shows a <**table**> tag along with attributes and values for a table that is 300 pixels wide with a 1-pixel border.

Table B.1 contains some common HTML tags and explains their use.

```
<html>
<head>
<title>Untitled Document</title>
<meta http-equiv="Content-Type" content="text/html; charset=iso-8859-1">
</head>

<body bgcolor="#FFFFFF" text="#000000">
<table width="300" border="1">
  <tr>
    <td> </td>
    <td> </td>
  </tr>
  <tr>
    <td> </td>
    <td> </td>
  </tr>
</table>
</body>
</html>
```

Figure B.1
Once you understand the building blocks of HTML—tags and their attributes—you can read a page of HTML code and begin to see what's happening.

Table B.1   Basic HTML tags

Tag	Purpose	Example
<**html**> </**html**>	The opening <**html**> tag starts the HTML document by invoking the HTML language. This tells the browser that interprets the text to expect HTML and display the Web page accordingly. The closing <**/html**> tag appears at the very end of the document.	
<**head**> </**head**>	The <**head**> tag appears just below the <**html**> tag. The <**head**> tag surrounds the identifying information for the page. Within the <**head**> tags appear the meta tags assigned to the page, the title that will appear in the title bar (between <**title**> </**title**> tags), and any scripting. The HTML code within the <**head**> tag can be as simple as a <**title**> alone or as complex as a long string of meta tags and lines of JavaScript.	
<**body**> </**body**>	The <**body**> tag indicates the beginning of the page content. The closing </**body**> tag appears at the end of the page, before the closing </**html**> tag.	
<**h1**></**h1**>	Not to be confused with a <**head**> tag, a *heading* tag indicates heading-style text. Between the opening heading tag and its closing tag partner, type the text of the heading. With heading tags, the number indicates the heading level: **h1** is a Heading 1 style, **h2** is Heading 2, and so on. When you assign heading levels, remember that the lower the number is, the larger the text will be.	<**h1**>Big Sale This Week Only!</**h1**>
<**p**> </**p**>	The<**p**> tag indicates a paragraph break, which inserts a blank line. If you want to create vertical space between paragraphs of body text, graphics, or tables on your page, insert a <**p**> tag (don't forget the closing tag). Whenever you press Enter in the Dreamweaver Design view, a <**p**> tag is inserted, along with its closing tag mate </**p**>.	
<**br**>	When you don't want a full blank line but do want to move down to the next line on the page, insert a <**br**> tag for a line break. You use no closing tag with the <**br**> tag.	

(continued)

Table B.1   Basic HTML tags *(continued)*

Tag	Purpose	Example
<**center**> </**center**> <**right**> </**right**> <**left**> </**left**>	The content that falls between the opening and closing <**center**> tags will be centered horizontally on the page. This content can be text or a reference to an image. You also can use <**left**> or <**right**> tags to align the text with the left or right margins.	
<**img src=** "_____">	An *image source* tag indicates the use of a graphic and tells the browser which graphic file to display. Replace the blank line with the name of your graphic file.	<**img src="/images/flower.jpg"**>
<**a href=** "_____"></**a**>	An <**a href**> tag indicates a hyperlink—to another page within your site, to an entirely different Web site, to a file for download, or to an email address. In the example, the phrase *Buy Books!* appears as a text link and takes the user to the Amazon.com Web page.	<**a href="http://www.amazon.com"**> Buy Books!</**a**>.
<**table**> </**table**>	The <**table**> tag heralds the start of a table. This tag is followed by <**tr**> (row) and <**td**> (column) tags; Both the <**tr**> and <**td**> tags have closing mates, </**tr**> and </**td**>. The table ends with the </**table**> tag. The example sets up two-column, two-row table. The ** **; code indicates a nonbreaking space. The **width="4"** code indicates the pixel width of the table. If you were to resize the table in the Dreamweaver's Design view, that number would change accordingly.	<**table width="4"**> <**tr**> <**td**> </**td**> <**td**> </**td**> </**tr**> <**tr**> <**td**> </**td**> <**td**> </**td**> </**tr**> </**table**>

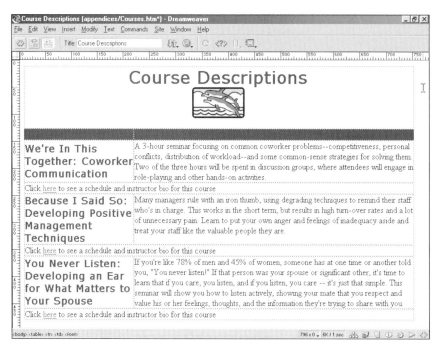

Figure B.2

Dreamweaver makes creating a simple page like this one easy—with a background color, text in both heading and regular paragraph styles, and a graphic image that links to another page.

Sometimes, it helps to see the whole forest, and then focus in on one of the trees. Toward that end, Figure B.2 shows a Web page in Dreamweaver Design view, and Figure B.3 shows that same page in Code view—you can see what's on the page and its underlying HTML code.

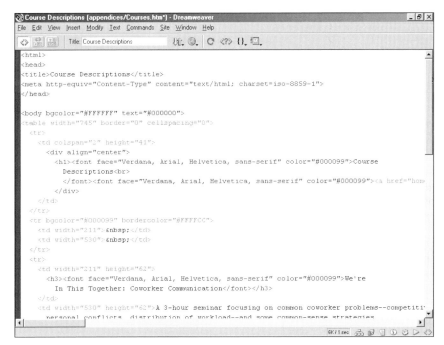

Figure B.3

The simple page consists of some simple tags; by comparing what you see on the page to the code that created it, you can begin to understand how HTML works.

Using Dreamweaver to Learn HTML

Dreamweaver provides a great environment for learning HTML—you can use the Design view (the default WYSIWYG view) to insert and format your page content, and then observe the resulting HTML code. When, for example, you type some text, insert a graphic, apply bold formatting, or change a table cell's width and then look at the HTML code that those actions created, you can quickly begin to see "what's going on."

Another excellent tool for learning HTML within the Dreamweaver application is the Reference panel. Click the Reference button on the toolbar (in either Code or Design view), and the panel opens, as Figure B.4 shows.

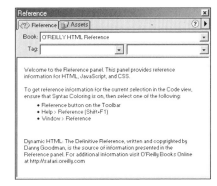

Figure B.4

Use the Reference panel to look up tags, attributes, and values, and discover ways to write cleaner, more efficient HTML code.

To use the Reference panel, follow these steps:

1. Click the Reference button on the toolbar, or choose Window|Reference. The keyboard shortcut to open the Reference panel is Shift+F10.

2. In the Reference panel, click to select the reference material you want to use.

3. In the Tag drop list, scroll to select the tag you want to read about, as Figure B.5 shows.

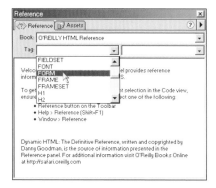

Figure B.5

Choose from a list of different HTML tags.

4. The Description drop list to the right of the Tag list changes, depending on which tag you choose. After you select a tag, click the Description list to see the associated attributes and values you can set for that tag.

5. Read the descriptive text in the main display area of the Reference panel (see Figure B.6). This text contains a description of the tag's purpose, samples of its use, and tips for avoiding problems associated with the tag, such as typical errors people make when they're using attributes and values.

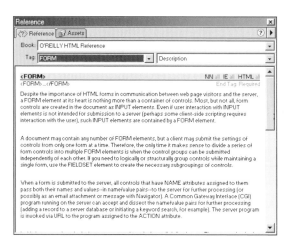

Figure B.6

While not the most inspired prose you'll ever read, the HTML reference material Dreamweaver provides is thorough and generally accurate

Viewing and Editing HTML with Dreamweaver

Dreamweaver 4 offers you more choices for viewing and editing your HTML code than you found in previous versions of the software. On the new toolbar, the first three buttons give you your choices for viewing the Dreamweaver environment:

- *Code view*—This view displays a full screen of your HTML code, obscuring your page entirely, as Figure B.7 shows. Any palettes (such as the Properties Inspector) are dimmed, and you can close them if they're in the way.

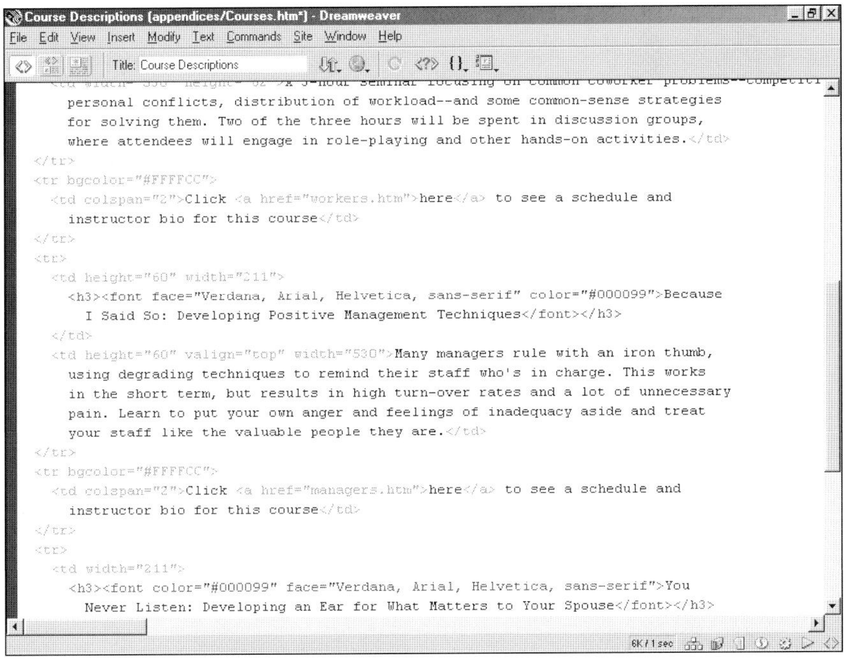

Figure B.7
Just the code, Ma'am.

- *Design and Code views*—This view splits the screen, showing both the page and its HTML code. Through this view, you can select items on the page and see the associated code selected in the Code view portion of the screen, as shown in Figure B.8.

- *Design view*—If you prefer to work in a WYSIWYG environment, and you either don't know or care to see the code, this view gives you an entirely graphical interface with no intervening references to HTML. As Figure B.9 shows, however, the code sneaks in, just a little—for whatever item is selected on the page (or wherever your cursor is), the associated tags appear on the strip across the bottom of the page.

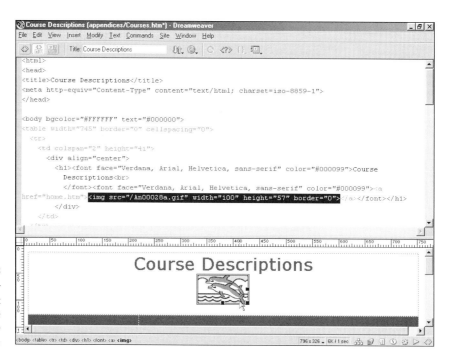

Figure B.8

Do you need to see the code for an element on your page? Select the element, and look in the Code view side of the window to see the relevant HTML.

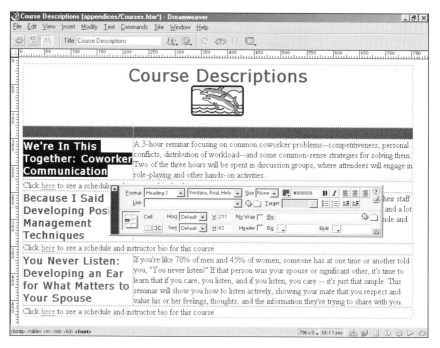

Figure B.9

If your cursor is in a table column, the <**td**> tag appears at the bottom of the window.

The first two views obviously show you the HTML code for the page currently displayed, and the third shows you just your page in a WYSIWYG environment. You can quickly view your code from within Design view by clicking the Code Inspector button in the lower right corner of the screen (which opens a separate HTML window, as Figure B.10 shows), or by switching to one of the Code views.

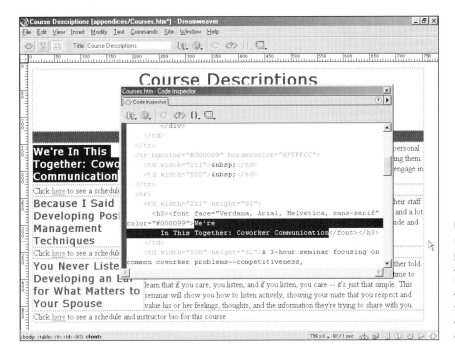

Figure B.10

If you want to see both your page and your HTML, but not in a split screen, use the Code Inspector to see the code in a window you can resize and move, thus customizing your experience of both the WYSIWYG and HTML aspects of your page in progress.

Learning from Other People's Code

If you want to see the HTML code for a page you're viewing on the Web, you can view the code in a separate window. If you're browsing with Internet Explorer, choose View|Source. If you're a Netscape user, choose View|Page Source.

You can learn a lot from other people's code. On the one hand, if their page is poorly designed or doesn't work properly—images are missing, error messages appear, the layout looks like something went wrong—you can view their code and learn from their mistakes. On the other hand, if you like someone's page—the layout, the way they've set up a table and arranged its contents—or you wonder how they achieved a particular effect, you can learn from that, too. You can also borrow their code, copying it from the window that appeared when you chose View|Source (or View|Page Source).

To borrow someone's code for learning purposes, select the code in the source display window (see Figure B.11), and copy the code into your Dreamweaver code view, or into a text editor such as NotePad.

Is doing this—copying someone else's code—wrong? Not really. HTML code isn't proprietary programming and, as long as you don't also "borrow" the graphic images from the page (animated GIFs, clip art, photographs), you aren't taking anything that wasn't essentially public domain. Look at it this way—borrowing code is the sincerest form of flattery—if someone's page has a layout you want to use, copy that person's code, and insert your own text and graphics. You should never borrow the content (the individual's paragraph text, graphics, sounds, or movie objects), because that's copyright infringement in most cases. The code, however, is not copyrightable—the designer of the page you're viewing might even have borrowed the code from someone else.

I Want It All

Do you want all the code for the page you're viewing? if so, don't bother copying and pasting. Just save the page to your local drive, giving the page a new name. You can then open the file in Dreamweaver, replace the graphics and text with your own, and make any other necessary edits. To save the file, use the File menu in the code display window, and choose Save As.

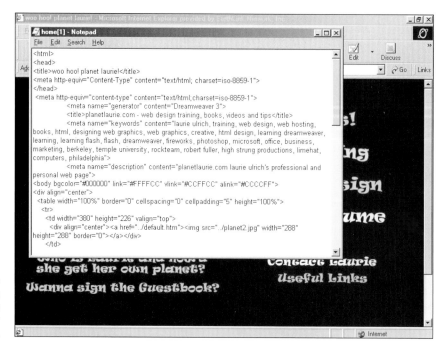

Figure B.11

You can scroll around in the page code, viewing everything that went into making the page you're viewing through your Web browser.

Appendix C

The Basics of Macromedia Fireworks

In this Appendix, you'll learn just enough about Fireworks to get into trouble. Well, not really, but doesn't that sound like more fun than "you'll learn the basics of a program that allows you to create Web-compatible illustrations and animations"? Both statements are true, and hopefully, with this Appendix in hand, you'll be able to get a jump-start on using Fireworks to add snazzy graphics to your Dreamweaver-designed Web pages.

What Fireworks Does

Fireworks is an application for creating Web graphics. You can create buttons and drawings and retouch photographs—essentially build and edit any graphic you can imagine. While Fireworks is a separate application, related to Dreamweaver only by the common manufacturer and some built-in connections (such as the capability to double-click a Fireworks-made graphic in a Dreamweaver file and automatically open Fireworks to edit that graphic), many people purchase the Dreamweaver/Fireworks "Studio" package and, therefore, have both products.

Identifying Fireworks's competitors in the Web graphics market is a good way to start a description of what Fireworks does. If you've ever seen or used Adobe PhotoShop or Jasc Paint Shop Pro, you have a general idea—all three products provide a set of tools for drawing lines and shapes, painting and illustrating with brushes and pencils, filling shapes and areas with color and interesting textures, applying artistic filters to alter the appearance of images, and re-touching photographs and graphics created in other applications.

By default, Fireworks creates PNG images, the latest entry into what is now a trinity of acceptable Web graphic formats—formerly, JPEG and GIF images were the only formats that Web browsers could reliably display. The W3C (World Wide Web Consortium) has recently accepted PNG files (pronounced *ping*), and the latest versions of the two main browsers—Internet Explorer and Netscape—display PNG images successfully.

You can also export images you create in Fireworks in a variety of JPEG and GIF formats. You can adjust the quality (and therefore file size) of the exported graphic, and you can choose to make the image Progressive (in the case of JPEGs) or Interlaced (in the case of GIFs). If you haven't read Chapter 4, check it out—you'll learn the terminology, requirements, and tips for good design using Web graphics.

A Tour of the Fireworks Interface

The Fireworks interface consists of several elements; each element serves as actual drawing and editing tools or gives you options for controlling how the tools work. As Figure C.1 shows, the interface includes a variety of on-screen tools, menus, and palettes to work with.

The main elements of the interface are as follows:

- *Menu bar*—Click the menu names and see a list of commands, many of which are accompanied by keyboard shortcuts. Use the Window menu to choose which on-screen elements are visible (see Figure C.2).

- *Toolbox*—This group of buttons represents Fireworks' drawing and ma-nipulation tools (see Figure C.3). The tools let you create shapes and lines, and paint, fill, erase, move, resize, and select elements of your images.

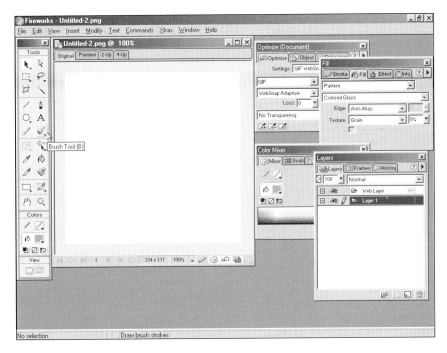

Figure C.1

Roll your mouse over any tool to see the tool's name, which usually gives you a good idea of what the tool does.

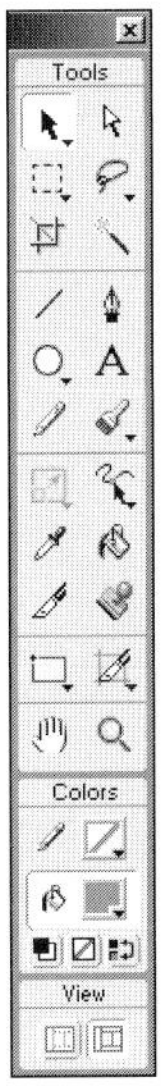

Figure C.2

(Left) The Fireworks Menu bar includes a list of commands and their keyboard shortcuts.

Figure C.3

(Right) The Fireworks Toolbox offers drawing and manipulation tools.

- *Toolbar*—The toolbar (which runs horizontally below the menu bar, as Figure C.4 shows) offers the standard Open, Save, Print, and Clipboard (Cut, Copy, and Paste) tools.

- *Floating Palettes*—Using the floating palettes, adjust the size of the paintbrush, pencil point, or eraser you're using, select an interesting texture or

Figure C.4
The Fireworks toolbar.

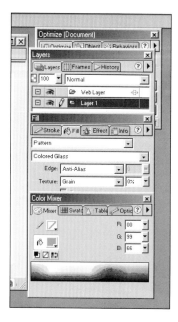

Figure C.5
The Fireworks floating palettes offer numerous options.

picture fill for a shape or area you've created, and control the layers within your image. The three main palettes are Layers, Fill, and Color Mixer as shown in Figure C.5.

- *Image Window*—When you open an existing or create a new image (File|New), it appears in a window that you can leave *restored* (in a smaller window that you can move around) or maximize to fill the window. You can zoom in on the image to tinker with fine detail, or zoom out to see the image in the size it will be on your Web page. Figure C.6 shows an image in progress.

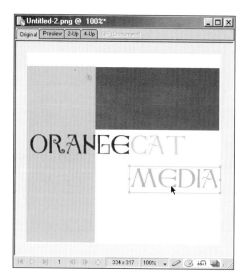

Figure C.6
Create and edit dazzling images in the Fireworks Image window.

Creating Web Graphics with Fireworks

To create a Fireworks graphic, you must open a new image window, and then use the drawing and editing tools to complete the image. To start a new image, follow these steps:

1. Choose File|New from the menu bar. The New Document dialog box opens, as Figure C.7 shows.

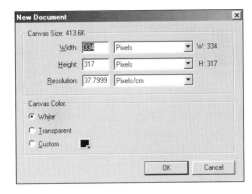

Figure C.7
Get the right start on your new image by setting the stage properly.

2. Enter the Width, Height, and Resolution you want for the new image. You can change from measuring the image in pixels to measuring it in inches or centimeters.

3. Choose your Canvas Color. The default color is White, but you can change it to Transparent, or pick a Custom color by clicking the palette box, which displays a palette of Web-safe colors.

4. Click OK to confirm your settings and close the dialog box. The new, Untitled image window opens, as Figure C.8 shows.

Figure C.8
A blank image window awaits your creativity.

Figure C.9

From a very simple image to a large or complex button, Fireworks gives you the tools to make your vision a reality.

Once you have a blank image window in front of you, you can begin drawing your image. You can use the Toolbox to draw shapes and lines, paint, and type text. Figure C.9 shows an image in progress.

Through the image window, you can view your graphic in four ways—the original, a preview of how it will look online, and optimized for the Web in 2-up and 4-up configurations. Figure C.10 shows the 4-up view of a GIF image.

Figure C.10

Check out how your image will look in whichever Web-safe format you've chosen, such as GIF, JPEG, or PNG.

Manipulating Drawn Shapes and Lines

As you draw shapes and lines, you can choose the color for your fill, outline, or stroke from the color tools at the bottom of the Toolbox. Depending on which part of the drawing is selected (a shape or a line), the fill or stroke color tool will be activated. Figure C.11 shows the palette of fill colors displayed for a selected rectangle.

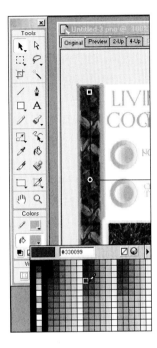

Figure C.11

Choose from a palette of Web-safe colors for your shape or line.

While part of your image is active, you can also use the palettes to change the way tools will work on that element. For example, if you've selected a shape, you can choose from a variety of fills in the Fill palette, as shown in Figure C.12.

You can also change the way the paintbrush and pencil tools work, choosing from a variety of Stroke options, as shown in Figure C.13.

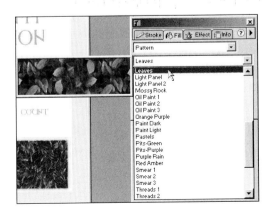

Figure C.12

(Left) Pick a fill—solids, gradients, textures, or patterns—for your selected shape.

Figure C.13

(Right) Does your design cry out for the look of having been drawn with a crayon? You'll find that option in the Stroke palette's list of options.

Using Text in a Graphic

You can add text to your graphic by clicking the Text tool, and then clicking on the image where you want the text to begin. The Text Editor dialog box opens (see Figure C.14), through which you can choose the font, color, style, size, and alignment for the text. You type the text in the large white text box, and use your mouse to select the text before you make changes to its appearance using the dialog box tools.

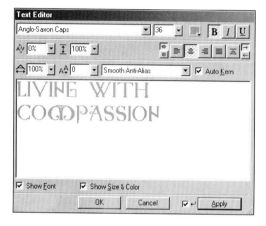

Figure C.14

Create graphic text objects with ease using Fireworks' Text Editor dialog box.

The Text Editor dialog box also lets you control the horizontal and vertical spread of your text, and clean up the curves and lines of your text, by applying various Anti-Alias settings. The default is smooth, and that's great for most fonts.

Saving Your Fireworks Creations

By default, Fireworks saves your graphic in PNG format. If you choose Save or Save As from the File menu, you can simply save your file by giving it a name and choosing a folder and drive on which to store it. If, however, you want to save your image in a GIF or JPEG format, follow these steps:

1. Choose File|Export Preview. The Export Preview dialog box opens, as Figure C.15 shows.

2. On the Options tab, click the Format drop list to choose a format in which to save the file. Be sure to check Progressive (for JPEGs) or Interlaced (for GIFs) if that effect is desirable for your particular Web application.

3. As necessary, you can choose an export area (to export only part of an image), zoom in on your image, or choose to view your image in one to four windows within the dialog box. You will find these options along the bottom of the dialog box, above the Export and OK buttons, as Figure C.16 shows.

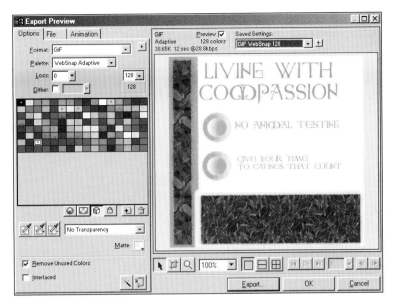

Figure C.15
The large and complex-looking Export Preview dialog box gives you a wide range of options for saving your image in JPEG or GIF format.

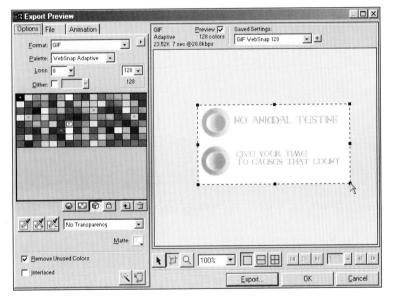

Figure C.16
You can export a part of your image if you don't want the entire graphic to be saved in GIF or JPEG format.

4. Click the Export button to open the Export dialog box, from which you can choose where to save your file and what to call it. The format you chose in the Export Wizard dialog box (which remains open behind the active dialog box) is the selected format, which is indicated by the extension automatically applied to the file name, as you see in Figure C.17.

5. After you select the location for your file and give the file a name (don't bother retyping the extension, Fireworks will apply that for you), click the Save button. The image is saved, and the Fireworks original remains open in the Fireworks window.

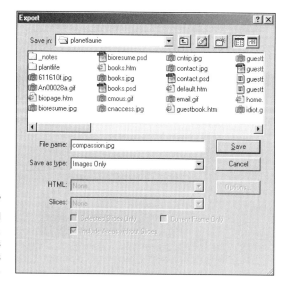

Figure C.17
Give your file a name, and choose a place to save it. Remember not to use spaces in file names if your image is bound for the Web.

Creating Animations

Creating animations is a rich topic, and you'll want to explore this aspect of Fireworks more thoroughly on your own. In the interest of having a jump-start on the process, however, you can follow these basic steps to create a simple rotating image:

1   Create an image. The image can include shapes, lines, and text.

2. Choose Commands|Animation|Rotate. A prompt appears, indicating that a multiframe animation will be created. Click OK to proceed.

3. At this point, Fireworks renders the image, creating a frame for every step in the rotation. You can see the frames by clicking the Frames tab on the Layers palette (the palette name will change to Frames as soon as you click the tab). Figure C.18 shows the frames created to rotate graphic text on a white background.

4. To see the effect that results, choose File|Preview In Browser, or simply press F12 to open a browser preview in the application you have set as your default. Figure C.19 shows the word *Spin!*, spinning in place in an Internet Explorer window.

5. Export the image as an Animated GIF, and you can use it on any Web page. To do so, choose File|Export Preview. The format (Animated GIF) will be selected by default because the image was animated through Fireworks.

6. Click Export to save the file with a name and to the location of your choice.

Back to the Drawing Board

If you want to save the Fireworks original image, which will include all the separate layers and settings you chose through the palettes, you can do so, giving the file the same name as the JPEG or GIF version you exported. Retaining this version of the file makes edits easier if they are required. If, for example, you've created and exported an image that contains text, and you find later that the text is misspelled or needs some other change, you can go back into the Fireworks original version of the file, edit the text layer, and then re-export the file as a GIF or JPEG, replacing the first file.

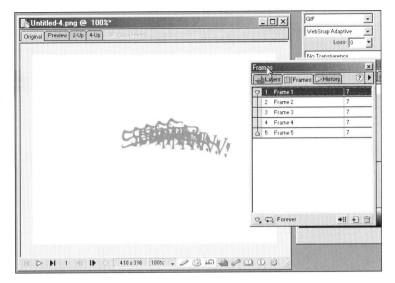

Figure C.18

You don't need to create your own frames or plan the steps involved in spinning the image—Fireworks does all this for you.

Figure C.19

In just seconds, your image can go from static to one that rotates.

Now, Go Explore!

With just these basic clues about the general operation of Fireworks, you should be able to get started building images for your Web pages. Fireworks has an extensive set of tools that go beyond the intention of this appendix, and if you plan to use Fireworks as your primary image creation and manipulation tool, you should invest in a book about Fireworks. I suggest *Fireworks 4 f/x and Design*, from The Coriolis Group, Inc.

In addition, you can rely on Fireworks's own Help files—the information is thorough and accurate, and you can easily navigate the Contents, Index, and Search components of the Help interface. Good luck, and enjoy Fireworks.

Appendix D

Using Project Files for This Book

The CD-ROM that accompanies this book contains files you'll need to complete some of the book's projects. This Appendix lists what they are and how to access them.

Project Files

The files for relevant chapter projects are stored in folders that are named to match the chapters and project numbers. Table D.1 lists the chapter folders, chapter titles, and the project folders you'll be using.

The Color Studio Section

In the Color Studio folder, you'll find the HTML files for many of the Web pages from that section of the book, along with the images included on several of those pages. Each page is in a separate subfolder that corresponds to the image.

I encourage you to borrow any of the code and reuse the images either in your own work or simply as part of the learning process. Observe the underlying HTML code, see how the pages are laid out, and try to recreate the pages on your own. You may even want to redesign them to suit your own taste and style, and I'd love to see your finished products. My email address is listed at the end of this Appendix, and I look forward to hearing from you.

How to Use the CD-ROM

After inserting the CD-ROM, access its files by clicking Start|Run and typing "D:Run" (substituting your CD-ROM drive for *D:* where applicable). Click OK. View the contents by clicking the Explore CD icon. You can also access the files through Windows Explorer or My Computer (click your CD-ROM drive). Table D.1 lists the folder and subfolders for each chapter's project(s).

To copy a file or folder from the CD-ROM to your local drive, simply select it and choose Edit|Copy. Select the drive and folder you want to copy to and choose Edit|Paste. Once files are copied to your local drive, you can access them any time using the graphics and Web-page files to complete the projects in this book or reusing them in your own work. If you prefer, you can open the

Table D.1   Project folders on the CD-ROM.

Chapter	Chaper Title	Project Subfolders
Chapter 3	Working with Text	Project 3A, Project 3B
Chapter 4	Effective Use of Graphics	Project 4A, Project 4B
Chapter 5	Connecting with Hyperlinks	Project 5A, Project 5B
Chapter 6	Structuring a Web Page with Tables	Project 6A, Project 6B
Chapter 7	Controlling a Page with Frames	Project 7A
Chapter 8	Positioning Page Content with Layers	Project 8A
Chapter 9	Using Color Effectively	Project 9A
Chapter 10	Creating Forms	Project 10A
Chapter 11	Working with Dreamweaver Assets	Project 11A, Project 11B
Chapter 13	Using Multimedia Objects	Project 13A

Web pages directly from the CD-ROM by double-clicking the HTML files—this action opens the browser you've set as your default application for accessing the Web and displays the selected page.

If you have questions regarding the images or Web-page files on the CD-ROM, please send me an email at **laurie@planetlaurie.com**. You can also visit my Web site, **www.planetlaurie.com**, and click the Coriolis link on the Books page for access to all the files that are on the CD-ROM. They're on my site in case you don't have the CD-ROM at your disposal—you may have lost it, or be reading a used or borrowed copy of the book that no longer contains the CD-ROM.

Index

S

W

If you *like* this book, you'll *love*...

Fireworks® 4 f/x and Design

by Joyce Evans

Media: 2 CD-ROMs

ISBN #: 1-57610-996-8

$49.99 (US) $74.99 (CAN)

Learn how to produce professional-level images, buttons, animations, navigation bars, and graphical interfaces for the Web. This guide goes beyond teaching the functions of Fireworks by providing real-world projects that can be effectively incorporated in a professional Web site. This book includes two CD-ROMs containing Special Comstock Photography with over 12,000 comping images, trial versions of Dreamweaver®, Flash®, and FreeHand®, as well as sample artwork to use in the projects. The foreward for this book was written by J. Scott Hamilin, director of Eyeland Studio and author of *Flash 5 Magic*.

Illustrator® 9 f/x and Design

by Sherry London

Media: CD-ROM

ISBN #: 1-57610-750-7

$49.99 (US) $74.99 (CAN)

Features new information and projects on styles and effects, how to prepare your images for the Web, as well as other enhanced features. With real-world projects, readers learn firsthand how to create intricate illustrations and compositing techniques. Readers also learn how to work seamlessly between Illustrator® and Photoshop®.

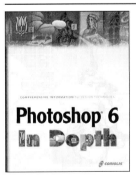

Photoshop® 6 In Depth

by David Xenakis and Benjamin Levisay

Media: 2 CD-ROMs

ISBN #: 1-57610-788-4

$59.99 (US) $89.99 (CAN)

Takes the mystery out of the new Photoshop® functions! Readers will learn layering, channel selection, color corrections, prepress integration with other applications, and how to prepare images for the Web. The linear format in each chapter addresses individual topics, allowing readers to select according to their needs and skill levels. This book includes two CD-ROMs, with three bonus chapters: "Third-Party Filters," "Preparing Graphics for the Web," and "Using ImageReady".

GoLive™ f/x and Design

by Richard Schrand

Media: CD-ROM

ISBN #: 1-57610-786-8

$49.99 (US) $74.99 (CAN)

From basic designs to advanced rollover techniques, *GoLive™ 5 f/x and Design* takes you on a tour of the hottest features of this high–end Web design program. Learn about Cascading Style Sheets, get ideas on how to create eye-catching forms, find out how to build dynamic sites by using today's cutting-edge technology, and then discover how the author builds an entire site using the techniques discussed throughout the book. The CD-ROM contains dozens of demo and free programs, special discounts on memory upgrades exclusive to this book, and original seamless backgrounds for use on your own Web sites.

Flash Forward with Coriolis Books

Flash-Guru™

The future of Flash training

Founded by **Jon Warren Lentz**, author of the Flash 5 and Flash 4 Bibles, **Flash-Guru**™ is a new vision of Flash knowledge sharing based on the concept of an expert community.

Flash-Guru™ has brought together some of best minds in the Flash world, united in a common endeavor: to develop and deliver a library of superior training materials.

Flash-Guru™ courses are built upon real-world projects by authors who know how to develop course materials for the web.

Flash-Guru™ instructors will develop a broad curriculum of original, compelling, long-form tutorials that cover the full breadth of Flash topics, areas of deep specialization, and the advanced ranges of the integration of Flash with other technologies.

Whether you are an absolute beginner or an accomplished Flash designer, the goal of **Flash-Guru**™ is to provide you with the training you need to take your Flash artistry to the next level.

At **www.Flash-Guru.com** you will get the information and training you need in a hands-on, quality-controlled learning environment.

"Jon Warren Lentz, together with Nik Schramm and Jeffrey Bardzell, has applied the concept of 'learner-centered design' to the creation of a knowledge-sharing web environment that's designed to support the learning goals of the participants, and that's flexible enough to take into account their motivation and lifestyle. The result, Flash-Guru, is a model of instruction that applies equally well to both lone designers and corporate groups." — **(Bill Turner,** author of **Flash 5 Cartoons and Games F/X)**

Flash-Guru, the future of Flash training for IT and motivated individuals.

Starting in May 2001.

What's on the CD-ROM

The *Dreamweaver 4 f/x and Design* companion CD-ROM contains elements specifically selected to enhance the usefulness of this book, including:

- *Web pages*—The HTML files for the pages included in the color section to help you learn from the existing code as you build your own pages.
- *Graphic Images*—The files you need to create the projects, including JPEG and GIF versions of original artwork and photographs.
- *Text Files*—To help you build content quickly, you'll find text documents from which you can cut and paste to build the projects.
- *Multimedia Files*—To assist you in developing the project for the multimedia chapter, a Flash movie and sound file are included on the CD. You can use them as sample content as you learn to build your own pages and incorporate multimedia objects.

Note: The following software (not included on this CD) is required to complete the projects and tutorials.

- Macromedia Dreamweaver 4
- Flash plug-ins (so you can run the Flash movie included on the CD-ROM)

System Requirements

Software

- Windows 98, NT4, 2000 or higher.

Hardware

- An Intel (or equivalent) Pentium 100MHz processor is the minimum platform required; an Intel (or equivalent) Pentium 133MHz processor is recommended.
- 32MB of RAM is the minimum requirement.
- Macromedia Dreamweaver requires approximately 35MB of disk storage space.
- A color monitor (256 colors) is recommended
- Sound card and speakers (recommended, but not required)